FROM FIZZLE
TO SIZZLE

FROM FIZZLE
TO SIZZLE

The Hidden Forces Crushing Your Creativity
and How to Overcome Them

Anthony D. Fredericks Ed.D.

BLUE RIVER PRESS

INDIANAPOLIS, INDIANA

Fizzle to Sizzle: The Hidden Forces Crushing Your Creativity
and How to Overcome Them

Copyright © 2022 by Anthony D. Fredericks

Published by Blue River Press
Indianapolis, Indiana
www.brpressbooks.com

Distributed by Cardinal Publishers Group
A Tom Doherty Company, Inc.
www.cardinalpub.com

ISBN: 978-1-68157-210-9

Cover Design: Korab Designs
Interior Design: Glen Edelstein
Editor: Dani McCormick

Printed in the United States of America

10 9 8 7 6 5 4 3 2 1   21 22 23 24 25 26 27 28 29 30

Dedication

To **Jack and Linda Sommer** -
For their warm friendship, sincere support,
"Souper Tuesdays," and effervescent humor...
but, especially for the friendship!

Selected Books by Anthony D. Fredericks

ADULT NONFICTION

THE SECRET LIFE OF CLAMS:
The Mysteries and Magic of Our Favorite Shellfish

WALKING WITH DINOSAURS
Rediscovering Colorado's Prehistoric Beasts

WRITING CHILDREN'S BOOKS:
Everything You Need to Know From Story Creation to Getting Published

HORSESHOE CRAB:
Biography of a Survivor

ACE YOUR TEACHER INTERVIEW (3RD ED.):
158 Fantastic Answers to Tough Interview Questions

DESERT DINOSAURS:
Discovering Prehistoric Sites in the American Southwest

THE ADJUNCT PROFESSOR'S COMPLETE GUIDE
TO TEACHING COLLEGE:
How to Be an Effective and Successful Instructor

CHILDREN'S BOOKS

DESERT NIGHT, DESERT DAY
UNDER ONE ROCK: BUGS, SLUGS AND OTHER UGHS
THE TSUNAMI QUILT: GRANDFATHER'S STORY
A IS FOR ANACONDA: A RAINFOREST ALPHABET
NEAR ONE CATTAIL: TURTLES, LOGS AND LEAPING FROGS
MOUNTAIN NIGHT, MOUNTAIN DAY
TALL TALL TREE
I AM THE DESERT

CONTENTS ||||||

PART FOUR

PART FIVE

INTRODUCTION
Sesame Seed Spread, Creative Decay, and a Regeneration

1.

Not long ago my wife gave me a shopping list and sent me off to the grocery store to pick up some essentials. As I scanned the list while entering the store, I noted "sesame seed spread" about half-way down the list. I wasn't familiar with this commodity; thus, I wasn't quite sure where it might be located in the store. I could have approached the Customer Service desk and asked one of the nice employees (with their distinctive red vests emblazoned with "Can I help? Yes, I can!" in large gothic letters on the back) where I would find sesame seed spread, but I decided to ask myself a question instead. "What if I was sesame seed spread, where would I live in this store?"

It's not a question destined to rattle the foundations of western civilization or force Congress to enact a new piece of nutritional legislation, but it would give me a chance to deal with a conundrum in an imaginative and dynamic way. And so, in my mind, I began to conjure all sorts of possible answers. Here are some of the responses I generated:

If I were sesame seed spread, I would live:

➤ With my nutty friends in the nut section.
➤ In the spice aisle because, well, because...I sound like I should be a spice
➤ Next to my distant cousins - the pantheon of peanut butter products.
➤ With my natural (though frequently chilly) relatives

- butter and margarine
➤ I'm pretty special - I have my own unique section next to my whole wheat cracker friends.
➤ In between the mouse poisons and charcoal briquettes, because no one has ever heard of me before so they put in a place that nobody knows about and nobody can find.
➤ With the cake mixes and frostings - because I sound like something that should be spread on assorted pastries
➤ With the jams, jellies, marmalades, and other sweet condiments for toast.

I wound up with about a dozen different possibilities for where I would live if I was, in fact, a container of sesame seed spread. None of those locations was necessarily right or wrong. The intent was to free my mind to look for options, rather than come up with an absolutely correct answer. In other words, I was trying to insert something between the asking of a question and its potential response. I was inserting the generation of possibilities.

And so, I imagined my search. First, I trekked over to the nut section and searched through shelves crammed with roasted almonds, sunflower seeds, brazil nuts, tasty pecans, walnuts, sinfully delicious macadamia nuts, mixed nuts, unsalted sunflower seeds, deluxe cashews, bulky bags of pistachios, and other assorted cans and jars of nut products and foods masking as nuts (peanuts). No sesame seed spread!

Next, I traveled over to the cracker section - thinking that if someone was purchasing sesame seed spread, they would need some sort of edible "device" onto which they could place the "spread." I searched amongst the whole wheat crackers, oyster crackers, potato and rice crackers, saltines, cheese crackers, multigrain crackers, graham crackers, and crackers with more flavors than your local delicatessen (Savory Onion, Mediterranean Herb, Tuscan Cheese, Asiago and Cheddar, Rosemary and Sea Salt). Alas, no sesame seed spread was to be found!

Perhaps (I imagined), sesame seed spread must be in the Dairy Section sitting beside buttery spreads such as salted butter, unsalted butter, sweet cream butter, organic butter, omega-3 butter, whipped butter, olive oil butter, butter with yogurt, butter with canola oil, butter with calcium, and then all those "foreign" butters - Irish butter, Finnish butter, European butter, and (since I live in Pennsylvania) Amish butter. Perhaps it was hiding near all its cousins - the margarines with their amazing concoctions of vegetable oils and nitrogen gases. Again, I struck out!

Then, I imagined rolling my cart over to the peanut butter section of the store to see if that would be a most likely place for a container of sesame seed spread to reside. I visually roamed over seven eight-foot long shelves overloaded with jars of crunchy, smooth, P.B.&J., organic, natural, reduced fat, unsalted, honey roast, super chunk, and peanut butter with all manner of sinful additions (chocolate, granola, strawberry, pretzels, graham bites, and grape jelly). Besides all the appellations of peanut butter there was an intriguing collection of sunflower seed spread, almond spread, cashew spread, and hazelnut spread. Then, there, at the very end of the second shelf of that coterie of delightful spreads was a short row of 16-ounce jars of sesame seed spreads (or Tahini as it's known in the Mediterranean and Middle East). I had discovered my destiny!

My imaginative journey through a grocery store was certainly not life-changing and it is unlikely to alter the arc of human history. Nevertheless, my initial question about where I would live in a supermarket if I were a container of sesame seed spread was a most pleasant mental diversion on a Sunday afternoon. It propelled me into a creative state of mind, got my neurons firing over something as mundane as a condiment for toast (or a veggie dip), and engaged me in a fanciful adventure.

Creativity is intelligence having fun.
ALBERT EINSTEIN

2.

So, who's the most creative person in the world? A four-year-old child, of course. Four-year-olds are known for asking an endless array of questions ("Why is the sky blue?" "How do birds fly?" and "Why does Mommy keep having so many babies?"). But, by the time that four-year-old has turned into a nine-year-old, her natural creativity has been significantly reduced. And, then, that nine-year-old grows up into a 22-year-old, graduates from college, gets a job, and discovers that her once dynamic creative spirit has completely fizzled.

What happened?

Simply put, our natural sense of creativity has been swept out of our minds by a system of societal myths, educational practices, workplace habits, and everyday expectations more concerned with conformity than with fostering creative expression. We have been "educated" to be mentally compliant; we have not been trained to generate a plethora of creative solutions when faced with intellectual challenges or job-related problems. In so many ways, our thinking has become "McDonald's-ized" - it's standardized, predictable, and convenient. "Thinking outside the box" is not what we do well.

Truth be told, we don't need to be creative every single minute. We don't need to be creative when shopping for a new refrigerator, we certainly don't need to be creative when we're filling our car with gas, and we don't have a need for creativity when we're cheering our local high school football team. We have certain routines and certain ways of behaving that make those tasks bearable, or even enjoyable. That's part of our "comfort zone." They aren't tasks we have to do any deep thinking about and certainly they are tasks that don't require a whole lot of mental input.

However, there are times in our daily schedules when we need something new (mentally speaking), when we need a different way of doing things, an innovative outlook, an unusual approach...times when we would benefit from a new idea. Perhaps our boss has assigned us a brand new project, or we're faced with a personnel conundrum that just has us flummoxed, or we're looking for a new way to understand our child's homework assignment, or we're searching for a certain condiment in our local grocery store. We need some sort of creative approach or dynamic answer that will increase our productivity, or give us a new way of seeing the world.

And so, we purchase an array of books and read a succession of internet articles looking for an essential nugget of innovative thinking

– How can I begin generating lots of creative ideas? Many of us think that creativity experts have some "inside secret" that gives them an advantage. In a way, they do. They are able to over-ride the mental barriers to creativity so they can utilize proven methods and dynamic strategies for jump-starting their brains and firing up their "mental generators." Big box bookstores have entire sections devoted to the subject of creativity - a response to our never-ending quest for more innovative thinking in our lives.

Yet, a big question still remains: What causes us to be "non-creative" in the first place? We were creative souls when we were very young; but, now, in our adult years we find ourselves wrestling with issues, conundrums, and challenges that demand creative thought; but we often discover that our creative "wells" have dried up. Why? Interestingly, it's a question that's never been asked before; and, even more important, one never answered in all the "How to Be More Creative" books (more than 60,000 on Amazon.com) and all the "Becoming a More Creative Person" articles (more than two billion on Google) currently available.

However, this book is different. It is both an examination of the hidden forces that influence our thinking and impede our creativity and also about how those all-too-powerful forces can be curtailed, reduced, and eliminated. We know, for example, that very young children are, by nature, quite creative beings. They draw pictures with red grass, flying horses, invisible monsters, and soaring medieval castles (surrounded by a crocodile-infested moat) in the heart of Baltimore, Maryland, Albuquerque, New Mexico, or Portland, Oregon. Up until the age of five their imaginations are at a fever pitch - there are no barriers to their creativity - anything is possible!

Then, between the ages of five and fifteen something happens to their creative spigot. Their training and education becomes standardized and routine. Their creative powers have been curtailed and sublimated to an educational curriculum that prizes memorization over imagination and rote learning over creativity. As a professional educator, I'm interested in how this happens; but equally important, how can these (inevitable) events in our lives be addressed and confronted? Is there something in the way we were raised, educated, or employed that has such a profound effect on how we approach the inevitable challenges and problems of daily living? And, equally important, is there something we can embrace and incorporate in our day to day living that will mitigate those oppressive forces?

The ultimate truth is that an understanding of creativity is also an understanding of hidden obstacles - the miseducation, myths, societal barriers, and workplace practices that often influence our thinking and quash our inventive desires. Ultimately, knowing the barriers, blockades, and barricades to creative thought prior to reading about and implementing great creativity strategies can help make those improvement strategies more effective in the short run and permanent in the long run.

In essence, this is a book about persistent and unseen forces...and how they can be subdued, quashed, and nullified.

Discovery consists of looking at the same thing aseveryone else and thinking something different.
ALBERT SZENT-GYÖRGYI

3.

Imagine the following: You wake up one morning with a severe pain radiating down your entire left side. You have an intense migraine headache, you're feverish, and your equilibrium is off-kilter. Your vision is blurry, you can barely stand upright, and there seems to be blood flowing out of your nose. You call your best friend who rushes you to the hospital. After a series of tests, two doctors come in to the emergency room, and one of them says, "We've figured out what's wrong and we're going to rush you in to emergency surgery. Not to worry, but you'll be back to normal in a few weeks. We'll see you soon in the operating room." And off they go.

Now, consider this: You get in your car one morning to begin your daily commute. As you back out of the garage, smoke starts pouring from the exhaust. The car shakes uncontrollably and a screeching sound emanates from somewhere deep within the engine. It is obvious the brakes are not working and the steering wheel is completely non-functional. You coast to a stop and immediately call your friendly service station. They haul the car into their shop and perform a series of diagnostic tests. After two or three hours, the manager of the repair shop calls you at work and says, "We've located the problem and we can probably have it fixed in about three or fours days. It's pretty severe, but not something we haven't seen before. The bad news is that it's going to set you back about $3,750. I'll give you a call as soon as we're done." (End of call.)

"Whoa!" (you might say to yourself).

It's clear that something is missing from each of those vignettes. In both cases, neither your doctor nor your car mechanic told you what was wrong. In both cases you were left "out in the cold." Each time a diagnosis of systemic problems in your body and in your car was made...but you were never informed about what they were. In other words, something was wrong, something was going to be fixed, but you had no idea what those abnormalities were. In both cases, a critical piece of information was missing.

If, indeed, we put a premium on creativity as an essential part of our personal and/or professional success, then it stands to reason that we need to understand why we have struggled with our creativity "demons" in the first place. I believe we spend too much time searching for creative solutions to all the challenges in our lives without fully comprehending the reasons why we may be struggling with creativity to begin with. In short, what caused us to get to this point in our lives? Without knowing the answer to that query, all the creativity strategies in the world aren't going to help us fully embrace a change in mindset or an alteration of our creative perspectives to any measurable degree.

For a moment, think what might happen if we knew the reasons for our lack of creative spirit before embarking on a mission of creative self-improvement. We would understand what often strangles our creative spirit when faced with a demanding task. We would be able to chip away at the personal barriers that consistently hamper our thinking. We would be able to reroute our thinking from past (inefficient) practices to innovative and imaginative thinking that solves, rather than creates, problems. We would know what influences us and thus select the appropriate techniques and strategies that address not a single problem, but a multiplicity of challenges.

> *Real knowledge is knowing the*
> *extent of one's ignorance.*
> - Confucius

4.

You may be wondering what types of changes are necessary in order to mitigate some of the events of your life...events that have depressed your personal creativity. By the same token, if you work with youngsters, as either a parent or educator (or both), you may be wondering how you can nurture and support the inherent creativity of kids in a warm and supportive environment. Alternatively, perhaps you are a manager, CEO, president, or leader of a business or volunteer organization and are curious about the processes and practices that will enhance the "creativity quotient" of the people under your supervision.

This book examines four critical components of our lives - our upbringing, education, work environment, and personal beliefs. To address those life events, Chapters 3-15 are each divided into two parts. Each chapter begins with an examination of stories, empirical research, psychological insights, insightful anecdotes, and expert explanations for why our inherent creative spirit has diminished over time. This initial section of each chapter seeks the answer to the one question we all need satisfied ("Why is creativity such a challenge for me?"). Here, you will discover penetrating enlightenments and commanding data about why you feel creatively hampered. In so doing, you'll discover some fascinating and interesting insights about your thinking and how you tackle (or not) everyday problems and personal issues.

The second part of each of those chapters ("How to Sizzle") offers a range of creativity enhancements, solutions, techniques, activities, and possibilities. They are practices that underscore the ultimate reality of a creative life: Creativity is not something done to us; rather, it should be something we do for ourselves. It's important to note that although the strategies within a chapter are designated for a particular part of our lives (our education, for example), I invite you to consider all of them as proven possibilities for the challenges you face every day. For example, the "What-if" strategy is located in the "Education" section of the book because it has such powerful ramifications for teachers and students (at any grade). However, it also has incredible implications for our adult lives, too. In fact, I find this particular strategy one of my most used - one I employ whenever I'm stuck on a significant issue or problem. Simply by asking a series of 'What-if' questions, I've solved some very difficult challenges in both my personal and professional life.

By the same token, "Take a Hike" is a strategy found in the section on upbringing, simply because it is something kids do naturally. Children love to explore new territories, venture into different landscapes, and hike through long forests. Children do this quite easily, but as adults, we often eschew this all-too-common activity as something we have little time for in our crowded and overburdened schedules. But, by making walking a regular part of our daily routine - particularly when faced with an intellectual challenge - we are able to generate a wide range of potential possibilities. Just like kids do!

Consider this book as a round-trip voyage: what's been holding you back and what can move you forward. It's designed to help you comprehend the invisible forces weighing you down (the diagnosis) and, in turn, offer you the techniques and strategies (the prescription) to tackle personal and professional challenges with a dynamic, innovative, and creative regeneration.

Expect the unexpected or you won't find it.
HERACLITUS, GREEK PHILOSOPHER

PART ONE
Brain Ripples/
Brain Waves

1.
Creativity Blues

A line is a dot that went for a walk.
- Paul Klee

1.

In the middle of this page is a box. Inside the box are two dots: one on the left and one on the right. Please get a blank sheet of paper and a pen or pencil. Draw two circles in the middle of the paper as in the following diagram:

Using your pencil or pen, connect the two circles.
Now, turn the page to see how you did.

IF YOU DID THIS	THIS IS WHAT IT MEANS
	You connected the dots in the same way as would about ninety percent of the general public.
	You responded as would about five percent of the general public.
	You responded as would about two percent of the general public.
	"There's no way I could come up with this. I'm just not creative!"
	"There's no way I could come up with this. I'm just not creative!"
	"There's no way I could come up with this. I'm just not creative!"

2.

Revisit your drawing of the circles (and the way in which you connected them) and you may note something. If you are like many people, you will have responded in a most predictable way. In essence, you responded in a way that was comfortable, familiar, and certain. Most likely, you saw that a straight line from the dot on the left to the dot on the right would be the simplest and quickest way to respond to the directions. Perhaps you were thinking of that familiar axiom, "The shortest distance between two points is a straight line." Or, perhaps you were thinking of a recent trip you took in which you had to get from one point (your home) to another point (the doctor's office) in the quickest amount of time. So, instead of taking a scenic route or any back roads, you drove in as straight a line as you could. Connecting the two dots with an equally straight line seemed to be the most reasonable and certainly the most logical way to respond to the directions (Of course, you may also have been unfairly influenced by the quote just under the chapter title.).

For most of our lives, we have been trained or "conditioned" to do many tasks in a very predictable and time-efficient manner. Maybe we really wanted to draw a hammock between the two dots, but our brain told us to do something else: Do it the way we have been conditioned to do it or do it the way everyone else will do it. Without realizing it, we suppressed our "creative mind" in favor of our "logical mind."

The chief enemy of creativity is "good sense."
PABLO PICASSO

Let's examine that concept a little further.

EXERCISE

Look at the figure below. How many squares do you see?

There are _____ squares.

Most people will see sixteen squares in the figure. Interestingly, much of your education has been structured so that you will answer the question above with a single (and most satisfactory) response: sixteen. In other words, you have been mentally trained to seek out the one perfect answer to any single question (one question = one answer). If you got sixteen, then pat yourself on the back - you answered the question correctly.

But did you?

Take another look at the figure. Forget about sixteen similarly-sized, equal-dimensioned tiny squares. Look for squares of different sizes (large, small) or different dimensions. For example, a square could be composed of four smaller squares all together (two squares by two squares). Or, a larger square could be composed of nine smaller squares (three squares on a side). Squares could appear in the upper left-hand corner of the illustration, in the lower right-hand corner, or just about anywhere. In other words, by changing your perspective you have become a little more creative (at least with an illustration of squares). Your new view of the illustration above had nothing to do with what you inherited from your parents, rather it had a lot to do with how you were "educated" to view the world. By the way, there are thirty squares (don't forget the one big square surrounding all the other tiny squares.).

EXERCISE

In the illustration below, there are six lines (imagine each line to be a toothpick). Your challenge: Eliminate three lines (take away three toothpicks) to leave four.

At first glance, you are probably thinking the puzzle above is an impossible problem. "There is NO WAY to remove three toothpicks from six toothpicks and leave four toothpicks," you might say, quite emphatically. But look again, that's not the problem. The problem was to remove three toothpicks to leave four. For most of our lives we have been taught to look for the most obvious answer - the most correct answer. As a result, we often read questions far too literally. In looking at the problem, you probably thought that the word "four" referred to the <u>number</u> of toothpicks. But, let's ask the original question in a slightly different way: "How else can I make a four?" or "What else is a four?" Those questions should get you thinking "outside the box." Now, it's possible to solve the problem. Remove the toothpick at the top, the one on the bottom, and the one on the right side of the illustration. What do you have left? Four (the Roman numeral "four")!

> *Creativity requires the courage to let go of*
> *certainties.*
> ERICH FROMM

3.

Consider the following scenarios:

A. Deshaun was an outstanding student at UCLA. As an economics major, he was known as a dedicated scholar, a passionate participant in all his classes, and a "rising star" to all his professors. He had several job offers long before graduation and eventually decided on a firm in Seattle near his soon-to-be-retired parents. Several weeks after he began, his supervisor called his department together for a meeting. The fourteen people seated around the table were informed that revenues were falling and that a new marketing plan was needed in order to gain more clients. Deshaun was "volunteered" to chair a small group of six co-workers tasked with coming up with a new outreach plan for the department. After the meeting, Deshaun looked at his fellow teammates and said, "I have no idea where to begin. I'm just not creative!"

B   Tiffany grew up in the Florida Panhandle. She was well

connected with the local community and proudly served on several boards and local charities. One of the groups she was most passionate about provided trips, excursions and outings for special needs children in the local area. The group survived on an annual fund drive and donations from a few businesses in the area.

Tiffany's passion for the kids and the organization's goals was clearly evident and it wasn't long before she was elected as president. The new responsibility meant she was in charge of raising funds for the group and ensuring that an increasing number of kids were offered daytrips not provided by other community groups. One day, over a caramel macchiato at the local Starbucks, she confided to her friend Tamisha, "I have no idea where to begin. I'm just not creative!

C.   Kay Lynn had long ago decided to be a "stay-at-home" mom. Her husband was the assistant manager at a hardware store in Cheyanne, Wyoming. Kay Lynn wanted to be home to raise their three kids. Later, she could get a part-time job and help with the bills; but for now, her primary focus was the kids.

One day, her oldest son came home from school with a homework assignment. The school history fair was scheduled in three months and every student had to come up with a project that demonstrated a grasp of basic historical research. Kay Lynn was completely stumped by the assignment and later that evening she expressed to her husband, "I don't know how I'm going to help him. I'm just not creative!"

Interestingly, one of the most prevalent psychological misconceptions or societal myths is that we are either born creative or not. That is, there are two kinds of people in the world: the creative ones and those who couldn't come up with a creative idea if their life depended on it. Because of our own frustrations in generating creative thoughts, we have conveniently grouped people into the creative "haves" and the creative "have-nots" (a dichotomy we'll explore in greater detail later in the book).

We often look at creative types as "strange" or "unusual."[1] They do things we cannot, they think things we don't, and they envision possibilities we could never conceive. They were born creative and we were not. The Leonardo da Vincis, Pablo Picassos, and Jane Austins of the world are "different." They were gifted with a set of genes that we did not get. They are in a different category, a different world, and a different universe. Because we don't have those creative genes we'll never rise to their level; as a result we satisfy our egos by stating that, "I'm just not creative" when faced with work-related challenges or personal hurdles.

An article in Harvard Business Review underscores this belief. During seminars and training sessions, a team of researchers regularly ask managers and executives around the world how many of them believe they are creative. Typically, less than 50% of the hands go in the air. Although the researchers admit this is not a scientific sample and methodology, their subsequent survey data strongly suggests that those who believe they are not creative typically do not engage in any creative endeavors.

This conclusion is supported by a study involving the creative productivity of engineers at a major oil company. Executives of the company were concerned about the lack of creative output on the part of these employees. They decided to bring in a team of psychologists to see if they could determine any significant differences between those deemed to be creative and those categorized as "non-creative." Their goal was to obtain a set of situations and practices that would lead to higher level of creative production on the part of the "non-creatives."

Over the course of three months, the team of psychologists asked a battery of questions focused on childhood experiences, family influences, academic performance, geographical preferences, and even favorite colors. After a thorough analysis of all the data gathered, they concluded that a single factor clearly separated the two groups:

The creative people thought they were creative; and the less creative people didn't think they were.

These results suggest that when we believe ourselves to be "non-creative," we seldom put ourselves into situations that allow us

---

1 The words "peculiar," "odd," "offbeat," and "weird" also come to mind.

to engage in creative endeavors or creative thinking. If we believe that we have low "creativity quotients," then we often don't allow ourselves to engage in imaginative activities, take creative risks, play with possibilities, or look for alternate answers. Just by saying, "I'm not creative," we give ourselves permission to reject creative possibilities.

Interestingly, though, all of us are creative souls early in our lives and it is our upbringing, schooling and work environment that often determine the degree or comfort we have with creative thinking. In short, it is what we have experienced throughout our lives that often determines what we can create. Creativity is never a matter of "I have it," or "I don't have it." It is, most often, the result of hidden forces firmly entrenched in our growth and development. Kaufman and Gregoire convincingly support this contention when they state:

> *...we are all, in some way, wired to create and that everyday life presents myriad opportunities to exercise and express that creativity. This can take the form of approaching a problem in a new way, seeking out beauty, developing and sticking to our own opinions (even if they're unpopular), challenging social norms, taking risks, or expressing ourselves through personal style.*

[With all due apologies to these two authors, allow me to rephrase their initial sentence: "...we are all, in some way, wired to create and that everyday life frequently presents myriad obstructions, barriers, and blockades to that creativity."]

The hard reality is that most of us have been exposed to a tsunami of "creativity crushers" that have found a permanent lodging in our heads - a residency sufficient to block creative expression in our school work, our job, how we raise our kids, how we solve problems at work, and how we face some of life's inevitable challenges. These inhibitors have become sufficiently cemented into our consciousness such that we find ourselves encased in a mental "box" - one seemingly inescapable. We resort to an all too common response (both to ourselves as well as to others): "But, I'm just not creative." In short, we bemoan the fact that we are not creative without a full comprehension of what changed us from who we were (as kids building forts out of cardboard boxes or as superheroes out to save the world) to what we are (as adults wrestling with intellectual challenges and everyday conundrums).

4.

So, what's happening? Why aren't we more creative? Why do we fret and worry when we're asked to create some new product, new procedure, or new strategy, and our minds just won't cooperate. Why do we moan and groan and beat our heads against the wall? Why do we spend long nights (and equally long days) steaming and stewing over a problem with no apparent solution in sight? What got us to where we are now?

This book is about how we have been educated and influenced to see things. It's about the reasons why our natural creativity (the "stuff" we had as a kid) has been shackled, manacled, handcuffed, bound, and chained (now that we're adults). It's about the impediments that get in the way of creating dynamic new ideas in our businesses, home lives, social interactions, play-time, and problem-solving.

But, this book is also about the methods, techniques, strategies, and personal habits we can introduce into our daily activities that can mitigate the effects of all those "depressants" on our creative spirit. It's about ways we can reverse the inevitable consequences of our upbringing, our education, our work environments, and our personal beliefs and achieve a level of creativity that can dramatically and positively affect our lives and work.

In other words, when we understand the reasons why our "creativity spigot" has been reduced to a slow drip, we can begin to effect a dynamic change in our perspectives and in our thinking. When we have the diagnosis, we can effect the prescription. Efficiently. Dynamically. Permanently.

2.
Invisible Influences

Don't let the bastards grind you down.
- GENERAL JOE STILWELL

1.

2.5 million years ago the cranial capacity of our prehumen ancestors was about 36 cubic inches. Of course, life was much simpler then. The challenges faced by those early relatives were relatively simple (obtaining food, staying warm, finding shelter). Over time, as humans evolved, there was a concomitant evolution of the human brain. Today, we humans have a brain capacity of roughly 73-85 cubic inches. Quite naturally, the challenges we face today are significantly different and arguably more challenging than those faced by hominoids scattered across the Paleolithic landscape.[2]

It could be inferred that the capacity for creativity expanded exponentially in concert with the expansion of the human brain. Suffice it to say, our cognitive powers (deductive reasoning, idea generation, problem solving, experimentation) have evolved to a significant degree over the millennia. However, we are still challenged. Although few of us need to locate a new place to forage for berries or build a communal cookfire, we still need to deal with problems and conundrums that will have a profound effect on our children, our work, and our lives.

But, as we will explore throughout this book, there are forces that frequently mitigate against solutions or conditions that hamper our natural creativity. As a result, we feel constrained, restricted, inhibited, and limited when faced with a question, conflict, problem, or

---

2 Trying to figure out why the Denver Broncos can't contend for another Super Bowl is a good example.

confrontation. We are aware that our creative spark has been tempered or extinguished altogether. We were playful and creative as children, but as adults, we become conscious of the fact that what we may have enjoyed as children has been considerably sublimated and quashed.

In his seminal book, "The Origins of Creativity," the preeminent biologist and naturalist Edward O. Wilson, asks, "What, then, is creativity?" For Wilson, it is the innate quest for originality. "The driving force is humanity's instinctive love of novelty - the discovery of new entities and processes, the solving of old challenges and disclosure of new ones, the aesthetic surprise of unanticipated facts and theories, the pleasure of new faces, the thrill of new worlds." He goes on to confirm a basic and inherent focus of human life - discovery and exploration. His thesis is based on a common assumption - one proven by decades of psychological research. That is, all humans are inherently curious, passionate explorers, and filled with lots of "whys?" In short, we are driven to explore and thus driven to create.

Least we think that creativity is the province of a few or a human development years, as opposed to eons, in the making, Wilson provides substantial evidence that this trait has been evolving for almost one hundred thousand years. Suffice it to say, humans have been wrestling with the concept of creativity for a long time. As such, it has been viewed as a power, a force, a process, and, of course, a conundrum.

Early humans, in their rush to escape a would be predator, as well as modern day individuals eager to woo new clients for their entrepreneurial enterprise, have all considered creative possibilities. The Paleolithic woman attempting to save her life while pursued by a saber-toothed tiger intent on some prime meat needed some sort of creative escape (an acacia tree with low-hanging branches, a stony escarpment with a deep cave, an abandoned termite mound) just as much as an entrepreneur designing an on-line store featuring beauty secrets for young girls needs a way to capture ever-changing desires. They are both products of their own creative spirit...or lack of that spirit.

But, just as some of our hominoid relatives lost that foot race with a starving and very rapid feline, so too does the 30-something wring her hands and beat her head against the wall when attempting to design a web site that will appeal to the often fickle buying needs of pre-teenagers.

That creativity has been a constant of human civilizations is both clear and constant. That it also defines who we are as *homo sapiens* - rational, thinking, and cognizant individuals - is both a biological and psychological certainty. However, the evolution of creativity comes with a caveat. That is, there are forces at work that tend to suppress our natural creativity - conditions that have a negative impact on our ability (and agility) to invent creative responses to our immediate environment.

Interestingly, that process starts early in our lives. The exigencies of life as promulgated by adults (our parents, relatives, and teachers) are pushed on us at a young age. We are steered towards expected behaviors and standardized thinking. Our creative impulses (in which the "results" are seldom sure or certain) are crushed rather than encouraged. We grow up into adults who celebrate those early years, but bemoan their evolutionary and psychological extinction. Creativity guru Sir Ken Robinson puts it this way, "Creativity is the greatest gift of human intelligence. The more complex the world becomes, the more creative we need to be to meet its challenges. Yet many people wonder if they have any creative abilities at all."

This book seeks to explore some of the most prominent (albeit invisible) forces that negatively affect our ability to generate creative thoughts and solutions ("I'm just not creative!"). It also offers a cornucopia of techniques and strategies to overcome those invisible forces - offering opportunities that can transform us back to the once creative individuals we were as children. For the sake of convenience, I have divided the book into four large categories: childhood, education, workplace, and daily living. The implication is that creativity depressants (and necessary creativity enhancements) occur systematically throughout our lives, from the time we are born up to the present day. That we should recognize them concurrently is a testament to their overwhelming significance in our personal lives.

2.

Childhood. Every year, thousands of kids sit in psychologists' offices and take a test. The test isn't designed to determine if they have any psychological issues or personality disorders. Rather it is a test to determine just how creative they may be. Known as the Torrance Tests of Creative Thinking (TTCT), it is a 90-minute series of discrete tasks that, over the years, has been taken by millions of children worldwide in at least fifty languages. Following is a small sample of the types of questions (not the actual questions) that appear on the test:

Question #1
Say, "Here are some drawings. When I say 'Go' take your pencil and try to make each figure into something else. You can make your drawings big or small, simple or with lots of detail. It's all up to you.

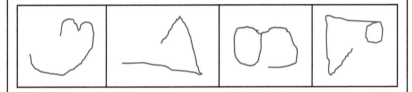

Question #2
Say, "Look at this drawing. How do you think this happened? What do you think will happen next?"

Question #3
Say, "How many different ways can you think of to use a chair?"

Question #4

Say, "Suppose you could have one super power. What would it be? Why would you want to have that particular super power?"

Question #5

Say, "Listen to this nursery rhyme. How would you solve the old woman's problem?"

There was an old woman
Who lived in a shoe.
She had so many children,
She didn't know what to do.

You will quickly note that this exam is quite different from the typical standardized tests ("fill in the bubbles") you took in school. In essence, there are no pre-determined responses - children are welcome to suggest a multiplicity of answers. The test is scored using thirteen criterion-referenced measures which include: emotional expressiveness, story-telling articulateness, movement or actions, expressiveness of titles, syntheses of incomplete figures, synthesis of lines, of circles, unusual visualization, extending or breaking boundaries, humor, richness of imagery, colorfulness of imagery, and fantasy.

Kyung Hee Kim, a researcher at the College of William & Mary, analyzed more than 272,000 scores of both children and adults who had taken the tests between 1966 and 2008 in all regions of the United States. She discovered that creativity scores were on the rise between 1966 and 1990. Since, then, a significant and continuous decline in scores has occurred - most notably in children from Kindergarten to sixth grade - a decline that has not abated in the intervening years.

"Americans are less creative today than they were twenty-five years ago. Furthermore, this decline continues with no end in sight - Americans continue to become less creative over time," Kim writes. She goes on to state, most emphatically: "To me, the most troubling aspect of this decreasing creativity is its prevalence in young children who should be actually improving their creative attitudes and skills. Not only that, but years after the study came out - despite all the concerns expressed by politicians, educators, and business executives - not much has changed. In fact, the decline in creativity continues unabated."

3.

Education. John Barrel, an educator in New Jersey, outlines a series of expectations that students have about how classrooms are run and what students do in those classrooms. See if these sound familiar to you:

➤ The teacher "teaches" and the students "sit and listen" or "learn" passively.

➤ There is one "right answer" to any question, and it is in the textbook or the teacher's head.

➤ The answer to most questions can be given in one or two words, and the teacher won't challenge you to go much deeper.

➤ Books and teachers are always "right," and we learn only from them, not any other resource in the room, such as classmates.

➤ If we wait long enough, a teacher will answer his/her own question, and we won't have to do much work. The teacher is the only one worth listening to.

➤ If we ask enough questions about a difficult assignment,

we can get the teacher to make it a lot easier and less demanding.

➤ If I memorize enough facts, I can get a good grade.

➤ Most tasks and tests will demand recall of isolated pieces of information, and I will not have to show how ideas are related.

Barrel calls these conditions the "hidden curriculum" - or that set of assumptions and expectations students traditionally have about education. As you look over these statements, you'll quickly notice that they are, for the most part, indicative of passive classrooms. By that, I mean they are the result of teacher-directed learning environments in which students have little input, little involvement, and little engagement.

More disturbing, is the fact that these "practices" sufficiently inhibit and quash creative thinking such that, as students progress through the educational system, their curiosity and innovative thinking (that was so much a part of their childhood), becomes increasingly diminished as they advance from grade to grade. As a result, students infer several "principles" about their educational experiences.

First, students often believe that getting the right answer is more important than thinking about a diversity of possibilities. By focusing only on single right answers, they frequently self-inhibit the creative-thought process. Second, students often believe that they must play by an inviolable set of rules - those established by the teacher. True, there are principles and rules that are essential to a well-functioning classroom. However, students often internalize these and think these rules of order are also rules of thinking, too. Third, many students are very concerned about a "fear of failure." That is, students' self-concept is affected when they get too many wrong answers. Thus, when students believe they might get a wrong answer, they are reluctant to venture any type of answer. Their creativity and thinking "shuts down" and they are hesitant to suggest any type of solution to a problem.

In 2012, the research firm StrategyOne conducted a cross-international study of five thousand adults from five different countries (the United States, England, Germany, France, and Japan). One thousand people in each country were surveyed about their views on creativity.

When the results came in they revealed a global creativity gap among all five countries. The research showed that approximately 80 percent of all the people surveyed felt that unlocking creativity is critical to economic growth. The belief was that economic engines are powered primarily by creative energy and without that "fuel" there is very little progress. By the same token, nearly two-thirds of all the respondents (irrespective of country) felt that creativity is valuable to society. It is something that society embraces, reveres, and celebrates. It is necessary for both personal and national advancement.

But, something else also surfaced from that survey: a striking minority – only about 25 percent – believe they are living up to their own creative potential. When queried, those same individuals indicated that the biggest culprit for that lack of creative spark was their country's education system. In the United States, 62 percent of the respondents felt their creativity was stifled by the education system. Even more interesting was the fact that in each of the five countries surveyed, more than half of those surveyed feel that creativity is being quashed by their education systems.

Ken Robinson puts it this way: "One of the problems is that too often our educational systems don't enable students to develop their natural creative powers. Instead, they promote uniformity and standardization. The result is that we're draining people of their creative possibilities and, as this study [by StrategyOne] reveals, producing a workforce that's conditioned to prioritize conformity over creativity."

4.

Workplace. For a moment, imagine you are the Product Manager for a very large company that manufactures a range of clocks - everything from minute timers to alarm clocks to enormous clocks on enormous towers in enormous cities. It has been brought to your attention that the alarm clock division is suffering mightily. Your biggest competitor - the Justin Tyme Clock Company - has increased its market share by 53 percent over the course of the past three quarters. Your division, on the other hand, has seen profits plummet by 21 percent over those same three quarters.

You decide to call an emergency meeting of your R&D folks to see what can be done. You gather all eight people together in the Board Room at 9:00 on a Monday morning and with desperation in your voice (your job is on the line, after all), and a dozen donuts on the table, you announce the following:

"Listen up, everyone. We're in serious trouble. The folks over at Justin Tyme are killing us with their new line of alarm clocks. Their profits are soaring while ours are tanking. If we don't do something quickly, we're going to have to close down the division and put a lot of people out of work."

"So, here is what I want you to do. I'm going to divide the eight of you into two teams. I want each team to spend the day brainstorming for any and all possibilities for a new, innovative, and exciting new alarm clock that will take the market by storm. Each team will submit their best idea to me by 9:00 tomorrow morning. The team with the best idea will earn a bonus of $5,000 to be divided equally between all members. Ready? Let's go!"

A typical scenario? You bet! But, if you take a close look at the paragraph above, you'll see that the speaker (you) has pushed three common myths about creativity onto your employees (brainstorming, "immediate inspiration," and a financial reward). Unwittingly, you have significantly depressed, minimized, and crumpled the creative output of your workers in less than 100 words. It is highly unlikely that any significant creative product will result from this "meeting of the minds."

While there is considerable value placed on creativity (by society in general and our boss specifically), there are also contradictory workplace forces in play which tend to sublimate and eradicate our creative desires. There are, not surprisingly, several beliefs, practices, and habits deeply ingrained in our professional lives that mitigate against creative expression. The things our supervisors believe, the ways in which managers assign tasks, and the comments we make to each other in the workplace often influence (negatively) how successful (or not) we are in engaging our creative side to address common issues or inevitable challenges.

Conclusions drawn from several research studies demonstrate common patterns in many sectors of the business world. Michael Roberto, Director of the Center for Program Innovation at Bryant University outlined them as follows: "Experts reject ideas and prefer to defend the status quo. Technical specialists exhibit closed-minded behavior when newcomers challenge the conventional wisdom or question established practices. Newcomers experience pressure for conformity. Leaders create an environment where people with new ideas fear speaking up. The organizational culture does not promote experimentation and risk-taking behavior. Rewards and incentive systems focus on efficiency and productivity, and they discourage learning and exploration."

Author Derek Thompson writes, "...in the past sixty years, something strange has happened. As the academic study of creativity has bloomed, several key indicators of the country's creative power have turned downward, some steeply." Thompson goes on to detail how research and development spending has declined by two-thirds as a share of the federal budget since the 1960s. What is most concerning is the realization that many corporate managers are complaining about a decided lack of creative enterprise, but are equally reluctant to address (and correct) the attendant issues that have led to this creativity chasm. It would be similar to seeing large clouds of smoke coming from the exhaust pipe of your car, but never finding the time (or having the inclination) to take it into your mechanic's shop for some repair. In time, your car will do something you really don't want it to do: it will stop!

A few years ago, GE interviewed a thousand senior business executives in twelve countries. They found that "95 percent of respondents believe innovation is the main lever for a more competitive national economy and 88 percent of respondents believe innovation is the best way to create jobs in their country." But the most stunning findings were about the kinds of innovation that will be the most important - and the differences between the innovations of the past verses what they are likely to be in the future. A remarkable 69 percent of the respondents agreed that "today innovation is more driven by people's creativity than by high-level scientific research." And 77 percent agreed, "the greatest innovations of the 21st century will be those that have helped to address human needs more than those that had created the most profit...." Most significant was that 58 percent of all respondents said, "more 'out of the box' thinkers on the team was the number one factor in helping companies innovate."

A Conference Board report stated: "U.S. employers rate creativity/ innovation among the top five skills that will increase in importance over the next several years, and stimulating innovation/creativity and enabling entrepreneurship is among the top ten challenges of U.S. CEO's." In a subsequent McKinsey & Company global survey, 84 percent of executives say "innovation is extremely or very important to their company's growth strategy."

Although business leaders are increasing their demands for more innovative people, current thinking points to the sobering conclusion that corporate creativity is on the decline. In many cases, it appears as though the prevalent solution to this creativity crisis is nothing more than a lot of hope, patience, and best wishes.

5.

Daily Living. You are constantly influenced by forces both invisible and unknown. Your attraction to a potential life mate, your preference for one car model over another, and even the brand of cereal you buy are all dictated by unseen powers over which you may have little control.

But, be careful! That brand of cereal you buy may not be the result of its taste or how many times it is advertised on Saturday morning cartoon shows. It may be influenced by the floppy-eared rabbits, swashbuckling pirates, and perky little leprechauns on the front of the box.

Particularly when they look at you.

Researchers at the Cornell Food and Brand Lab demonstrated that the characters on the front of cereal boxes are drawn in such a way as to create eye contact with potential customers. That eye contact is designed to help build brand loyalty with potential customers. The researchers examined over eighty-five different characters on sixty-five brands of cereal. They discovered that the cereals on the top shelfs in the cereal aisle of a grocery store have characters staring straight ahead or slightly up in order to make eye contact with adults. The cartoon characters that populate cereal boxes on the lower shelves have their gaze focused slightly downward in order to create eye contact with youngsters.[3]

In one of the tests, the researchers showed one of two versions of a Trix cereal box. One version had the rabbit looking down; the other test had the rabbit making direct eye contact with youngsters. The results revealed that brand trust was sixteen percent higher and the connection to the brand was ten percent higher when the rabbit made eye contact. The implication is that when the Trix rabbit makes eye contact with you, then you are more likely to put that rabbit (and the box on which he appears) in your shopping cart...or, at least your child will gleefully toss that box into the cart. If a character on a box higher on the shelf (presumably on a box of healthy and nutritious cereal) makes eye contact with you, then you might be inclined to include that box in your cart, too.

It is clear that we are manipulated by forces we cannot see. In large measure, we've been influenced by our parents, our teachers, and our work environment to set aside our natural creativity in favor of a predictable, standardized, and convenient way of thinking. Our inherent creativity (what we had as kids) has been sufficiently compromised that we believe that it no longer exists - that we have self-assigned ourselves to a class of people known as the non-creatives. "But, I'm just not creative!" we lament. The creative pursuits of our youth are suppressed in our (adult) quest to raise a family, hold down a job, pay our taxes, and fit into society.

The basic theme of this book is that we were all once creative, we have all experienced unseen forces that quash those instincts, and we all have the potential to regain the creative spirit of our youth. With that in mind, let's take a look at a fascinating research project initiated in 1968. As part of the study, researcher George Land administered a creativity test to 1,600 four and five-year-olds. The test had been specifically designed to identify innovators for engineering and design positions at NASA. Land administered the test two more times to the

3 The researchers also confirmed that cereals specifically targeted to children are placed at about twenty-three inches off the ground while cereals aimed at adults are placed at forty-eight inches off the ground.

same groups of children - when they were ten-years-old and when they were fifteen-years-old.

The scores of the children were compared with a sample of over 250,000 adults who also took the assessment. An examination of the percentage of test-takers who scored at the highest level of creative imagination in each of the two samples revealed some interesting information. Ninety-eight percent of the five-year-olds scored at the highest levels of creativity; thirty-two percent of the ten-year-olds did; and ten percent of the fifteen-year-olds did. Most striking was that only two percent of the adults attained the highest level of creativity.

This revealing study demonstrates that many adults have lost their creative impulses over time, but it also hints that they still have the raw materials to regain that creative spirit. The conclusion to be drawn is that when our creativity is not nurtured systematically over time, it diminishes. The good news for all of us is that we have the capacity to regain that spirit.

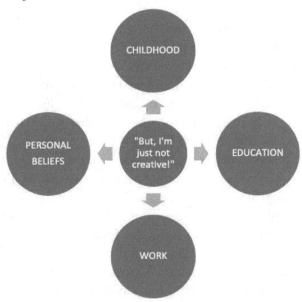

Creativity involves breaking out of established
patterns in order to look at things
in a different way.
- Edward de Bono

PART TWO
Once Upon a Time
We Were Children

3.
Parental Persuasion

The creative adult is the child who has survived.
- URSULA K. LE GUIN

1.

In the summer of 2018, I was diagnosed with a compressed nerve in my neck. My orthopedic surgeon scheduled me for an MRI in order to pinpoint the precise location of the problem and provide necessary data for some upcoming surgery. As you may know, an MRI uses a strong magnetic field and radio waves to create detailed images of specific organs and tissues within the human body. If you've ever had an MRI, you know they are noisy, confining, and somewhat uncomfortable. But, they are also lifesavers. And, for that, we can thank Isidor Isaac Rabi.

Isidor was born in 1898 in what is now Poland. He and his family emigrated to the United States and settled on the lower east side of Manhattan. As a youngster, he was always interested in science - reading science books and building his own radio sets. In 1916, he entered Cornell as an electrical engineering student, but quickly switched over to chemistry. He also developed a fondness for physics. He continued his studies at Columbia University where he was eventually awarded his doctorate.

In 1929 Columbia offered him a faculty position. His early interest in the magnetic susceptibility of certain crystals led him to research and develop techniques for using nuclear magnetic resonance to discern the magnetic movement and nuclear spin of atoms. For his distinguished career, Rabi received many awards and honors. These included the Elliot Cresson Medal from the Franklin Institute, the King's Medal for service in the Cause of Freedom from Great Briton, the Barnard Metal for Meritorious Service to Science, the Niels Bohr International Gold Medal, the Four Freedoms Award from the Franklin and Eleanor Roosevelt Institute, and the Vannevar Bush Award from the National Science Foundation, among others. It was for his work on nuclear magnetic resonance that he was awarded the Nobel Prize in Physics in 1944.

After his acceptance speech for the Nobel Prize, he was asked about some of the major influences in his life. He told the story about how he grew up in Brooklyn. When his friends all came home from school, their parents always asked them, "What did you learn in school today?" However, when Isidor came home from school each day, his mother always asked him, "Izzy, did you ask a good question today?" He told how that single question from his mother every day helped him develop the inquisitive mind necessary for academic success and his eventual scientific discoveries.

It has often been said that parents are a child's first and best teachers. Without question, our parents provide us with the basic foundation on which successful learning experiences can be built. The support, encouragement, patience, and understanding of our parents have a profound effect on both our academic and social development. Indeed, when parents are involved in the academic affairs of their youngsters, students' scholastic achievement mushrooms significantly. This is equally true for elementary students, middle school students, and high school students.

As parents ourselves, we also want to protect our children from the injustices of the world, from physical and emotional harms, and from the inevitable failures we all experience in the course of growing up. Sometimes we take that protection to the extreme, unconsciously instilling in our kids a sense that there are creative people in the world and that there are other people who are not, or cannot be, creative. Let's take look:

Eight-year-old Landon loved science. He devoured science books in the library, was an active and energetic student in all the science activities his teacher, Mrs. Morrison, shared in class. He constantly talked about new scientific exploration and discoveries he found on the internet. He was almost jumping out of his skin when his teacher announced the school's first science fair to be held in February.

Landon was particularly fond of geology and he decided to create a simulated volcano that would erupt (using vinegar, red food coloring, and baking soda) in a cataclysmic display of volcanic power. The science fair judge was a Biology professor from the local college, so Landon knew his project would get a thorough scientific evaluation.

Landon worked for several days on his project and he and his father transported it to the school on the designated date. He set it up on a table, arranged some plastic dinosaurs around the base, and got his materials in order. During the judging process, the professor walked throughout the gym writing notes about each of the eighty-six projects. Landon noticed about five other volcanos, several solar system models, some live animals (butterflies, worms, ants), and a smattering of the usual electricity and mechanical projects. He was confident he was going to get, at the very least, a blue ribbon, and was seriously hoping he just might get the "Best of Show" trophy.

When the judge announced the winners, not only did Landon not get the trophy (it went to a girl who demonstrated the reaction of earthworms to various types of soil pollutants), he did not even receive a ribbon. Landon was devastated. When his parents picked him up, they knew they had to say something.

What would you say?

Carol Dweck, in her book *Mindset* (which we will discuss in later chapters) says that, "There is a strong message in our society about how to boost children's self-esteem, and a main part of that message is: Protect them from failure!" She cautions that while such a response may help a child in the short term, it has serious repercussions for that child in the long term - particularly in regards to his creative spirit.

So, let's take a look at what Landon's mother said: "Landon, I know how you feel. You are very disappointed that you worked on your science fair project and didn't win a ribbon or trophy. However, you know, you haven't quite earned those awards yet. There were many students there who worked longer and harder than you did. There were students who put a lot of time and effort into their projects. So, if this is something that is important to you, then it will be something you will need to work on...something you will really need to work for."

Landon's mother then asked him a very critical question, one we often forget to ask our children when they pursue an academic challenge. Here was her question: "Landon, what do you think you will need to do in order to succeed in next year's science fair?" This question is critical on several levels: 1) It shows Landon that the responsibility for success is up to him, no one else; 2) It gives Landon choices - he is the one who will decide the level and amount of work necessary for success; 3) It sends a powerful signal that his success is in his hands - a judge, a parent, a teacher, or another student does not determine it. This is self-determination at its best; and 4) Landon's creativity is not based on what others think, but rather is determined by his own investment in an academic task.

Educators often refer to this as constructive criticism. It does not judge, it does not demean, it does not blame. It says to children that their creative spirit is alive and well and that it is up to them to use it in academically satisfying ways. By using adult logic or unfairly shielding our children from inevitable failures, we are doing more harm than good. If we fail to encourage the personal responsibility essential to creative efforts, our children may grow up to become adults unwilling or unable to engage in innovative problem solving.

2.

Unlike driving a car, hunting for deer, fishing for rainbow trout, or just getting married, there is no license required to be a parent. We may read bestselling books ("How to Be the Perfect Parent and Raise Perfect Children Who Grow Up to Become Perfect Adults"), consult an ever-increasing array of internet resources ("Potty Training in 327 Easy Steps"), and turn to our friends for advice ("Joyce, Brenda here. The baby's been smiling at me a lot lately - do you think anything's wrong?"), but for the most part, we "fly by the seat of our pants" and learn while on the job. Such is the nature of parenting.

Consider that what we say to our kids has long-term repercussions in both their personality development as well as in their interactions with others.[4] Our advice, discipline, and counsel has a profound effect

---

[4] Like this creative tweet from @maryfairybobrry (posted 5:05 ? Aug 10, 2019): 8 - "Mom, where do babies come from? Me - "From backrubs Honey."

on how our children develop social, personal, and academic skills. Child psychologists agree that emotionally-charged comments, over time, can actually change the structure of children's brains. Ultimately, those comments can also significantly impact our children's creative spirit. Here are some of the things parents sometimes say to their children - inadvertent comments that have a decided influence on kids' innate creativity.

"You're so smart" - When your child does well on a homework assignment, gets a 100 percent on a spelling test, or submits a paper with glowing comments and a big bold **A+** at the top, you want to verbally reward her by commenting on how smart she is. Your intent is to boost her self-esteem and let her know that she has have been positively recognized for her efforts. Actually, the opposite is usually true. When a child is told she is smart she tends to internalize that label and, as a result, she feels compelled to defend this label. As a result, she may shy away from challenging academic tasks simply because if she did poorly on those tasks she wouldn't be deserving of the "smart" label. She often takes the easy way out and eschews challenging academic tasks for fear of not being "so smart." As a result, her creativity suffers because she is less likely to take risks and more apt to play it safe.

"Good job" - Variations on this include "Well done," "Excellent work," "You are a terrific student," and "That's what I mean by good work." In small doses these are not particularly detrimental to a child's creative spirit. But, they are frequently so overused that they send the wrong signal - a feeling of always being judged by others. Instead of pleasing themselves, children who receive a lot of these judgmental comments often feel an obligation to please others. Doing something that gets the approval and praise of others becomes more important than doing something according to one's own initiative. Being creative doesn't always get accolades; being compliant frequently does. If there is no one around to praise a child, children often lose the incentive to do anything at all. Their creative spirit has been sublimated in favor of (their need for) a verbal commendation.

"Why didn't you get an A?" - It's perfectly OK to have high expectations for our children, but we shouldn't expect perfection every time they are engaged in a learning opportunity. When parents utter this comment, what children hear is something like, "I guess I'm never going to be good enough in the eyes of my parents. Every time I try something, I'll probably disappoint them." Their creativity suffers greatly because the message they hear is "Learning about something implies mastery of that subject." Creativity, on the other hand, is all about exploring possibilities, not necessarily becoming an expert in those topics when first encountered.

"You're making me sad." - Growing up is often challenging and difficult. So much to learn and so much to understand. Why should we impose our personal feelings on our children? Comments like this tell the child that they are responsible for their parents' happiness (or lack of happiness). That's a pretty heavy burden for any child to carry... often throughout their lives. Most of all, it's unfair and undeserved. Creative impulses are stopped dead in their tracks because of the possibility of a negative reaction from parents.

"Why can't you be more like your brother/sister?" - Comparisons are always dangerous, particularly for young children. When a child is compared to a sibling, neighbor child, or classmate it usually sets up the other child as an ideal model - a model that your child will never emulate or aspire to. This, as you might expect, instills a sense of inadequacy in your child and typically makes her feel as if she will never be good enough. Fostering creativity is more successful when children are invited to work towards their own unique potential, not the "standards" of other children.

"That's not good enough." - Imposing our own standards of performance on children can be detrimental to their initiative and drive. It tells kids that perfection can only be achieved when we satisfy the wishes of others, rather than satisfying our own self-initiated objectives. Kids quickly get the idea that others' expectations are more important than their own. As a result, creativity diminishes exponentially.

"You're smarter than that." - A certain way to tell kids they aren't good enough is to equate intelligence with creativity (If you're not smart, then you can't be creative.). Telling kids they aren't smart enough restricts their self-concept as well as their willingness to try new things. It imposes a synthetic label on children that, quite frequently, lasts throughout their lifetimes.

"You can do better." - Again, we set artificial standards when we tell our children that their performance doesn't always meet our expectations. While this comment sounds like praise on the surface, underneath it gives children a sense that they are out of control; that their creative desires should be sublimated in favor of the wishes of others. Often kids infer that they are not perfect and that they will never be perfect. So, why try?

"You're doing that wrong." - Learning is not about achieving perfection; it's all about becoming engaged in an experience including experiencing all its attendant mistakes, gaffes, boo-boos, stumbles, and mis-directions. Creativity is not about being right the first time we try something. It's also about persistence in the face of the inevitable "hiccups" that naturally and normally occur when we try something new. Creative people are not perfectionists; rather they are persistent to a fault. They'll keep trying in spite of the hurdles along the way.

"I really don't think you can do it." - This effectively stops any creative effort in its tracks. What kids hear is, "I don't believe in you," or "I don't have any faith in your abilities." This comment effectively saps their strength, promotes discouragement, shuts down their determination, cancels their motivation, quashes their tenacity, and nullifies their creative spirit. In essence, it tells kids that creative expression is not important and will, most likely, go unrecognized.

'You're such a disappointment." - Wow, what a label to hang on kids who are just setting out to explore the world and examine new learning opportunities! This single comment may do more to stifle creativity than any other. It tells children that no matter what they do, they'll always be a failure...so why even try? All the incentive for creative exploration is virtually sucked out of their lives - never to return. Making mistakes is not a life sentence; it is a unique part of the learning process.

"Can't you do anything right?" - Learning is often a bumpy road. We fall down a few times when learning how to walk, we tap (or hit) things when learning to drive, and we make some inappropriate comments in the early chapters of our personal relationships. Eventually we learn from those mistakes. However, when children hear words like "never," "everything," and "anything" they get the message that not only did they mess up in one activity, but that they also mess up in all activities. As you might imagine, this sublimates their desire to investigate, explore, and examine the world around them. Why take a chance learning about something if there's an equal chance you are going to be called out about that experience.

Inadvertently, and often unconsciously, we use statements such as those above as ways of helping our children develop into productive and successful adults. The reality, however, is that statements such as these are often detrimental in terms of initiative, developing personalities, self-concepts, and educational success. In many ways, these statements place a label (or a series of labels) on children - labels that have a long-term impact on their creativity and innovative thinking.

Pam Nicholson, a certified parenting educator with The Center for Parenting Education cautions that assigning labels to children (via verbal comments) has significant effects on their developing personalities and overall emotional health. She mentions four hazards: 1) Labels stick to children. Children are taking in information all the time. A label becomes something permanent in a child's mind because it was "assigned" by a (supposedly) knowing adult; 2) Labels speak to children. A child assigned a specific label ("Are you always that lazy?") will perceive herself as such and live down to that label; 3) Labels cost children. Labels can damage the parent-child relationship over time. Often, parents tend to see their child through the lens of that label; and 4) Labels are difficult to remove. Labels often achieve permanency. We often see ourselves according to the labels others have assigned us. We frequently carry that label throughout our lives.

What is equally compelling is the idea that once we have been assigned a label (either positive or negative) it's difficult to break away from it. It becomes difficult to explore other options, examine other possibilities, or pursue other interests. Labels inhibit our creativity because they often put us in a class that is not creative ("Why can't you be more like your brother?") or assign us to a group that becomes, not only self-fulfilling ("You obviously don't have the 'smarts' for math."), but often permanent. How many of us remember a label we were given - either from our parents or a teacher - a label we have carried with us well into adulthood?

For many children, those labels become psychological boxes: inhibiting, restrictive, and crushing. They tell children what others perceive them to be (rightly or wrongly) and, eventually, what they will believe themselves to be - not only in childhood, but as they grow and mature into adults. As you will note, most of those labels are creatively restrictive. In essence, they say that utilizing your creative talents may not be a viable option for you. You are expected to perform *this* way, not *your* way. Dr. Thomas Armstrong, with the American Institute for Learning and Human Development, unequivocally puts it this way: "Creativity can't thrive in an atmosphere of judgement."

Go back to the list of parental comments in this section and ask yourself a few questions. How many of those comments were part of your childhood? How many times did your parents use those phrases during your upbringing? How do you remember those comments? With anxiety? Fear? Trepidation?

3.

Danika was seven years old and had just received a package of 1000 multi-colored wooden craft sticks for her birthday. Her father (Jerry) knew how much Danika loved her doll Rapunzel (with the requisite long hair and complementary jeweled crown). Danika let it be known that Rapunzel should have a "tower" to live in and so the bundle of craft sticks gave her the opportunity to construct a tower to her own specifications.

But, the craft sticks were tricky. As soon as Danika got them stacked up (on their sides) to a height of about 10-12 sticks, the pile toppled over, leaving Danika frustrated and upset. This happened time after time. Her cat Muffin laid at the end of her bed and watched all of these proceedings with an overwhelming sense of aloofness and indifference.

After several days had passed, Jerry walked into her room as Danika quietly began another new tower only to see it fall over once again. Jerry sat cross-legged on the floor and took a small handful of craft sticks. He began building his own tower alternately laying the sticks in a criss-cross pattern at a 90 degree angle. His "tower" grew as Danika watched in rapt attention.

The next day, Jerry had to work on a leaky pipe under the kitchen sink, so Danika brought her craft sticks into the kitchen and piled them on the table. She began to build a new tower, but watched, as time after time, the towers continued to fall over. Jerry offered verbal support, but never came out from under to sink to build the tower for her.

On Saturday, Jerry and Danika got in the car and went for a drive throughout the city. They talked about the various buildings they saw along the way and how they might have been constructed. Near the downtown area was an historic log cabin preserved from Revolutionary War times. Jerry parked the car nearby and the two of them went for a stroll around the classic building. They talked about how the building might have been constructed and why the logs were in certain configurations. Jerry encouraged Danika to ask questions and to look at the all the surrounding buildings as various models of what good construction might entail. When they returned home, Jerry contacted a young architectural student in the neighborhood who talked with Danika about some simple construction techniques that architects use when designing new buildings.

Return to Danika's bedroom. Danika, slowly but surely, became more adept in building her tower. She was able to interlock the craft sticks in a unique pattern that allowed her to create a tower that began to soar ever upwards. One foot. Two feet. Three feet. The tower stood firm and with Rapunzel placed next to it on one side and Danika on the other, it made for a most delightful "selfie." Muffin was noncommittal, but Jerry had an enormous smile on his face. So did Danika.

This is the ending we hope for whenever our children encounter any learning task. We want them to be successful. We want their dreams to come true.

But, oftentimes we get in the way. Oftentimes we put verbal or psychological barriers in front of our children and, as a result, we impair or interrupt their creative instincts. Jerry was careful not to do that. Let's take a closer look.

Jerry invited Danika to ask her own questions. Oftentimes we believe that as adults we should be asking all the questions. When we do so, we take away the element of "ownership" from our children. When children are given chances to ask questions, they are given opportunities to "possess" the challenge. In turn, they are more motivated to solve the challenge via their own initiative. As a result, creativity is enhanced when children are given an opportunity to embrace that challenge as theirs. Without that ownership component, children become dependent on others to solve their problems.

As parents, we often have a tendency to think that, as mature adults with a bevy of lifetime experiences, we always know what's best for our children. We're older and thus smarter, so let's just eliminate all the frustration and angst from any new venture by telling them exactly what they should do and how they should do it. We'll certainly save lots of time and aggravation. But, as you might imagine, we also create a monster along the way: we take away a problem-solving opportunity. By injecting a "father knows best" attitude, we tell children that adults will always "save the day" with their enormous bank of knowledge. Children are denied the opportunity to learn things for themselves. The teacher (Dad) will always be around to tell us how to do it.

As we will learn later in this book, many challenges in our lives have multiple ways of "solvability." There's seldom a single right answer (usually the answer in the parent's head) to solving an issue or conundrum. Jerry knew this instinctively, and so took his daughter on a "field trip" around the city so she could see a wide variety of construction examples . He gave her the opportunity to talk with a college student to understand some basic architectural principles. He never said which way was the best, or which way was the "only way" to build a tower for a doll with very long hair. He gave Danika an opportunity to look for herself, ask for herself, and decide for herself any potential options. More important, he gave her the time to try out those options on her own.

Viewing life through creative eyes can be an integral part of the maturation process. But, let's face it: it's difficult to create the conditions that make that happen in our busy, hectic lives. We want to help our children become successful adults, but often we get in the way of that process. We tend to want to do too much for them - imposing our adult views (and adult knowledge) when, in fact, they need time and opportunity to discover those for themselves. In many ways, creativity needs support, rather than direction. As parents, we're often prone to tell our children what to do, thus robbing them of valuable opportunities to discover the intrinsic role of creativity as a normal and natural way of viewing (and solving) the world.

In 1987 a group of researchers in California began a long-term study of the homes and families of creative children. They also looked at the contrasting attitudes and behaviors of parents whose children were deemed to be less than creative. The following table represents the beliefs and practices of parents who had a negative impact on children's innate creative spirit:

PARENTS OF LESS CREATIVE CHILDREN

Attitudes These Parents Have:

➤ I teach my child that in one way or another punishment will find him when he is bad.
➤ I do not allow my child to get angry with me.
➤ I try to keep my child away from children or families who have different ideas or values from our own.
➤ I believe that a child should be seen and not heard.
➤ I feel my child is a bit of a disappointment to me.
➤ I do not allow my child to question my decisions.

What These Parents Did When Trying to Teach Their Child a Task:

➤ Tended to over-structure the tasks.
➤ Tended to control the tasks.
➤ Tended to provide specific solutions to the tasks.
➤ Were hostile in the situation.
➤ Were critical of the child; rejected the child's ideas and suggestions.
➤ Appeared ashamed of the child, lacked pride in the child.
➤ Got into a power struggle with the child; parent and child competed.
➤ Gave up and retreated from difficulties; failed to cope.
➤ Pressured the child to work at the tasks.
➤ Were impatient with the child.

Psychologist Teresa Amabile at Harvard Business School, in responding to the study, writes:

"Homes that nurture creative children are homes where both adults and children have 'creativity habits.' Very creative people have formed the habit of questioning what they see, taking new perspectives, finding new ways of doing whatever they do, and just simply creating as often as they can. You can make creativity a habit by constantly asking questions such as: How can we do this differently? Is there another interpretation? What does this mean? What else might it mean?"

Mihaly Csikszentmihalyi, a distinguished and respected psychologist, provides convincing evidence that the encouragement a child receives from parents and other adults in her world is considerably more influential (in terms of creativity development) than her basic academic talent. In his book, *The Systems Model of Creativity*, he provides a wealth of empirical research demonstrating that when parents and other adults do not devote time and energy to youngsters' overall development, they also significantly depress creative inclinations necessary in both work and life. Additional research, conducted in 2012, carries this one step further and demonstrates a direct relationship between parental style and the development of creativity. The investigators discovered that a permissive parenting style (with encouragement) had a positive effect on creativity development while a more authoritarian parenting style (often characterized by negativity) tended to depress creativity to an appreciable degree.

The implication is clear: when we, as parents, fail to offer our children psychological support in combination with opportunities to become actively engaged in the learning process, there is a negative impact on the development of their creative thinking abilities. The long-range consequences are also clear: what we say and do as parents often determines whether our children will view themselves - later in life - as creative individuals.

But (as you might expect), there are other factors that also impact the creative inclinations of our children.

Like cardboard boxes!

4.
How to Sizzle: 1 - 9

1. 3-2-1. Over time, children often get the idea that education is the accumulation of knowledge, rather than a process of utilizing that knowledge in making sense of the world in which they live. One way you can help your children think beyond the memorization of simple facts is to challenge them each day with the "3-2-1 routine." Here's how it works: When your kids get home from school take five minutes and ask the following:

A. 3 - "What are three questions you asked today?"
B. 2 - "What are two things you learned today?"
C. 1 - "What is one thing you would like to learn more about?"

Make these questions a regular and planned occurrence and your children will discover that learning can be a creative exploration of information. Equally important, they will begin to understand that education is not necessarily something that is done to them, but also something that offers an opportunity to take an active role in the learning process. That "ownership" lays a solid foundation for future creative journeys.

You might want to take this idea one step further and invite your children (particularly those in middle school and high school) to ask you a critical question when you get home from work ("Hey, Dad, what questions did you ask at work today?"). What a great way to role model for your kids!

2. Yes Over No. According to at least one children's counselor, the average child hears about 432 negative comments (or words) every day vs. 32 positive comments (or words). For a moment, image if 93 percent of the feedback you received at work every day was negative. Would you be discouraged? Frustrated? At a loss to do anything creative? When you think about it, comments such as "No, you can't do that," "Don't go in there," and "That's not a good idea" are uttered far too often. "No" statements put kids into a box: "yes" statements allow kids to explore outside that box. Think about how many times you give negative responses to your children. Is it to an excess or is there a balance between the negative and the positive? You may want to do some self-recording of your responses - keep on ongoing tally. What comments could you modify or adjust? Instead of saying, "No, you can't do that," what might be an alternate approach - one that doesn't employ the word "no."

3. Process Over Product. Often, when kids do academic assignments (including homework) they are frequently focused on the final product ("I've got to get this project done by tomorrow." "I have to do 25 multiplication problems and then I'm done." "As soon as I read Chapter 8 I can go out and play with the guys."). A focus on the products of our work, rather than the processes necessary to do that work often diminishes the creative work necessary for successful accomplishments. The object, in both school and our professional lives, is to get something done. Without attention to the thinking that goes into those efforts, we have significantly diminished the importance of creative intervention in accomplishing our ultimate goals. As your children initiate projects, or work on homework assignments, consider asking some of the following questions:

➤ "What will you need to do in order to complete this successfully?"
➤ "Tell me about the steps you will need to follow for this assignment."
➤ "This seems like a challenging assignment. What will you need to think about to get it done?"

➤ "Please help me understand some of the ways you could solve this issue."

➤ "Everyone learns in a different way. Which way do you think will work for you?"

4. Check Your Comments. Be aware of how you respond to your child's academic work. Comments such as "You're so smart" and "Why didn't you get an A?" actually depress a child's future achievement. They also tend to foster a more external locus of control, which, in the long run, will have consequences in their professional lives. Instead, invite your children to self-assess: "How do you think you did on that math test?" "What is causing you the most difficulty in Chemistry? How might you meet that challenge?" When children are offered opportunities to self-assess they develop the confidence to proffer their own thoughts and ideas - a good first step to a creative life.

5. Reduce The Verbiage. Not surprisingly, when kids and adults are together, adults do most of the talking, explaining, and teaching. In many situations, adult talk takes up 80 percent of the time together. Think about the last time the family took a car trip or visited relatives. Who did most of the talking? Who initiated most of the questions? Who came up with most of the answers? Instead, offer children more opportunities to ask questions, suggest solutions, solve problems (verbally), discuss interpretations, share ideas, and initiate conversations. Support and encourage their verbal skills. Oh, talking while they're playing a game on their iPhone or while you're responding to a text message don't count.

6. Family Dinners. It has often been said that the most important piece of furniture in any home is the dining room table. This is a place where family members can just talk about their day, inject their own opinions about the world they see, and listen to the thoughts and musings of others. The free flow of ideas, without condemnation, is a terrific stimulus for creative thinking. This is also a wonderful opportunity for children to get and receive acclimation for their contributions - particularly when parents invite them to share their views of the world or ask them questions that have no right or wrong answers ("What are some ways you would design that new space vehicle?" "I wonder what those buffalo do when there are no humans around."). Make family dinners (and family conversations) a regular and normal part of the day. No cell phones, no TV, no music - just a good meal and some good conversation. The results, over time, are transformative.

7. Give Kids Choices. Don't tell your children what they should do or think all the time. Offer them choices whenever practical. "Would you like to go to the park, the museum, or the lake today?" "Do you think we should get a dog, a cat, or a bird for a pet?" "What would you like for dessert tonight: ice cream, a cookie, or an apple?" All children can benefit intellectually from making their own choices. Often, when our choices are restricted, our creativity is too. When children feel comfortable in making choices throughout their lives, they will also feel comfortable in creative endeavors as well. They will begin to understand that life is not about getting right answers all the time (as determined by others), but also about creating, inventing, and initiating their own answers. The more choices kids have while growing up will help them immensely in making creative decisions as adults. Kids (and adults) will learn that selecting from a pantheon of possibilities is an important part of the creative process.

8. Give Them Time. Perhaps the most important resource you can give your children is time. Creativity is fostered when kids have lots of free time - time to create, imagine, play, think, wander and do things without a lot of adult supervision or direction. It also means a lot of time without commercial products (toys, games, cell phone apps), but rather sufficient opportunities to turn common objects such as kitchen utensils, hardware from the garage, old sheets and cardboard boxes, scraps of wood, discarded clothing, or a large ball of string into all sorts of imaginative playthings. Consider getting a very large box (labeled as the "Imagination Box") and tossing in all sorts of used or discarded items every now and again. Invite your children to reach in, select one or two items and play with them for a while. What can they invent, what can they imagine, and what can they make up on their own?

9. Positive Everyday Comments For Your Kids.

➤ "You really worked hard on…. You must be very proud of yourself."

➤ "Look. You're getting better at…."

➤ "Can we start over?"

➤ "I know we can fix this together. Tell me what you're thinking."

➤ "I love you and know you are doing the best you can."

➤ "It looks like you're having a difficult time. Can you tell me about it?"

➤ "Everyone makes mistakes. That's how we learn."

➤ "Your opinions matter to me. Tell me what you're thinking."

➤ "We are a team and I will always have your back."

➤ "Thank you for reminding me how much fun it is to learn."

➤ "Your ideas are unique. Tell me more."

➤ "It was really helpful when you…."

➤ "It looks like you're learning a lot about…."

➤ "OK, if we start over?"

➤ "What do you think you learned from this?"

➤ "Maybe today's not the right day. Can we try again tomorrow?"

➤ "Yup, learning is all about asking lots of questions."

5.
Creative Endeavors

*I don't think outside the box; I think what can
I do with the box.*
- Anonymous

1.

One December, our son, his wife, and their 17-month-old daughter (Amelia) journeyed from Colorado to visit us in Pennsylvania for about a week. Since they were limited in regards to the number of toys they could bring along, we decided to create some playthings that would keep Amelia engaged and entertained while she was with us.

My wife and I had just purchased an oversized storage cabinet which arrived in a very large cardboard box, now residing in the basement. As we looked at the box just prior to the visit, we both came to the same conclusion: "Let's transform the box into a house." So, we turned the box upside down and with utility knife in hand, we cut out a small door on one side and a window in each of the two ends. We didn't decorate it or add any frills to this cardboard dwelling.

As soon as Amelia arrived, the first thing she noticed was the box (Of course, it was "conveniently" placed in the middle of the living room.). It became her constant plaything the entire week she was with us. Dolls went in and out of the house on a regular basis. A large stuffed Santa sat on the roof and "guarded" the house from all manner of nefarious creatures. Pop-Pop (me) stuck his head in the windows and through the open door - playing an endless series of "peek-a-boo" and other games.

We provided Amelia with a box of crayons and she "decorated" the house as only the imagination of a 17-month-old can do. There were scribbles along one wall, lines and circles over the roof, and an apparently incoherent (to adults) series of marks, scratches, and figures that adorned the interior walls.

During the entire visit, the cardboard house was a constant source of joy and pleasure for our granddaughter. She never tired of the imaginative activities invented on the spot. She was able to crawl in and out of the house at will - becoming a character just like the stuffed bear, over-sized Minnie Mouse, and several cat toys that occasionally took up residence in and out of her cardboard house.

She had simply created her own environment - a private universe inhabited by inanimate objects that took on imaginary personalities, did impossible tasks, and moved in creative ways. The fact that her grandfather was a co-conspirator in these escapades only served to heighten the fun and frivolity. In her mind, it was the best toy ever created. She never stopped giggling. She never stopped playing.

The cost of one cardboard box: $0.00. The value of imagination: priceless.

I'm sure you'll agree that the natural uninhibited playfulness of children is a joy to watch. When kids are engaged in activities they can self-direct and control, their imaginations soar and their creativity mushrooms accordingly. This is elastic thinking - thinking unfettered by the logic or practicality of adults. As adults, we are conditioned (often by social norms) to focus on practical matters, such as paying our bills on time, stopping at octagonal red traffic signs, and watering our house plants on a regular basis. But, for children, anything is possible and anything goes. A cardboard box becomes a house, a funnel becomes the nose cone for a supersonic rocket, and a cat (most reluctantly) becomes a fierce jungle creature who pads around a tropical landscape. Kids are, by nature, uninhibited and free...until they turn into adults.

It is during that maturation process that children are creatively affected by numerous events that assail their inherent creativity. Those situations can have negative consequences as those same children grow up, get educated, enter the work force, and deal with a range of intellectual challenges and problems.

Let's take a look.

2.

*You can discover more about a person
in an hour of play than in a year of
conversation.*
—PLATO

Noted child psychologist Jean Piaget once said, "Play is the work of childhood." It's something kids do naturally and without inhibition. Gather a group of kids together in a park or on a playground and they will naturally turn to play as a way of entertaining themselves and engaging in meaningful social activities. Play is both physical and mental fun - an uninhibited way of discovering the world around that is both satisfying and fulfilling.

But, play also appears to help kids become more creative. In one classic study, researchers divided ninety preschool children into three separate groups. The first group was invited to play with several common objects including a collection of paper clips, a pile of paper towels, a wood board, and a screwdriver. The second group of children watched an experimenter play with the four items and then they were asked to duplicate exactly what the experimenter did. The final group was given some paper and drawing instruments and invited to illustrate anything they wanted without ever seeing the paper clips, paper towels, screwdriver, or wooden board.

Each of the groups participated in their assigned activities for approximately ten minutes. At the conclusion of each set of activities, the children were asked to come up with some creative ways on how the items could be used (other than the standard and expected uses). The experimenters noted that the group of children who played with the four items came up with, on average, about three times as many creative uses for the items as did children in the other two groups. The conclusion drawn was that play is an essential ingredient in the development of creative thinking.

The value of play in our lives and on the development of creative thinking has been validated by other researchers who have shown how it is instrumental in healthy brain development, particularly with regards to the promotion of new ideas and ways of pursuing those ideas. Play, particularly free play (play without rules or restrictions), encourages kids to initiate and create innovative activities, imaginative scenarios, and dynamic possibilities. In many ways, play challenges a child's developing brain in ways that organized and formal games cannot. Fantasies are invented (warding off a fire-breathing dragon), kingdoms are created (a castle surrounded by a moat filled with very hungry alligators), and space exploration travel is possible (establishing a human colony on the surface of Neptune, with the usual assembly of protoplasmic aliens).

Yet, despite all the benefits of play on the enhancement of creative thinking, it is being significantly reduced in the lives of children. Data from the American Academy of Pediatrics shows that children's free-time play dropped by a quarter over a 16-year period. Perhaps even more disturbing is the fact that as the federal government and school districts advocate for higher scores on standardized tests, more than thirty percent of American schools have eliminated recess or are considering eliminating it from the elementary curriculum. The Academy also notes that a national survey of 8,950 preschool children and parents found that only 51 percent of children went outside to walk or play once per day with either parent.

In place of recess, schools are spending more time on test-taking skills, structured academic activities to beef up overall test scores, and added instructional tasks geared for "at risk" students. For many districts, recess time is considered wasted time. It can't be tested, it saps valuable instructional time, and it's risky.

The reduction in recess time and the concomitant escalation of instructional time denies children significant opportunities to discover, use, and strengthen their creative powers. More information may be crammed into their heads with more hours devoted to formalized instruction. But, kids have less opportunities to use that knowledge in innovative and imaginative ways. The imaginative time is being reduced such that creativity is sublimated in favor of content. Children are thus deprived of experiences that mesh with and enhance their developing brains.

There is convincing evidence that a play-deprived childhood is a first step on the road to a creativity-deprived adulthood. Play is not a compliment to childhood, it is an essential and necessary ingredient of childhood. Play allows curiosity, imagination, and innovation to develop and grow. That growth establishes a critical foundation upon which future creative endeavors can stand and prosper. Without play, a child's cognitive growth is stunted and her creative opportunities limited.

And, as we'll learn later, the same holds true for adults.

3.

I was trying to daydream, but my mind kept wandering.
- STEVEN WRIGHT

Go into your memory bank and recall a time in school when you were daydreaming. Perhaps it was during a particularly boring lecture in a high school history class. Or, maybe you were drifting off while your fourth grade teacher shared some meaningless information about photosynthesis in science class. Or, perhaps your mind wandered all over the place during a required assembly when the principal droned on and on about how to walk in the hallways.[5]

Maybe you recall an incident or two as an adult when you daydreamed during a "necessary" and "very important" staff meeting (and you drifted off to a tropical island and a romantic encounter with a very attractive and very sexy movie star). Or, what about that time you were sorting through some mundane paperwork at your office desk (and you began thinking about that very sexy movie star). Or, how about the time when you were sitting by yourself in your department's conference room aimlessly toying with a container of Greek yogurt (and thinking about that very sexy movie star).

All too often, we think of daydreaming as something negative ("Young lady, isn't it about time you rejoined our little discussion here?" or "Earth to Tony, Earth to Tony! Come in, please!"). The thinking is that people who daydream aren't paying attention, they aren't mentally engaged, and they aren't processing any of the "required" information. But, what if I told you that frequent daydreaming may be a sign of intelligence and creativity?

---

5 Or, perhaps, like certain authors, you did all three.

When kids daydream, they often conjure up imaginary plots that have them sailing pirates ships across uncharted seas, galloping over a frozen tundra to challenge an evil ruler, piloting an enormous space vehicle to a distant world far beyond our own solar system, or assuming some incredible super power that allows them to magically disappear or toss lightning bolts from their eyes. When adults daydream, we often think about encounters with a sexy mov...well, never mind!

But, how does daydreaming aid our creative impulses? According to psychologist Eric Klinger it may be because the waking brain is never really at rest. Klinger posits that floating in unfocused mental states serves an evolutionary purpose. That is, when we are engaged with one task, mind wandering can trigger reminders of other, concurrent, goals so that we do not lose sight of them. Other researchers suggest that increasing the amount of imaginative daydreaming we do (or replaying variants of the millions of events we store in our brain) can be creatively beneficial simply because it allows our minds to wander across imaginative landscapes not normally a part of our logic or normal habits of convergent thinking. Daydreaming expands our horizons.

Daydreaming is an important mental activity, especially if we pay attention to it. In one study, researchers asked 122 students to read a children's story and press a button each time they caught themselves tuning out. The researchers also periodically interrupted the students as they were reading and asked them if they were "zoning out" or drifting off without being aware of it. They concluded that, "What we find is that people who regularly catch themselves - who notice when they are doing it - seem to be the most creative." The results also demonstrated that individuals scored higher on a test of creativity in which they are asked to describe all the uses of a common object, such as a brick. Daydreamers were able to compile longer and more creative lists. "You need to have the mind-wandering process. But, you also need to have the meta-awareness to say: 'That's a creative idea that popped into my head.'"

Another study, this from the Georgia Institute of Technology, also suggests that daydreaming may not be such a bad thing. The researchers suggest that frequent daydreaming may be a sign that you're really smart and creative. In this particular study, researchers measured the brain patterns of more than a hundred people while they were in an MRI machine. The participants were instructed to focus on a stationary fixation point for five minutes. The team used the data to identify which parts of the brain worked in unison. The prevailing research suggests that these same brain patterns measured during these states are related to different cognitive abilities. Once they figured out how the brain works together at rest, the team compared the data with tests the participants took that measured their intellectual and creative ability. Participants were also asked to complete a questionnaire about how much their mind wandered in daily life.

The results were, to put it mildly, quite interesting. There was a strong correlation between those individuals who reported more frequent daydreaming and their scores on intellectual and creative ability tests. The MRI results supported the conclusion that these individuals had more efficient brain systems. "People tend to think of mind wandering as something that is bad. You try to pay attention and you can't," said Eric Schumacher, one of the study's co-authors. "Our data are consistent with the idea that this isn't always true."

But, there is a cautionary note here. These findings demonstrate a correlation between our daydreaming and creativity, not a cause and effect. There may well be other variables at work. However, it's fair to assume that daydreaming, from a creativity standpoint, is a good thing. It's not something we should prevent as children and adults engage in intellectual tasks. Having one's head in the clouds is an opportunity to let an individual's creative powers develop and flourish. This is mental play at its finest - a potent exercise in which innovative thinking is supported and celebrated.

Raised in an environment of "Stop daydreaming and get back to work," kids often get the message that they shouldn't be using their minds to think creative things. Rather, the over-riding lesson is that thinking is reserved primarily, if not exclusively, for logical (not imaginative) thoughts. Thus, daydreaming is viewed as something to be avoided; something that has no place in a formalized educational setting. It's something bad for your brain. The message is clear: when you're not paying attention, you're not...well...you're not paying attention! How can you possibly learn? How can you possibly engage in any productive and meaningful work?

4.

Every child is an artist. The problem is
how to remain an artist once we grow up.
—Pablo Picasso

Imagine waking up one morning to find a glob of sticky goo stuck in your hair. And, then, as you get out of bed you trip on something you left on the floor. While in the bathroom, you accidentally drop your favorite blouse into the sink (while the water was running). And, then, at breakfast the only thing available is stale cereal. On your way to work you get an upset stomach and are on the verge of vomiting. Shortly after arriving at work your boss tells you that the project you've been working on isn't "up to standards" and your best friend refuses to talk with you because of something you said yesterday.

It's very clear that you are having a terrible day. A horrible day. A no good day. A very bad day!

If this scenario sounds familiar, it should. It's the basic plot line from a classic children's book: *Alexander and the Terrible, Horrible, No Good, Very Bad Day* by Judith Viorst (1972). In the book, the central character - a young boy named Alexander - is having a less than spectacular day. He gets gum in his hair, he trips over his skateboard, he doesn't find a prize in his breakfast cereal, he gets "smushed" in the car pool to school, there was no dessert in his lunch box, an elevator door closes on his foot, and a host of other tragedies made for a less-than-enjoyable day. Evil forces are definitely working against him.

But, one of the memorable moments in the book, revolves around art class. Viorst writes, "At school Mrs. Dickens liked Paul's picture of the sailboat better than my picture of the invisible castle (a blank sheet of paper)."[6]

I think we can all agree that exposure to the arts (music, art, dance, drama, design) exposes kids to various expressions of creativity. Youngsters get to see how others have interpreted the world around them in dynamic ways. So, too, are children exposed to models of creativity

---

6 Many years ago, after a read-aloud of *Alexander and the Terrible, Horrible, No-Good, Very Bad Day*, I showed a group of young students a blank sheet of paper and asked them what it was. Here are a few of their responses: a blizzard, the top of a polar bear's head, a painting to be hung in an igloo, a rectangular pool filled with white toothpaste, what a really tiny person sees when standing inside a mound of mashed potatoes, and (the kids' favorite) vomit from a snowman.

- individuals who have viewed their environment in innovative ways. Youngsters quickly learn that the ways in which art is expressed may differ from individual to individual - it is neither right or wrong, it is just...different.

Equally important, youngsters are offered opportunities to creatively express themselves in numerous ways. This is particularly true when they are introduced to the arts in an exploratory way - where they can experiment and venture into undiscovered territories. They can create their own individual pieces, their own individual interpretations. There is no "right" or "wrong" here, rather there are possibilities. According to at least one expert, arts education encourages children to ask questions ("What if I made the sky purple and red instead of 'same old, same old' blue?"), to use their imaginations ("Let's create a drum set from these empty coffee cans."), and to see learning as something more than memorizing facts and taking tests (In the classic children's book *Amazing Grace* by Mary Hoffman, a young black girl tries out for the (male, white) role of Peter Pan in the class play.).

The multiple advantages of arts education has been confirmed by numerous researchers. First of all, it stimulates children to explore the world in which they live in dynamic and expressive ways. It has been cited as critical in advancing a creative interpretation of events and conditions often cloaked in dry facts and dull presentations. Arts education enhances problem-solving skills - it offers youngsters the opportunity to tackle both intellectual and personal challenges in divergent ways. In so doing, it improves their judgement and demonstrates that there are often multiple perspectives in tackling an issue. Most important, however, arts education encourages inventiveness, fosters innovative thinking, and promotes divergent points of view.

For a moment, let's choose one element of arts education: music. Think about the music you like to listen to. For me, it's the rock and roll classics of the 1960s and 1970s. For my wife, it's the classical music she tunes to on our local NPR radio station. What's your choice: country western, hip hop, techno, rock, folk music, dubstep, classical, jazz, rhythm and blues, or electro? What is it about that genre that turns you on, gets you excited, releases all those positive endorphins, or makes your foot tap under the table at a local restaurant? What if I told you that, no matter what musical genre you prefer, the more you listen to it, the more you are impacting your creative thinking?

In a novel experiment, participants were asked to engage in several creativity exercises that measured divergent and convergent thinking. Individuals were divided into two groups. The first group completed their activities in complete silence; the other group listened to music during the various activities. The results demonstrated that individuals who listened to "happy music" (music they preferred) had significantly higher scores on measures of divergent thinking than those who had performed their tasks in complete silence. In other words, the "Happy Music" group generated more ideas, as well as more creative and innovative ideas (as rated by people unfamiliar with the study's aim). In writing up the results of this study, the researchers suggested that music "enhances the cognitive flexibility needed to come up with innovative solutions - the ability to switch between different concepts and perspectives, rather than seeing a problem from a rigid point of view."

Other studies have reported similar findings relative to arts education. In one four-year study, students participating in regular music classes were found to have changes in their brain structures that helped them transfer their motor skills to other areas. Another study found that when students practiced a specific art form, the efficiency of their attention network became more efficient and their fluid IQ scores increased dramatically. Scientists at Johns Hopkins University shared findings showing that arts education can help rewire the brain in positive ways. The prevailing conclusion among a vast majority of cognitive scientists is that arts education is a critical ingredient in the development and support of creative thought.

Why, then, are the arts being eliminated from our schools?

The reasons are threefold. First, budget cuts are a financial reality for most school districts across the country. Public investment in K-12 schools has declined dramatically in many states over the last decade. Worse, some of the deepest-cutting states have also cut income tax rates, weakening their main revenue source for supporting schools. And, often, the first to fall are arts programs. As of this writing, less than half the schools in Detroit, for example, have full-time arts instructors; two-thirds of New York City's elementary schools and half of American schools overall have no art or music teachers. Due to budget constraints, fewer schools today offer art classes today than a decade ago.

Second, there is an increasing emphasis on core subjects. Federal initiatives such as No Child Left Behind and Common Core State Standards have placed educational emphasis squarely on the improvement of math and reading scores on standardized tests. With the emphasis on improving test scores (which improves a school district's ability to secure more state and federal funding), school districts are reallocating their funds towards reading and math instruction - frequently at the expense of arts education.

Since the arts aren't tested (as a result of state and federal mandates) their funding has decreased significantly. The result is that arts education has been severely reduced in many schools and completely eliminated in others. Many youngsters go through their twelve years of public school education without ever having experienced an art or music class any time in their scholastic lives. The clear message to many kids is that creative expression or development is unimportant in their overall educational experience; thus, why should it be important in their adult lives?

Third, there is often a racial undercurrent in who receives the benefits of arts education and who doesn't. According to some recent data, minority children were two times less likely to have access to school arts programs than their white peers. The number of minority children receiving regular arts education while in school has been steadily declining over the last several decades. A recent survey by the National Endowment for the Arts (NEA) demonstrated that only 26 percent of Hispanics received any arts education, in comparison to 28 percent of African Americans and 59 percent of whites. Moreover, 3.9 million public elementary school students do not have access to visual arts classes and 1.3 million public elementary school students have no access to music classes.

These declines are both predictable and continuous. Many minority children attend schools in poor neighborhoods and in under-performing districts. This puts pressure on those schools to meet the same academic standards (via standardized testing) as do higher performing districts. Schools that fail to meet those standards are assigned to program improvement status that focuses academic improvement solely on the basics (e.g. math and reading), to the exclusion and elimination of arts education. With a reduction in funding coupled with a lack of administrative support, the arts become a pedagogical byproduct. They are often reduced and frequently eliminated from the curriculum. Once eliminated, they are rarely restored.

Eliminating or significantly reducing arts programs in American schools doesn't, in and of itself, reduce overall creativity. Rather, it reduces the <u>importance</u> of creativity in one's life. Many students quickly get the impression that thinking logically is much more important than thinking creatively. They sense that the purpose of school is to deliver lots of factual information and to make sure that they (the students) use that factual information to get high scores on standardized tests. Convergent thinking takes precedence over divergent thinking. The overriding consensus is that school curricula are, for the most part, based on helping students accumulate data, rather than manipulate data. Product is more important than process.

The consensus of researchers is that the reduction or elimination of arts education negatively impacts our embrace of creative thinking. But, here's the flip side: When we as parents, grandparents, teachers, day care workers, playground supervisors, camp counselors, and recreation leaders offer sustained and regular exposure to the arts throughout a child's life we can effectively mitigate the decline of art in our public schools.Think about it: Ventures to art galleries and museums, after-school art programs, along with regular opportunities to draw, illustrate, create and listen to music, dance, and participate in plays offer youngsters the chance to see art as an enthusiastic enhancement of creative thinking...and creative doing. Arts education - whether in formal school settings or informal family excursions - opens up creative possibilities and creative expression. Excluding it from childrens' growth and development is more harmful (from a creative standpoint) than beneficial. Former First Lady Michelle Obama puts it this way: "...Arts education isn't something we add on after we've achieved other priorities, like raising test scores and getting kids into college. It's actually critical for achieving those priorities in the first place."

The same holds true for butterflies and forests.

6.
How to Sizzle: 10 - 18 ‖‖‖‖

10. See = Be. Marian Wright Edelman, Founder and President of the Children's Defense Fund, once said, "You can't be what you can't see." In short, in order to be good at something we need positive role models in our lives. Without those models, we are often unsure of what it takes to be competent and successful in one's chosen field. Young girls, for example, need to see female scientists in action if they wish to become a scientist, too. Young baseball players need to see professional baseball players in action if they are ever to achieve success in baseball. A young musician needs to see trained and dedicated musicians in action to get a sense of what it takes to be a competent musician. The same holds true if we want our children to be creative throughout their lives: we need to provide them with multiple and sustained opportunities to see creative people in action. In short, take your child to an art gallery, a musical concert, a woodworking exhibit, or a tap dance recital to see what creative people do or create. Provide opportunities for your children to talk with creative people: carpenters, landscape architects, commercial artists, professional authors, glass blowers, guitar players, weavers, craftspeople, or even the next-door neighbor who knits caps for newborns at the local hospital. Offering your child numerous opportunities to view and discuss creative endeavors is a powerful stimulant for their own creative development.

11. Simple Lesson. Want to be more creative? Think like a child, not like an adult. Children are creative; adults are logical. Adults know what works and what doesn't work. Children, on the other hand don't know what they can and cannot do. So, they go out and try. Adults have a tendency to repeat things that don't work over and over again (or as a wise philosopher put it, "Insanity is doing the same thing over and over again and expecting different results each time."[7]). A child, on the other hand, doesn't know what works (and what doesn't) and so, tries it out just to see what happens. Pretend you're doing something for the first time. See what happens. Pablo Picasso was walking home one day and saw an old rusty bicycle seat and handlebars lying on the side of the road. He took them home, stuck them together, and created a sculpture of a bull. Just like a child would do. Climbing inside the mind of a seven-year-old (for example) sounds crazy, but there are lots of practical ramifications...and some very interesting research to back it up. A study by Darya L. Zabelina and Michael D. Robinson found that when participants were instructed to imagine themselves as seven-year-olds with copious free time, they performed significantly better in objective tests of creative thinking. The lesson: regression may be just as important as progression.

12. Simple Toys. Don't flood your home with lots of expensive and "educational" playthings. The simple fact is that most toys labeled as "Educational" seldom are. That's just a come-on to get you to purchase them. For the most part, they are used once or twice and then quickly forgotten. The best toys are the simplest. My three recommendations: a large empty cardboard box, a collection of wooden blocks, and an old sheet. Give them to your child and watch their imaginations run wild. In the same vein, invite your children to invent their own toys. What could they create with a several blocks of wood, a bucket of sand, a small shovel, and a hose? When kids have opportunities to create their own playthings, their creative spirit is both enhanced and celebrated. In short, don't always <u>buy</u> toys, invite children to <u>create</u> toys.

13. More Play Time. A recent study in England - commissioned by the National Trust - found that today's children spend half the time playing outside than their parents did. For many children, playtime is that part of the day when they're sprawled out on their bed playing

---

7 This quote is often mis-attributed to Albert Einstein. Interestingly, there is no evidence that Einstein ever said this.

games on their iPad or iPhone. Regular and sustained opportunities for physical play is critical to creative development and strong imaginations. Play allows children to invent, create, and innovate. Imaginary characters are developed, innovative rules are constructed, make-believe surroundings are invented, and pretend friends are conceived. Equally important: resist the current movement to reduce or eliminate recess in your child's elementary school. The consequences of a school day with no recess will have lasting effects on their creativity for years to come. As has been proven in study after study, a day without play can have serious repercussions for children's evolving sense of creativity both now and well into the future.

14. Beginning At The End. One semester, in a Creative Writing course, I challenged students by giving them a full and complete ending to a story (three paragraphs). I then invited them to write the beginning and middle of the story that would lead up to that conclusion. Next, I presented them with a two-paragraph middle of another story and invited them to write both the beginning and end of that particular story. Finally, I gave them the beginning and ending paragraphs of another story and asked them to write the middle part of that story (that would link together the beginning and end of the story). By the time class was over, students looked up at me – most with a smile on their face. They understood what I had done. I shook up their logical thinking (stories always start at the beginning, continue through a middle, and finish up with a satisfactory conclusion). As a result, the stories, while initially awkward to write, were more creative and decidedly more innovative. Young kids do this all the time - and are quite comfortable with the process.

Try the same thing with a project you're working on: write out the ending (your anticipated result) and then imagine the steps that would need to be accomplished to achieve that desired result. Write out what you think the middle of the project will entail. Set it aside and, then, a few days later return to your document and design the beginning and end. By shaking up your logic (or what your brain tells you is an accepted way of solving problems) you change your focus and help your brain see things that were hidden, or perhaps, illogical. Your stories (or projects) will be more dynamic and more clever.

15. Finger Paint. One of the best creativity stimulators you can share with your children is a set of finger paints. In fact, humans have been finger painting for more than 13,000 years (witness the cave drawings in Lascaux, France) – strongly suggesting that creative expression has been around for thousands of years. When children use finger paints it allows them to connect small motor skills, imagination, and other sensory functions into a piece of art that focuses more on the processes of creativity than it does the products. In short, what children create is less important than is the actual process of production. Finger painting stimulates creative expression – alerting kids to the power of their minds rather than the approval of parents or other adults. Finger painting allows them to create their own rules for expression. So too, does it give them "ownership" over their imagination and spirit of inventiveness. [Personal note: I have a finger painting done by my two-year-old granddaughter hanging in my office. It is vibrant, intense, and slightly surrealistic. I don't know what it is, but it sure is creative!].

16. Become The Idea. What if you became the product or idea you were working on? How would your perspective change? How would your immediate environment change? What new things would you see that you were not aware of previously? For example, imagine you are a trash can. How could you be easier to use? How would you clean yourself? How would you feel if everyone ignored you? Now, imagine yourself to be a jar of ground cinnamon. How would you stand out from all the other spices in the grocery store? What would attract attention to you specifically? How could you make sure you were noticed? Now, imagine you are a problem. How are you making life difficult for the people in the room? Why are you so persistent? How would you like to be changed? Enter a world of fantasy and become the idea and you'll gain new vision and new insights. For example, consider this quote from Albert Einstein: "When I examine myself and my methods of thought, I come to the conclusion that the gift of fantasy has meant more to me than my talent for absorbing positive knowledge."

17. Musical Perspectives. One of the best ways I know to generate lots of ideas – good ideas – is through music. I've often found that music, like art, can awaken the right side of the brain. When the right side is activated, then the left side feels "more comfortable" about its work. It tends to "do" better work. This is just a slight shift in perspective. It simply means that you should listen to lots of music – not necessarily the music you are most comfortable with – but rather the music that will stretch your senses and cause them to expand in some new directions. The trick is to immerse yourself in a style of music you wouldn't normally listen to. For example, I like old-time rock and roll (my playlist includes The Doors, The Eagles, Santana, Crosby, Stills, Nash, and Young, Dire Straits, Queen, The Traveling Wilburys, and Fleetwood Mac, to name a few), but typically don't listen to classical music or hip hop music. So, to get my creative juices flowing, I often listen to those styles of music so that my creative powers are awakened and stretched (I tend to be more perceptive with "unknown" music.).

18. Focus Your Daydreaming. You're in a business meeting and your mind wanders to the steak dinner you're planning for dinner tonight or the handsome "hunk" that just moved into the neighborhood or that Caribbean cruise you're hoping to take next year or to a thousand different things that have absolutely nothing to do with the content or direction of the meeting at hand. You catch yourself daydreaming (or your boss catches you with that faraway look in your eyes) and you mentally pull yourself back into the reality of what is going on in this all-important confab. You feel guilty for drifting or someone else makes you feel guilty for your cognitive detachment.

Interestingly, it is not unusual for us to spend between 25-50 percent of our waking hours daydreaming or mind-wandering during our waking hours. While daydreaming is frequently portrayed as a "mental black hole" where productivity is diminished or, quite often, extinguished, the opposite may, in fact, be true. According to researchers at the University of California, Santa Barbara, "...two types of daydreams - those that are personally meaningful and those with fantastical content - are associated with creativity."

The results of this extensive study of the daydreaming habits of 133 volunteers yielded the following results:

"In the lab, we found that participants who reported a greater tendency for meaningful or fantastical daydreams wrote more vivid and creative short stories. Outside of the lab, using experience sampling, we found similar results. Participants who often found their daydreams meaningful reported greater inspiration at the end of the day, and those who frequently reported fantastical daydreams reported more creative behavior."

The implications were straightforward. That is, the time we spend engaged in meaningful or focused daydreaming and the time we spend in thinking about fantastical alternative worlds might be ways of discovering new inspiration and renewed creativity. In short, daydream more about a project you are working on and you may open up the possibilities for increased levels of creative expression.

7.
Images: Natural and Artificial

Children need nature for the healthy development of their senses, and therefore, for learning and creativity.
— RICHARD LOUV

1.

When I was growing up in southern California, my father and I would take an annual fishing trip up into the High Sierra Mountains. Each August, we would pack up the car with camping equipment and fishing gear and head north out of Los Angeles on Highway 14. We would drive through the heat of the Mojave Desert, turn onto Route 395 and begin our ascent into the cool mountains of eastern California. This part of our journey took us through the poetic towns of Little Lake, Olancha, Lone Pine, Independence, Big Pine, and Bishop. We would eventually arrive at Mammoth Lakes and take a cabin for the night.

Early the next morning we would drive to the Mammoth Lakes Pack Outfit, hire a muleskinner, several pack animals, a few horses and set out for the remote reaches of Inyo National Forest. After a nine hour trek on sections of the John Muir Trail that wove in and among stands of lodgepole pines, pristine alpine lakes, and snow-capped mountain ridges, we would eventually arrive at Jackson Lake (AKA Grassy Lake). We'd set up camp and then, for the next two weeks we would walk long sinuous trails, fly fish crystal clear streams, search for wildlife both in the sky and across grassy expanses, swim in the cool waters of the lake, cook over an open campfire, sleep beneath the stars, and spend long hours listening to nature.

It was during these sojourns that my father and I invented "The Impossible Story." Each year the rules remained the same, although the stories always changed. The design was for one of us to begin telling a story with a brave and dashing hero as the central figure (e.g. "Jack Armstrong"). The intent was to create a set of circumstances from which it was virtually impossible for the hero to escape and then turn the telling of the story over to the other person. It was that person's task to extricate the hero from the impossible set of circumstance and then put him in another set of seemingly more impossible circumstances from which the other storyteller would have to devise an escape. Here is an abbreviated sampling of a story we may have shared one August night around a smoldering campfire in the majestic Sierra Nevada Mountains.

DAD: "Jack Armstrong was a pilot for an air transport company in Alaska. One day, while flying near the Arctic Circle, he noticed that he was low on gas. It was apparent that someone had sabotaged the plane; but there was no time to think about that because the plane had started a long slow dive toward the Arctic Ocean, an ocean inhabited by large and hungry sharks. Suddenly the fuel line ruptured and the tail of the plane burst into flames. Jack realized that he was going to crash into the cold, numbing waters of the sea below. Smoke began to billow into the cabin of the plane, making him dizzy and disoriented. The sharks circled below, the sea was unbelievably cold, and Jack was quickly losing consciousness." O.K. son, now the story is yours.

ME: "Jack crawled into the rear of the plane and quickly saw that the cargo consisted of thousands of handkerchiefs. Suddenly, he had an idea. Working quickly, he began tying the handkerchiefs together, and seconds before the plane crashed into the sea he was able to parachute to safety on a nearby deserted island. But then, he realized that he had no supplies and the frigid Arctic night was coming on. Suddenly, he felt a shaking beneath his feet. Looking down he saw that he was laying on the rim of an enormous volcano that was ready to erupt. The violent shaking knocked him into the mouth of the volcano - breaking both of his legs and his left arm. There was no way he could crawl to safety and he knew the volcano was set to explode within minutes." O.K. Dad, now it's your turn.

DAD: "Fortunately, his backpack landed beside him. With his right hand, he reached inside and carefully - and very slowly - pulled out...."

Each night, the story expanded with impossible episode after impossible episode. The plot became increasingly far-fetched and implausible as the main character was subjected to a never-ending series of events that would try the resourcefulness of even the most determined secret agent. We each tried to outdo the other in terms of drama, intrigue, and design. We reveled in the magic of these never-ending stories and in our desire to explore the outer reaches of creativity and inventiveness in a forested arena blanketed by millions of glimmering stars.[8]

We never knew how our stories would turn out or where they would take us, but that really didn't matter. What did matter was that we could enjoy some make-believe and fantasy, participate in an event without limits, and engage in a creative experience propelled by the majesty of a rippled mountain lake.

Little did we know we were engaged in an experience that had long-term implications...and a ton of research to support those implications.

2.

The Remote Associates Test (RAT) has been used by psychologists to assess various cognitive abilities linked to creativity. The test typically lasts forty minutes and consists of thirty to forty questions - each of which presents three cue words (that appear to be unrelated), but are linked by a fourth word, which is the correct answer. Here's an example:

---

8 It should be noted that we were creating these improbable tales long before the inception of the TV series *MacGyver* [1985-1992 and 2016-].

Cottage / Swiss / Cake
Answer: **Cheese** [cottage cheese, Swiss cheese, cheesecake]

Here are five other samples for you to try on your own. The answers are in the footnote at the end of the chapter.

1.	High / District / House	Answer:
2.	Wheel / Hand / Shopping	Answer:
3.	Catcher / Food / Hot	Answer:
4.	Food / Forward / Break	Answer:
5.	Dress / Dial / Flower	Answer:

How did you do? Did you find some items easier than others? Did you discover one or two items that were absolutely frustrating and, thus, unsolvable?

Several years ago, a fascinating study was conducted with the RAT. The researchers were interested in determining if there was any connection between exposure to nature and creativity. They selected fifty-six Outward Bound students - both males and females - and divided them into two groups. The first group took the Remote Associates Test before taking four-day hiking excursions in Alaska, Colorado, or Maine. The second group took the test after having spent four days on the trails of Alaska, Colorado, or Washington.

The results were startling: participants who took the test after four days in natural settings showed a 50 percent improvement in their creativity scores. Yes, 50 percent! The researchers concluded that "...there is a real, measurable cognitive advantage to be realized if we spend time truly immersed in a natural setting. The current work demonstrates that higher-order cognitive skills improve with sustained exposure to a natural environment."

Ruth Ann Atchley, a cognitive psychologist, and one of the researchers on this project, notes that modern-day humans are beset by a host of mental distractions and threats. She states, "They sap our resources to do the fun thinking and cognition humans are capable of - things like creativity, or being kind and generous, along with our ability to feel good and be in a positive mood. Nature is a place where our mind can rest, relax, and let down those threat responses.

Therefore, we have resources left over - to be creative, to be imaginative, to problem solve - that allow us to be better, happier people who engage in a more productive way with others."

Recall times in your youth when you escaped to a quiet environment (a treehouse, a fort in the woods, a slow flowing stream) just to be alone; just to contemplate an event in your life or a decision you had to make. You may have remembered how things seemed to slow down, how the air became peaceful and contemplative. Your mind was quieted, your pulse was lowered and your thoughts turned inward. Without all the usual distractions, you were able to refocus and recharge. The bombardment of stimuli was stilled and boundaries to your thinking were diminished. A "wide open space" (AKA: Nature) offered you an unfettered opportunity to think and, perchance, to solve.

Robin Moore, an expert in the design of learning environments, has written that these natural settings are essential for healthy child development because they stimulate all the senses and integrate informal play with formal learning. According to Moore, multisensory experiences in nature help children build "the cognitive constructs necessary for sustained intellectual development," and stimulate imagination by supplying the child with the free space and materials for what he calls children's "architecture and artifacts." He also emphasizes that "natural spaces and materials stimulate childrens' limitless imaginations and serve as the medium of inventiveness and creativity."

In short, nature excites our creative impulses. Nature propels us into imaginative frames of mind and dynamic ways of approaching the world. Consider our early human ancestors who evolved in East Africa over two million years ago. Theirs was an unknown environment - one that demanded creative solutions to a myriad of challenges. Tracking down a herd of hairy beasts, securing a habitation that offered both shelter and security, and surviving climatic variations that were random and often dangerous required a multitude of decisions and creative solutions. Not all of them worked, but in evolutionary terms, enough of them did to ensure that the species was able to expand and populate enormous tracts of North Africa, Europe, and Asia. To survive in nature *Homo sapiens* needed creative solutions, learned over hundreds of generations, that propelled them both physically as well as intellectually.

Today, children are subjected to vastly different kinds of environments - both natural and artificial. The wide open grasslands, thick steamy jungles, and parched savannas of our ancestors have given way to the asphalt-covered playgrounds of urban America and sterile gymnasiums of both private and public schools. The contrasts are not only visual, but are also creatively influential in ways our Pleistocene relatives could never have imagined.

To prove that hypothesis, researchers in the United States, Sweden, Canada, and Australia examined the way children played in both green areas as well as manufactured areas. Not surprisingly, they found that a more natural schoolyard stimulated more creative forms of play, including more fantasy and make-believe. A greater sense of wonder also evolved from the play observed in green areas versus that in more structured environments.

Those creative pursuits involved playing with action figures and dolls; role playing on imaginary battlefields and planets, and in mythical landscapes with fairies and queens; elaborate jump-rope routines; constructing buildings or objects from loose materials, and exploring the environment. Children set free in a natural world examine possibilities and embrace experimentation more so than they would in an arena of manufactured jungle gyms and steel-ribbed monkey bars. Early *Homo sapiens* also examined possibilities and embraced experimentation...and survived quite well!

We take our kids to an urban park for a picnic and a game of catch, we help them build towering sandcastles on a vast stretch of beach, and we vacation in a national park to gaze at vistas both awesome and beautiful. We may think those natural environments are only creatively beneficial for youngsters, but a series of qualitative interviews with Danish professionals tapped into adults' creativity, their individual relationships to nature, as well as their experience in nature's ability to stimulate their creative impulses. Chief among the findings was the fact that nature does, indeed, influence our creativity. This is true for adults as much as it is for kids. Nature seems to be part of our genetic code - no matter our age or evolutionary standing.

For example, imagine a time when you walked alone on a beach or took a stroll along a forest trail. Your mind was (temporarily) freed from the constraints of an overburdened schedule and a seemingly endless parade of deadlines. You may have concluded, as did another group of researchers, that nature has the ability to evoke a creative way of thinking by making us more curious, able to embrace new ideas, and stimulating us in becoming more flexible thinkers. "Nature is the great visible engine of creativity, against which all other creative efforts are measured," said Terrance McKenna in a talk in the early nineties. "Nature's creativity is obviously the wellspring of human creativity. We emerge out of nature almost as its finest work of art. The productions of nature. And human creativity emerges out of that."

I don't suppose that walking around a city with a metal cap on your head and various wires plastered to your forehead would be a fun way to spend a weekend. But, a group of researchers in jolly old Edinburgh, Scotland did and they discovered something quite remarkable as a result. They gathered together a group of average citizens (presumably individuals who are not self-conscious about multiple wires draped over their heads), attached each of them to a mobile electroencephalography (EEG) machine, and sent each of them out on a 25-minute walk through one of three different environments. One was a shopping street, another was a path through green space, and a third was a street in a busy commercial district. As each person strolled through their designated space the EEG equipment provided continuous data on five different channels: labeled excitement (short-term), frustration, engagement, long-term excitement (or arousal), and meditation.

It quickly became evident that when the subjects moved through the green space area they exhibited lower arousal, engagement, and frustration. They also showed higher levels of meditation in those same areas. So, what's the connection to creativity. Well, when our prefrontal cortex (the region of the brain involved in planning complex cognitive behavior, decision-making, and personality expression) is quieted, our brain's default mode turns on and is activated. As a result, flashes of inspiration and insight hit us. According to the authors, "It's akin to an 'imagination network': it's activated when we're not focusing on anything specific, and instead we're engaged in mellow, non-taxing activities, such as walking in the woods. Our minds are allowed to idly wander or to dip into our deep storehouses of emotions, ideas and memories." Time in nature flips a switch - turning on our creative juices and "electrifying" our innovative tendencies.

Clearly, time spent in nature has a most positive and decided beneficial effect on our creative inclinations. For both children and adults, there is certainly both empirical research in concert with anecdotal evidence to support that notion. If that is, indeed, the case, then we need to ask ourselves a critical question: Why are we reducing the amount of time kids spend outdoors?

3.

In 2005 Richard Louv published a groundbreaking book - *Last Child in the Woods*. In it, he presents overwhelming proof that there is an increasing divide between our children and the natural world. In many cases, according to Louv, we are instructing children to avoid contact with nature: you can get hurt outdoors, there are all sorts of dangerous critters in the woods, we don't have time for playing outdoors - we have to improve our test scores, theme parks are more fun than running through an open field, and all the entertainment you ever need can be found on a cell phone.

Louv identifies this abstinence from nature as "Nature Deficit Disorder" - a condition suffered by modern-day youngsters who are excluded from the mental, physical, and spiritual benefits of nature via legislation, false beliefs, and technology. Yet, as Louv emphatically proves, "Nature inspires creativity in a child by demanding visualization and the full use of the senses. Given a chance, a child will bring the confusion of the world to the woods, wash it in the creek, turn it over to see what lives on the unseen side of that confusion."

Despite those benefits, there is compelling evidence that our children are spending less time playing outdoors or engaging in unstructured play in their backyards or neighborhoods. According to a study by researchers at the University of Maryland, there has been a reduction of 50 percent in the proportion of children (ages nine to twelve) who spent time in activities such as hiking, walking, fishing, beach play, and gardening. The data also showed that children's free play and discretionary time in a typical week declined a total of nine hours over a twenty-five year period. These days, the figures have not

changed to any appreciable degree - there is an increasing and significant decline in the amount of time devoted to outdoor play today
than there was when our grandparents were youngsters.

Those findings are further substantiated by another team of
researchers at Manhattenville College in New York. Their data revealed
that children spend less time playing outdoors than their mothers did
when they were young. The scientists surveyed 800 mothers, whose
responses were compared to the views of mothers interviewed a generation ago. The results were eye-opening: seventy-one percent of today's
mothers said they recalled playing outdoors every day as children, but
only twenty-six percent of them said their kids played outdoors daily.
"Surprisingly, the responses did not vary a great deal between mothers
living in rural and urban areas," one of the researchers reported.

This growing body of research underscores a disturbing disconnect
between what we know intuitively and what we see on the other side
of the front door - children are walking away from woods, fields, open
spaces, rivers and streams in increasing numbers. Sadly, those exits are
often orchestrated by well-meaning adults; including parents, teachers,
community, and recreation leaders. Parks are being fenced in, trees (for
climbing and treehouses) have warning signs posted on their trunks,
barbed wire is strung around open fields, and kids are told, "Don't go
outside, there's a lot of dangerous critters out there." As a result, kids
are spending considerably more time indoors than ever before.

Erika Christakis, in her penetrating piece in *The Atlantic*
(December 2020), underscores both the relevance and significance of
nature in the lives of youngsters. She states,

> "Years of accumulating evidence reveal concretely
> measurable benefits of nature-based learning and outdoor
> time for young children.... Yet despite what we know about
> nature's positive impact on mental health, attention span,
> academic outcomes, physical fitness, and self-regulation,
> outdoor time is too often seen as a quirky and marginal
> add-on, rather than as central to the learning process itself."

What's the practical lesson here? Does nature impact creativity?
Absolutely. Yet, when we deny our children a regular exposure to nature

as part of their everyday experiences, we also deny them an opportunity to use and extend their creative capacities. As they grow up and enter the workforce, this nature/creativity connection becomes even more critical. As young adults begin their careers, they push nature to the sidelines; instead, concentrating their mental efforts on "keeping up with the Jones's" and shifting their occupations into higher gears. Time outdoors - even with its attendant impact on creative inclinations - is something we find difficult to schedule.

This is equally true for both young and old.

Louv passionately makes the point that America's genius has been nurtured by nature. He asks, "What happens to the nation's intrinsic creativity, and therefore the health of our economy, when future generations are so restricted that they no longer have room to stretch?" On one hand, the answer is scary; on the other, it's prophetic. If more nature = higher levels of creativity, then why are kids leaving the wilderness of forests, parks, and mountains for the sterile sanctuary of the indoors? What's taking over our childrens' time such that they are eschewing nature in unprecedented numbers?

The answer will not surprise!

4.

I'm so thankful I had a childhood before
technology took over.
- ANONYMOUS

As I write this, there are approximately 4.88 billion mobile phone users throughout the world (62.17 percent of all the people in the world are cell phone users). 121 million homes in the U.S. have a TV set and over two billion computers are in use worldwide. To say that we live in an age of technology would be to understate the super obvious. It would also be correct to assume that youngsters are subjected to this technology with increasing frequency and familiarity. According to one researcher, "Screen time is an inescapable reality of modern childhood."

And yet, an escalating number of disturbing studies connect delayed cognitive development in children with extended exposure to electronic media in concert with an absence from nature. The US Department of Health and Human Services estimates that American children spend an unbelievable seven hours a day in front of electronic media. Other statistics reveal that kids as young as two regularly play iPad games and have playroom toys that involve touch screens. In defiance of our ancestors, playing in nature has become an after-thought, rather than a right of passage for this generation of children.

Dr. Aric Sigman, an associate fellow of the British Psychological Society and a Fellow of Britain's Royal Society of Medicine, states that when small children get hooked on electronic media they can unintentionally cause permanent damage to their still-developing brains. Too much screen time too soon, he says, "is the very thing impeding the development of the abilities that parents are so eager to foster through the tablets. The ability to focus, to concentrate, to lend attention, to sense other people's attitudes and communicate with them, to build a large vocabulary—all those abilities are harmed." In short, the early and consistent exposure to screen time may have more negative consequences for youngsters' developing brains - educational, psychological, and sociological - than most parents are prepared for.

In the evolutionary history of human brain development, electronic technology is a fairly recent intrusion. This technological advancement runs counter to the hundreds of thousands of years children have been exposed to, and have enjoyed the benefits of, the natural environment. Nature offers kids all manner of stimuli critical to normal brain development. Exposure to the sights and sounds of the natural world, opportunities to communicate and connect with other human beings, and the influence of family interactions are all significant elements in developing appropriate cognitive and creative skills.

And yet, when young children spend an inordinate amount of time in front of electronic screens that developmental cycle is derailed. The results are not short-term, but may significantly influence the child's cognitive powers throughout her or his lifetime.

For the most part, the images on a computer screen or cell phone are created artificially. They're developed by a team of (adult) computer programmers according to a carefully laid out production plan. They do not emanate naturally from the imagination of a young child. They are someone else's images, not the child who is viewing them. They are artificial, not natural. They flash rather than soothe; they stimulate rather than calm. They are antithetical to the doctrine that creative exploration should be the personal generation of possibilities, not an electronic one.

By the same token, electronic media direct a young child to engage in multiple actions simultaneously. Children are forced into multitasking actions at a time when their developing brains are not prepared for such endeavors. The ability to transform verbal words into visual pictures, the skills necessary to turn words into sentences and sentences into comprehensible stories, and the need to engage in social contexts with other human beings are all sublimated by a "machine" that does all that necessary "brainwork" for a child.

Given the ubiquitous role of media in the lives of children, the American Academy of Pediatrics (AAP) has issued policy statements that address this issue. "Families should proactively think about their children's media use, because too much media use can mean that children don't have enough time during the day to play, study, talk, or sleep," said Jenny Radesky, MD, FAAP, lead author of the policy statement, "Media and Young Minds," which focuses on infants, toddlers and pre-school children.

The AAP recommends parents prioritize creative, unplugged playtime for infants and toddlers. For school-aged children and adolescents, the AAP strongly suggests that parents balance media use with other healthy behaviors. The consensus of pediatricians is that unregulated and unsupervised use of electronic media by young children can have a significant (and often negative) effect on critical thinking abilities and creativity enhancement.

Melissa Bernstein, one of the co-founders of Melissa & Doug (a company devoted to creating imaginative playthings for kids), wrote that, "Kids have more planned activities and passive entertainment at their fingertips than ever before, but less free time to dream, make-believe and focus on what they truly love." She, and a host of researchers, argue that electronic media robs kids of their natural instinct to imagine and dream. Someone else, via an app or game, has taken over that duty and instructed kids how to think and behave. Children don't discover the power of innovative thinking on their own - somebody has already done it for them.

In short, creativity becomes something that is externally managed, rather than organically developed via exposure to natural environments.

A cell phone, for example, puts a physical limit on children's play. Their so-called "playing field" is confined to a three-inch by six-inch screen. There are few or no opportunities to physically engage with their surroundings (actually running through an open field or skipping along the edge of a mountain lake). The world available for exploration becomes confined and limited, instead of open and free. Their minds have been squeezed into a mental (and metal) box instead of being released into a wide open and unconstrained environment - an environment that stimulates personal creativity.

Equally significant is the fact that cell phones, iPads, and computers also over-stimulate the developing brain. They bombard youngsters with visual stimuli and loud noises at a rapid pace. What young brains need more is calmness and time to ponder the world around them. A stroll through a forest of lodgepole pines will naturally generate creative possibilities more so than will any app. That stroll (at least in evolutionary terms) is more in line with a child's developing brain and creative potential than any electronic stimuli.

When youngsters are in a continual state of mental agitation they are unable to do the deep work associated with imagination, innovation, and creativity. Kids can shoot aliens out of the sky, but are prevented from initiating their own mental images of medieval castles with handsome princes on golden stallions or journeys through Amazonian rainforests populated with writhing anacondas and insatiable piranhas. A hike through a glaciated mountain pass or an afternoon under a leafy maple tree can create those images quite well.

Perhaps, most critical, in terms of creativity, is the fact that electronic media allow little chance for free time - time to imagine, create, conjure, invent, envision, or dream. Electronic devises take up time rather than provide time. The opportunity to create something on one's own is a necessary process - both from a historical standpoint as well as a personal one. Letting our children's minds play around with thoughts and ideas is a seedbed for creative problem-solving.

Denying young (developing) minds that opportunity hinders the mental practice of thinking about varied possibilities rather than the preordained choices offered on a computer screen, for example.

If we want our children to embrace creativity as a natural part of their growth and development perhaps we should offer them more opportunities to scamper across an open field, climb up into a treehouse, or just pick up seashells along the ocean's edge. Such activities offer more creativity training than does any "Try and slaughter as many gargantuan green gargoyles as you can in five minutes" computer game.[9]

9 Answers to the five RAT questions: 1. School, 2. Cart, 3. Dog, 4. Fast, 5. Sun

19. Reduce On-Screen Time. According to a 2016 report by Common Sense Media, kids, ages 2-5, spend 32 hours a week in front of a screen (TV, computer, iPad, cell phone) and kids 8-12 spend approximately six hours per day in front of a screen or monitor. For the most part, all the images children see on a screen are artificially created by others. In short, children often get the subtle message that creativity is something that is the province of adults (i.e. those who create all those screen images). Children need more opportunities to initiate their own unique imaginations. One of the best presents parents can share with their children is more crayons and less on-screen time. More time creating and less time watching on-screen productions establishes a solid foundation for creativity to prosper.

20. Get Out! Plan regular opportunities for kids to interact with nature. You don't have to schedule extensive journeys to National Parks (although that would be nice). A walk around the neighborhood, a bicycle trip through a local park or nature preserve, a car trip to a forest, lake, or nearby river, a stroll through a vacant lot (looking for insects or other critters), a vacation at the beach, are all valuable learning experiences. All are easy and inexpensive ways to expose children to the creative impact of nature. When nature is shared as a natural and normal part of growing up it also has the potential to be a natural and normal part of adult life, too. Kids will begin to understand and appreciate the role nature can have in their daily lives. Eventually they will begin to see how nature has solved some unique and distinct "challenges" (e.g. the design of a spider web, the splay of roots at the base of a tree, the opening and closing of flowers, the various methods of camouflage employed by certain animals). Nature's creativity stands as an example of how "challenges" are met in several unique ways.

Interestingly, some of the most inventive ideas have come from nature. Think about Velcro and how many clothing items you have that incorporate that magical material in their design and function. Velcro was "invented" when George de Mestral looked at the sticky hooked spine of the common burr and shouted "Eureka" (or some other suitable euphemism) and created a multi-billion dollar industry. I frequently take regular and extended walks through nature (a stroll through a park, a hike along a mountain trail, a walk beside a shimmering lake). Not only does this journey through nature free my mind and open up my senses; so too, does it give me some unique opportunities to recharge my creativity and ask interesting questions: What would a groundhog think about the creativity book I'm writing? If I was a goldenrod flower, what would I see that I'm not seeing now? Do the dips and curves and long stretches of a trail have a particular pattern I could incorporate into a new piece of furniture? Nature has lots of creative answers if we take the time to look for them.

21. Read Aloud - Every Day. Read a book to your children every day. Expose them to imaginative stories, science fiction, mysteries, space stories, fantasy, myths and legends. Give them opportunities to let their imaginations soar and their creative impulses to take flight. Check with their teacher or the local public librarian for recommended titles and authors. Make books regular presents for birthdays and other celebrations. It is from books that children get some of their initial introductions to imagination, innovation, and creativity. By making reading a regular part of their growth and development, you are helping to cement the value of creativity as an expectation rather than as a rarity. Reading to your children opens up brand new worlds and brand new possibilities. It provides a firm foundation upon which projects and challenges (encountered as adults) can be built. The biographies of many creative individuals are filled with stories of how books (and being read to from those books) were instrumental in the discoveries and inventions they made later in their lives. Read a book; create a genius!

22. Sharpening Their Focus. When kids have frequent opportunities to get out into nature, it opens their eyes to all the wonders of the outdoors - it encourages them examine, explore, and discover things right out their back door, across their neighborhood, in a nearby park, or perhaps on a family vacation. Those outdoor opportunities also encourage them to use the same skills naturalists do - skills that open up the possibilities for multiple discoveries and multiple adventures throughout the outdoors. Here are seven to share with your children on any outdoor excursion:

➤ **Observing** - Observing involves all the primary senses: seeing, hearing, smelling, tasting, and touching. ("Wow, look at how that flock of birds take off from the lake. Why do you think they do that?")

➤ **Classifying** - Classifying is the process of assigning a random collection of items to specific groups. ("I think this is a reptile...or maybe it's an amphibian. How could we find out?")

➤ **Measuring** - Measuring includes gathering data on size, weight, and quantity. It's something scientists do all the time. ("Do you think that tree is taller than anything in our back yard? How could we measure it?")

➤ **Inferring** - Inferring involves making an educated guess about something happening in the present. ("I bet the temperature is over 70 degrees right now. What do you think?")

➤ **Communicating** - Communication refers to the various ways people share information with each other. ("How do you think we could record these animal footprints?")

➤ **Predicting** - Predicting involves making educated guesses about something in the future. ("Based on the last few days, what kind of weather do you think we'll have later this afternoon? Why do you think that?")

➤ **Experimenting** - Through experimenting, ideas are proved or disproved. ("I wonder what will happen if we change the type of seed in this feeder. What kinds of birds will eat the sunflower seeds?")

23. Change Your Environment. My office is a comfortable place to work. On most days, I know where all my books are, where to locate articles or necessary research, where my coffee cup is placed, and even where to find the special purple marker I use to edit manuscripts. It's a very familiar place and as a result I often find myself falling into very familiar patterns of behavior and thinking. To get into new and different patterns of thinking I often change my perspective – I literally place myself in new environments in order to generate new insights and ideas. I take my laptop and notes and sit on a park bench, a mountain ledge, beside a cow pasture, or in a rustic cabin beside a meandering stream to work on a book manuscript. I'll spend some time in the front yard, at the dining room table, on the back deck, or, yes, in the bathroom. This change in environment gets my brain focusing on unusual items (I don't normally have a parade of cows marching through my office or a raucous group of squirrels scampering beside my desk.). By exposing myself to different views and different scenarios, my mind is re-energized and renewed. Try it, particularly when you are working on a most challenging project. You'll quickly see how your mind reacts...quite a bit differently...than the "same old, same old" way of thinking. Change your environment often and you'll see something more than the "tried and true."

24. Take A Hike. The philosopher Friedrich Nietzsche (1889) once wrote, "All truly great thoughts are conceived by walking." He may have been on to something, because two researchers at Stanford University have conclusively proven that walking increases creative ideation. They also concluded that "walking improves the generation of novel yet appropriate ideas, and the effect even extends to when people sit down to do their creative work shortly" after a walk. The researchers discovered that more than 80% of all the participants in their study were more creative during and after a walk than they were sitting down. Their very strong suggestion: the more we incorporate walking into our daily activities, the more creative ideas we are able to generate. Shane O'Mara in his absorbing book *In Praise of Walking* devotes an entire chapter (Chapter 7) on walking's impact on creativity. He provides expansive empirical research and insightful anecdotal evidence to demonstrate how "We can reach a more creative state...by being in motion." The bottom line: take a hike...every day.

25. Get Moving. Empirical research and anecdotal evidence have shown what we all know intuitively; that is, physical exercise has a positive effect on our creativity. This is one significant reason why recess is such an important part of a child's overall education. Physical movement and physical exercise can enhance creative potential - both during and after any form of movement. One of the most powerful forms of exercise - from a creative standpoint - is dancing. Dancers have many opportunities to express themselves, to interpret a form of music in whatever way they wish, and coordinate both mental and physical abilities in dynamic and satisfying ways (For an excellent example, check out "Old Movie Stars Dance to Uptown Funk" on You Tube. It's creativity in motion.). When we eliminate or reduce the amount of recess time in schools, we are also reducing a powerful opportunity for children to interpret, illuminate, and imagine the world around. Children need as much time to play (to dance) as they do to study. Physicality begets creativity.

26. Disconnect. Are you overwhelmed by the incredible amount of information bombarding you every day? Yeah, me too! Compelling research shows that the constant onslaught of text messages, Facebook postings, emails, news feeds, phone calls, advertising, spam, and other forms of information takes a significant toll on our mental state; and, by inference, our creativity. Researchers point out that when we are in a constant state of consumption (regularly taking in all that information) we have little mental power left over for production – that is, the production of creative ideas. Our brain is on overload and is deprived of its natural inclination to create (produce) solutions to problems or issues. We are mentally overwhelmed. The solution, though easy to profess, is quite difficult to enact: disconnect. That is, we need to provide ourselves with time and space to divorce ourselves from all the jibber-jabber, mish-mash, and chit-chat thrown at us on a daily basis. All that absorption leaves little time for creation; regular (read: planned) mental disconnects gives our brains time to relax and conjure ideas.

27. Trees And Forests. Sometimes we don't always see the details of life. We get caught up in all the "big pictures' of life and forget that life is a combination of unique and singular details that can help us focus more on what is important - shifting our gaze to all the parts that make up the whole. Or, to reverse a familiar saying, "sometimes we don't see the trees for the forest."

Here's a trick I use when I realize that I'm spending too much time with the "big picture" and not enough time with the details that make that picture possible. Go to your local Goodwill or Salvation Army store and pick up an old picture frame (If there's a picture in the frame, remove it so that you just have the bare frame. Go outside and pick a scene -- a scene that is beautiful (a summer sunset), interesting (a person wearing an unusual hat), colorful (turning leaves on a tree), or mysterious (an architecturally "strange" house).

Hold the picture frame in front of you to frame that specific scene. Now, visually eliminate everything outside the borders of the frame and focus your complete attention on the scene inside the boundaries of the frame. Do this for about five minutes concentrating your complete attention on all the specific details within the frame. Don't look anywhere else. What do you see? Do you see things within the frame with greater clarity? Are you more focused on the small items within the frames - the small items that make up the larger picture? Is your vision sharpened by this experience? Has your perspective shifted from the large picture to the small picture?

Do the same thing with a scene inside your house or place of work (a small portion of the living room, a corner of the garage, your desk at work, a section of the Break Room). What do you notice inside the borders of the picture frames? Are you seeing things you didn't notice before? Are small details surfacing that have been overlooked every other time you've looked at them?

Now, get a much smaller picture frame (e.g. a 3" x 5" index card with a 2" x 4" rectangle cut from the middle) and hold it up to a project you're working on. These may include a paragraph of a written report, a schematic of a new commercial product, a section of a spreadsheet, or a small portion of an advertising campaign. What do you see within the frame that you haven't seen before? Are you focused on something that wasn't clear before? Are you seeing something with new eyes?

I suggest you practice this strategy on a regular basis. Occasionally use the large frame to look at common scenes you encounter in your local environment. Focus on the details within that frame. Then, use a small frame to focus on the details of a work project. I'm certain you'll make some unique discoveries and see things with brand new eyes as a result. Sure, you may look strange to your colleagues, but you may discover some unique trees while they're still staring at the forest.

PART THREE
Our Common Education

9.
The Limits of Right Answers

*The dominant forms of education actively
stifle the conditions that are essential
to creative development.*
SIR KEN ROBINSON

You may recall suffering through standardized tests when you were in school. Also known as multiple-choice tests, they are a staple of classrooms every spring when hundreds of thousands of elementary and secondary students take them to determine how much they have improved academically over the course of the preceding school year.

Try these questions from a 3rd grade test:

1. Which of the following cities is the state capital of California?
   A. Los Angeles
   B. Sacramento
   C. San Francisco
   D. San Diego

2. Which of the following planets is closest to the sun?
   A. Mercury
   B. Earth
   C. Mars
   D. Neptune

3. (275 + 31) - (179 - 47) = ?

A. 471
B. 132
C. 174
D. 306

4. Only one of the following word pairs rhyme. Which one?
    A. Sand - Mad
    B. Pear - There
    C. Must - Last
    D. Thank - Monk

Here are the correct answers:
1. Sacramento, 2. Mercury, 3. 174, 4. Pear - There.]

If you are like most people reading this book you, most likely, answered those questions correctly. Your responses probably came from somewhere in your educational history. Perhaps, you were able to reach into one or more of your elementary or secondary education courses to come up with the answers to a social studies question, a math problem, a science fact, and a language arts category. It seems reasonable to expect that the retrieval of those responses was quick and was done without a great deal of thought.

While you were verifying the answers, you may well have mentally patted yourself on the back, smiled at your knowledge base, or celebrated the fact that you remembered some stuff from long ago.

Terrific!

Now, allow me to change those questions just a little. I am going to reframe them by playing around with the language. Here are your new questions:

1. Why is Sacramento the capital of California?
2. How could you determine the average surface temperature of each of the listed planets?
3. What are three different ways you could use to solve this problem?
4. Why do some word pairs rhyme and others do not?

If you are like most people, you probably found this new set of questions considerably more challenging. The first test gave you an opportunity to demonstrate a certain level of knowledge in four scholastic subjects. The second test challenged you to expand and elaborate that knowledge at a higher level of cognition. You were asked to tap into some mental functions that were more complex than those you used in the first test. The first test focused on getting the right answers; the second test focused on reasons and rationales beyond those right answers. The first test was easy; the second test not so much!

If you've ever watched the popular TV game show *Jeopardy!* (the original version debuted on Mach 30, 1964), you know we have a fascination with factual information. Watching Ken Jennings in 2004 (when he amassed $2,522,700 over his 75 episodes) and James Holzhauer in 2019 (his winnings totaled $2,464,216 over 32 episodes), and their ability to recall information from a multitude of fields - everything from anthropology to zoology - was both mesmerizing and consuming. We were in awe of their unique ability to recall so many different bits of information in a very competitive atmosphere.

Jeopardy! and other similar game shows underscore our fascination with people who know a lot of "stuff." If you have a lot of information in your head (or so the saying goes), then you must be intelligent. Intelligent people, we believe, know a lot of things. As a result, we celebrate them, we honor them, and we revere them. They are the epitome of what it means to be a learned person. They are intellectual gods.

They are also emblematic of our passion for the right answer. If you have a lot of right answers roaming around your head, then you must be smart. Smart people know a lot of stuff. Thus, by extension, the more stuff you can get into your head (and keep in your head), then the smarter you are. Much of our educational system is based on this simple concept: kids who know a lot of facts are well-educated; kids who don't know a lot of facts aren't well educated. And, how do we know if someone has a lot of factual information in their heads? We give them a factual information (or "right answer") test - a standardized test. Do well on the test and you've (obviously) learned a lot; do poorly on the test and you (obviously) didn't pay attention in class. High scores on multiple-choice tests are celebrated as a sign of a good education...a sign that you know a lot of "right answers."

But, as you might expect, there's a problem...a big problem...with that thinking.

There is a basic assumption that doing well on a standardized test is a sign of a well-educated person. There is a concomitant assumption that a well-educated person is also someone who can come up with novel ideas and innovative solutions to everyday problems. This relationship can be illustrated with the following formula: high test scores = high level of education = high level of creativity. That's the common thinking; but, just for a moment, think about this psychological reality: there is little correlation between the amount of knowledge we have (about a particular topic) and our ability to generate creative ideas. That is, having lots of knowledge (or "right answers") doesn't give us an unfair mental advantage in generating creative ideas.

Knowledge is only a foundation...a starting point. Using that knowledge in dynamic ways is what creativity is all about. If we're considered to be creative, we don't just sit on our knowledge (or rest on our laurels), we actively play with our knowledge. We religiously generate lots of new ideas - practical ideas, childish ideas, wild ideas, off-the-wall ideas, crazy ideas, foolish ideas, quiet ideas, loud ideas, obtuse ideas, weird ideas, and strange ideas (In short - a plethora of ideas.). Knowledge just gives us a starting point - it doesn't solve the problem!

When we're in a creative frame of mind, we move beyond our knowledge - we look for ideas in unfamiliar, strange, and never-be-fore-explored places. We break the rules, make up our own rules as we go along, or work without any rules at all. We ask questions that have never been asked - childlike questions, silly questions, imaginative questions, improbable questions, irrational questions, inconceivable questions, looney questions, and way-out-in-the-universe questions. Creativity is, quite simply, playing with our mentality. No limits. No bounds. No controls. Pure and simple: unadulterated mental fun. Creativity is all about turning your mind into a mental playground.

"But, but, but - don't you have to be intelligent to be creative?" (you may be asking). We'll get to the answer shortly, but first....

2.

By some estimates, the average student will take nearly 2,500 tests, quizzes, and exams during her school years (Grades K-12). For the most part, those measurement devices determine how much students know about a particular topic or topics. However, they are often misused and overused - instruments that often waste time and yield imperfect results. Do we need to know how well students are learning? Absolutely! But, giving lots of tests because...well...because we've always given lots of tests is hardly a justification. Let's take a look.

When teachers evaluate students, they compare one student's achievement with other students or with a set of standards. One very common example of formal evaluation is known as high-stakes testing. Simply stated, high-stakes testing is when students are given a standardized test, the results of which are rewarded in some way. Failing the test might have negative consequences (or rewards), too. For example, in California, students must pass the California High School Exit Examination to graduate. If they don't pass, they don't graduate. Thus, when some sort of reward system is attached to a standardized test, that test becomes a high-stakes test. SATs (Standardized Achievement Test) and ACTs (American College Testing) are good examples of high-stakes testing because the "reward" is often admission into college.

There are various types of federal legislation that require states to administer standardized tests to elementary and secondary students. Often students' achievement on these tests determines the amount of funding or financial reimbursement a school, district, or state will receive from the federal government. As with just about everything else, high-stakes testing has arguments for and against. Here are some arguments against high-stakes testing: 1) The content on the tests may not match the content taught in the classroom, 2) Educational decisions are often based on how well students do on a single test, 3) Students from lower socio-economic groups and from certain minority groups tend to do poorer on standardized tests, and 4) High-stakes testing often puts a lot of pressure on both teachers and students.

And, some arguments for high-stakes testing include the following: 1) Standardized testing holds teachers accountable for teaching what needs to be taught, 2) The tests allow schools within a district to be compared with each other. Schools may be rated good, average, or poor based on test results (This can also be a negative.), 3) The public can get a sense of how well a school is doing by reviewing the results of these tests, and 4) Some people argue that the tests foster increased student motivation. For example, if students want to graduate from high school, they need to pass the state exam.

Classroom teachers have little control over the use of high-stakes testing. Teachers may be required to administer these tests whether or not they agree with them. In fact, in many districts, these tests are also used to evaluate individual teacher performance. When a class does well on a test, then, that means the teacher did a good job teaching them. If students in another class do poorly on one of these tests, then (quite obviously), the teacher didn't do a good job teaching them.[10] Suffice it to say, these tests have an enormous impact on how teachers teach and what students learn.

And, as you might also suspect, all this testing puts a decided and myopic focus on "getting the right answer." Not necessarily a creative answer (or answers)!

3.

You just purchased a brand new car. It is beautiful; it is a work of art - something you've wanted for years, something you will treasure forever. It's sleek, fire-engine red, turbo-charged and the envy of every human being on the planet. It's an instant classic. And, most important, your neighbors will celebrate your good taste every time you drive out of the garage.

One day, with your "significant other" in the passenger seat, you set out for a drive in the country. You take the car through its paces, shifting easily between all five gears, speeding up to the triple digits, and hugging corners like it was born for the road. This is a masterpiece of driving excellence. With the wind in your hair and a perpetual smile

---

10 This logic, of course, assumes that all children in a class are educationally, socially, and economically equal. It also assumes all children learn at the same pace and at identical levels of motivation. As any classroom teacher will attest, this is more myth than reality.

on your face, the miles whiz by on a beautiful summer day.

But, then, something terrible happens. You get a flat tire. Deftly, you pull the car over to the side of the road and get out to survey the damage. Yup, there it is - the right rear tire is decidedly as "flat as a pancake" - a three inch nail unceremoniously protruding from the wall of your very expensive European tire.

"No problem," you say to yourself as you joyfully remove the tire iron and jack from the aerodynamically-designed truck and lay them on the ground beside the clearly deflated tire. Merrily whistling, you carefully remove each of the four lug nuts from the flat tire and lay them on the ground. You jack up the car and, with a huff and a puff, you lift the punctured tire off the car and place it on the ground. You gingerly roll the spare tire over to the side of the car and lift it onto the lug screws.

That's when you notice that something is amiss. The lug nuts are gone. Perhaps they were absconded by some alien life force, a wandering bear with a penchant for metallic objects, or an itinerant hobo looking for some nifty decorations to arrange around his campfire. But, no, it seems as though you carelessly set the lug nuts on an adjacent sewer grate where they disappeared into the deep dark abyss - forever lost and irretrievable.[11]

Now what?

After about ten minutes of beating your head against the side of your recently polished car and significantly annoying your "significant other," you are at a complete loss as to how to solve your current and most frustrating problem. As luck would have it (especially in stories like this), a young girl is pedaling her bicycle down that same road. She stops to marvel at your car and asks, "What's the matter?" You tell her your tale of woe and she silently smiles. "So, you lost all the lug nuts from your flat tire. No problem! I know how to solve this very easily," she says confidently. "Here, let me show you how to get the spare tire on your car so you can drive to the service station down the road and get the flat tire fixed."

And, in less than fifteen minutes you're back on the road (and your "significant other" is in a considerably better mood). So, how did the young girl solve your problem? (The answer is at the end of the chapter).

---

11 Oh, you also discover that both your cell phones are missing. But, that's another problem... and another story!

For more than two decades, I used a simple activity in one of my undergraduate education courses to help students (all future teachers) understand the fallacy of focusing all their instructional attention on having students get "The Right Answer." Students in the course were randomly divided into several teams of three to four members each. Each team was provided with nine miniature marshmallows and fifteen round wooden toothpicks. Each team was then challenged to construct the tallest free-standing structure possible with just those materials (A free-standing structure was defined as something that could stand on its own, it could not lean against or be supported by any other structure.). There was no time limit for this activity and students were free to solve this challenge in whatever way they could imagine.

In most cases, over nearly thirty years [sixty semesters] of teaching the course ("Teaching Elementary Science"), teams began with a simple concept: "What is a system that will use all these materials to create a structure that is taller than any other structure in the room?" Students came up with a plan, stuck toothpicks into the miniature marshmallows and watched as their structures took on the semblance of wobbly-footed, and decidedly surrealistic cell towers. Some of the "marshmallow towers" reached heights of ten inches, twelve inches, or more (If my memory is correct, the tallest reached a height of about fifteen and a half inches.).

I wasn't so much interested in how tall these structures were, but more so in the processes used to construct them. For the most part, these college students, primarily juniors and seniors, decided on a single prototype and then followed that prototype to the end. In short, they decided that there was one, and only one, way to solve the challenge. "Let's do it by creating a series of interlocking triangles," they said. "How about if we made some squares and linked them together," others said. "I got it! Let's build a small base and then construct a tall line of toothpicks." What became clear in these students' problem-solving skills is that they were focused on one, and only one, possible solution. They were looking for the single "right answer."

As University of San Diego professor Jennifer Mueller explains, in solving problems we often focus on searching for and identifying the one best solution. We place a premium on accuracy and correctness in decision making. We frequently question how a novel idea will be implemented and what obstacles might prevent successful adoption, rather than focusing on why it just might work. The how/best mindset represents linear thinking - one path, and one path only, must lead to an optimal solution.

Unsurprisingly, creativity suffers when people adopt a how/ best mindset. In contrast, Mueller finds that creativity flourishes when individuals embrace a why/potential mindset. People with this attitude tend to approach problems with the belief that multiple viable solutions exist. They do not look for the one perfect path (the one "right answer") to success. These individuals ask positive questions about alternatives: Why might this work? Why might this be a good idea? Why might we want to pursue this approach?"

Over those same thirty years, I've also conducted my marshmallow activity with another group of students. They were given the identical materials and the same instructions. Most interestingly, their structures were more diverse and, for the most part, their structures were considerably taller. No, they weren't mechanical engineers or professional architects. They were groups of first and second grade students!

Unlike the older adults, these young participants engaged in several problem-solving strategies. First of all, they didn't discuss and plan a prototype. They simply jumped into the activity ready to experiment with all sorts of potential solutions. Second, they were not afraid to engage in a trial-and-error approach. Sometimes their structures worked and sometimes they didn't. It was clear that they were unafraid of making mistakes. Making mistakes is how we learn how things aren't done and we can then move on to approaches that may possibly work. Third, they were open to all sorts of experimentation - they not only tried out ideas, they tried out lots of ideas. Unlike the adults, they were not locked into a "one size fits all" mentality. Anything and everything was possible. In short, their key to success was that they consistently looked for many possible options, rather than for a single right answer.

My "Marshmallow Challenge" has been verified dozens of times by designer Tom Wujec. Using a somewhat different set of materials (strands of spaghetti instead of toothpicks, a single marshmallow instead of several, along with some masking tape and string) he has challenged teams of business school graduates to create tall freestanding towers within an 18-minute time frame. In test after test, the constructions falter, buckle, and collapse and the average height in considerably below expectations.

He then assigns the same task to teams of Kindergarten students. The results, as you might imagine, are spectacular and much more successful than those of the grown-ups. Wujec speculates that business school students are systematically trained to look for a single right answer through careful analysis and focused deliberation. They eschew mistakes in favor of disciplined preparation. In short, they are trained as linear thinkers rather than as creative problem-solvers. [If interested, you can see this for yourself on a most interesting and revealing TED talk ("Tom Wujec: Build a Tower, Build a Team").

4.

For much of our lives we are predisposed to look for a single solution to a single problem (e.g. What is 2 + 2?). We have been "brainwashed" to think that for every problem there is one, and only one, way to solve that problem. Much of our educational experiences have been focused on learning the right answer or discovering the right answer. Seldom have we been offered the opportunity to consider that there might be a multitude of potential responses to any problem. The "one-problem, one-answer" syndrome has been thoroughly ingrained into our patterns of thinking.

But, what happens when students are invited to generate multiple responses instead of a single right answer? And so, I asked a group of fourth grade students to come up with as many possible solutions to the 2 + 2 = ? problem as they could. I did it by asking them this question: "What if there was more than one way to record the answer to 2 + 2 = ?." Here are some of the responses (out of the 54) they came up with:

6-2   22
√16   1+1+1+1

(2 x 1) + (2 x 1)	½ of 8
40% of 10	The number of corners in a square
What a golfer yells	How Lincoln began 'The Gettysburg Address"
6 x 6 ÷ 9	Number of runners on a relay team (track or swimming)
Always after 3	16 ÷ 4

As you can see, these kids were not "boxed in" by the artificial "requirement" of finding a single right answer (When you add the number 2 to another number 2 you will always get the number 4.). Rather, they were asked a question beginning with the two words: What if.... The results, you must agree, were diverse and quite inventive.

Ken Robinson puts this all into perspective when he writes, "... too often our educational systems don't enable students to develop their natural creative powers. Instead, they promote uniformity and standardization. The result is that we're draining people of their creative possibilities and...producing a workforce that's conditioned to prioritize conformity over creativity." In short, our educational system is focused more on getting right answers (thinking inside the box) than on promoting creative possibilities (thinking outside the box).

The implications can be staggering. Insight and logic support the notion that a focus on a one-right-answer mentality forces us into a "don't take any risks" mindset. Consumed with getting the right answer (a proven consequence of an over-emphasis on standardized testing) conditions us not to take chances. In turn, taking risks also means we are comfortable in making mistakes. Make too many mistakes and you get a low score on a test. Get a low score and you may deprive yourself of a college education (as a result of your SAT scores), a chance at graduate school (via your GRE scores), or an occupational advancement (via your score on the LSAT [law school] exam or MCAT [medical school] exams).

Simply put: we are not taught how to be creative; rather our education is focused more on "mental compliance" than it is on innovative expression. Dr. Robert Sternberg, a psychologist who has studied creativity extensively, agrees. He writes, "Creativity is a habit. The problem is that schools sometimes treat it as a bad habit....Like any habit, creativity can either be encouraged or discouraged." Michael Roberto, in his book *Unlocking Creativity* further cements this view when he states, "Our schools may be discouraging creative students in a variety of ways. A stream of research has shown that teachers claim to value qualities such as independent thinking and curiosity, yet they reward behaviors such as obedience and conformity."

Because of the prevalence of exams in our lives (recall the 2,500 figure mentioned earlier) we have a tendency to stay in a comfort zone: a focus on the right answer. Occasionally, we may be asked to voice a creative response to a question ("What do you think are some of the long-range consequences of our current trade policy with China?"), but are hesitant to do so on the belief that the questioner, or teacher, may be looking for a specific and particular response. Perhaps our creative answer is not the one the teacher was looking for. We may have stepped outside the bounds of what was expected and into the territory of the unknown. The objective of a lesson often becomes: Right answers get rewarded; wayward or unusual responses (e.g. creative responses) are often censured.

5.

Here are a few names you're likely to recognize: Oprah Winfrey, Sonia Sotomayor, Barack Obama, Queen Elizabeth, George Clooney, and LeBron James. These are all famous people - people whose names are (or have been) in the news, or who are discussed in newspaper articles, or who often appear on TV. They get a lot of press. But, here's a name you're probably not familiar with: Simon Kashchock-Marenda. Simon recently got a lot of press, had several articles written about him, and was featured on several news programs.

But, very few people know who he is.

Although it hardly seems like a line of research that would be classified as earth-shattering, Simon was keenly interested in discovering how artificial sweeteners (*Sweet 'N Low*, *Equal*, *Truvia*, *Splenda*, *Nutrasweet*) affected fruit flies. He began an experiment in which he fed various groups of fruit flies several different sweeteners over a period of several days. One of his initial discoveries was that all the flies fed *Truvia* died within six days.

He replicated the experiment again and got the same results: The flies fed on food laced with *Truvia* lived for an average of 5.8 days; the flies raised on other sweeteners lived for an average of 38.6 to 50.6 days. Simon hypothesized that there was something in the *Truvia* that was toxic to the flies.

Later experimentation found that a critical component of *Truvia* was the sugar erythritol. Equally important was the discovery that *Truvia*, which uses a stevia plant extract, has been approved by the FDA (in 2008) for human consumption, but that it also serves as a potent insecticide, particularly for fruit flies.

Simon's initial work with artificial sweeteners has spurred a flurry of additional research on the use of erythritol as a "human-safe" insecticide for crops. The commercial implications, as you might imagine, are enormous.

Oh, did I forget to mention that Simon was only eleven years old when he made his discoveries?

So, how was it, that a middle school student, with no formal training in the biological sciences, was able to determine a practical (and alternative) use for an artificial sweetener, when legions of highly trained professional biologists could not? Simply because he asked multiple questions (divergent thinking), rather than looking for a single right answer (convergent thinking). Or, as famed management guru Peter Drucker once wrote, "The most common source of mistakes in ... decisions is the emphasis on finding the right answer rather than the right question."

As we'll soon discover, the kinds of questions we ask youngsters determines, in large measure, how they think. And, that thinking is often "controlled" by a single word - a common word that focuses our attention on getting "the right answer."

Imagine you are an elementary school student. Here are a few questions you might be asked in various classes: "What is the answer to question number seventeen in your math book?" "Who was the third U.S. president?" and "What is the chemical symbol for salt?" What you will notice about all those questions is the use of a critical, and very focused, word: "**the**." By asking for "the answer" or "the chemical symbol" you are focusing the attention of the respondent on a single correct response - "**the**" answer.

As a result of all those "right answer" questions, there's something that happens in almost every classroom almost every day. Single answer questions are asked and students (who are either bored, frustrated, distracted, or unprepared) often answer "I don't know" or "Dunno." It's a common enough occurrence in any classroom that it is quite easy to recognize (I am certain, that you and me and hundreds of millions of other former students have used this "cop out" more than once or twice in our educational careers.)

When students respond with "I don't know," they are often saying that they don't want to make any kind of intellectual investment in the topic under discussion. That frequently comes from a fear of not knowing the right answer - particularly the "right answer" that is already lodged in the teacher's head or dutifully highlighted in a Teacher's Manual. It's also a convenient way of escaping from any intellectual pursuit - a way of telling the teacher, "I don't know what THE right answer is so, rather than making a fool of myself, I'm going to give myself a very convenient "out." In many ways, the student is telling the teacher, "I'm done here, go ahead and move on to someone else."

As a professional educator, I find this common occurrence unacceptable. A focus on getting the right answer shortchanges students - it denies them an opportunity to understand the ramifications of a concept, expand their thinking horizons, and engage in a supportive conversation that is both respectful and educational.

The message is both subtle and overwhelming at the same time. Students are being asked a question that has a single correct response - a response that the question-asker (or the makers of a test) have previously determined to be the right one. No other answer will do; only the right one will suffice. Come up with *the* one right answer and a student will be "successful;" come up with any other response and that student will have answered incorrectly and will be marked accordingly. By asking for "the right answer" a student's field of choices is narrowed. So too, is she forced to determine what is already in the question asker's head or what is in a Teacher's Manual or curriculum guide, for example. And, while that student is in school, how often will she be forced into this way of thinking?

More than eighty percent of her classroom time.

6.

Since 2001 and the passage of the Elementary and Secondary Education Act (ESEA) generally known as "The No Child Left Behind Act" (NCLB) we have been a nation focused on high stakes testing. In an effort to raise academic standards in all schools, to make teachers accountable for student achievement, to raise levels of college preparedness, and to reinvigorate the economic competitiveness of the USA we have subjected generations of students to a pantheon of standardized tests and exams that have presumably measured their academic progress at the expense of their creative thinking skills. How pervasive is this emphasis on testing? It has been estimated that test sales have grown from approximately $260 million annually in 1997 to over $700 million today - nearly a threefold increase.

What has all that money gotten us? Several things...both good and bad. On the positive side, we see that high-stakes testing results in changes in both instructional practice as well as curriculum reform. Instructional programs are more focused, directed, and specific. We know what needs to be taught, because we know what will be tested.

Unfortunately, there's also a downside of our current overemphasis on testing. In order to do well on the test (and thus increase a school's funding from both the state and the federal government) teachers are often prone to "teach to the test." That is, teachers now know what will be assessed on a standardized test and, in order to ensure high scores, they teach students materials specific to the tests in addition to teaching children how to take these, often intimidating, exams.

In Pennsylvania, for example, students in grades three through eight take the PSSAs (Pennsylvania System of School Assessment) each spring. According to the Pennsylvania Department of Education website, "The annual Pennsylvania System of School Assessment is a standards-based, criterion-referenced assessment which provides students, parents, educators and citizens with an understanding of student and school performance related to the attainment of proficiency of the academic standards." When students do well (when they get a lot of right answers), both teachers and schools are highlighted and celebrated; when they do poorly, their perception in the eyes of the public suffers.

And, so legions of classroom teachers initiate lessons that drill students on how to take standardized tests. That is, students are taught the strategies that will lead to a high number of right answers and, thus, higher scores on the test. The mechanics of test-taking are emphasized and the curriculum becomes narrowly focused so as to ensure that students will achieve high scores. How to get a high score on a once-a-year standardized test is favored over an eclectic broad-based education focused on creative thinking and interpretation. Quite often, the emphasis is more on the content covered (and test preparation) rather than deep improvements to instructional practice...or creative thinking.

The consequences are dire. Our educational focus is frequently short-sighted (get high scores on a standardized test at the end of the school year), and seldom long-range (instruct students how to use their new-found knowledge to solve real-world problems). Because schools typically don't test for creativity, it isn't emphasized. As Ken Robinson writes, schools are designed to "...promote uniformity and standardization. The result is that we're draining people of their creative possibilities and...producing a workforce that's conditioned to prioritize conformity over creativity."

And so students, and the public in general, get the notion that the ultimate goal of education is to get high scores on a test. Know a lot of stuff, do well on a standardized exam, and the prevailing thought is that you have been well educated. That may be true up to a point. The reality is that students are trained to get right answers, but receive few opportunities to engage their creative side. We exit school knowing how to take tests, but with insufficient emphasis on innovative thinking. Or, as Scott Barry Kaufman and Carolyn Gregoire state, "Unfortunately, our society increasingly allows children's creativity and imagination to fall by the wayside in favor of the...superficial learning evaluated by standardized tests - which only serve to increase extrinsic motivation, often at the expense of intrinsic passion."

As a result, many children are subjected to educational practices that quash their creative instincts. The inventor Marvin Camrus, who holds more than 500 patents, said it best: "I think little children tend to be creative, but the more education you get, the more the inventive spark is educated out of you."

We know how to get right answers, we're just not sure what to do after we get them.[12]

...if you think there's only one right answer,
then you'll stop looking as soon as you find one.
—ROGER VON OECH

---

12 Sir Ken Robinson's speech ("Do Schools Kill Creativity?") is one of the most watched TED talk ever. At this writing, it has been viewed more than 20 million times.

10.
How to Sizzle: 28 - 35

28. Put Standardized Tests Into Perspective. Keep in mind that there may be little correlation between the material assessed on a standardized test and the school curriculum. The tests and the curriculum are, most often, created by two completely different educational entities. In short, what is taught may not necessarily be what is tested. Also, remember that a test only records what a student knows at one point in time. Have a good day and you may do well on the test; have a bad day and you might not. Standardized tests are only one small part of a child's educational experience; they are not the *raison d'etre* for teaching (or learning). Even more important, scores on a standardized test have little relationship to one's creativity.

29. No Wrong Questions. On a Zoom meeting, a conference call, monthly department meeting, emergency session, or any other kind of group discussion try to avoid asking the following question: "What is the answer?' or "What is the solution?" By asking that question, you are severely limiting a multiplicity of responses simply because the group is now focused on finding **THE** answer or **THE** solution...rather than in generating a vast array of potential answers or solutions. More appropriate questions might include, "What are some possibilities here?", "How many different ways can we look at this?", or "What are some of the impediments we have to overcome." In short, ask questions for which there may be a wide variety of responses rather than questions which limit the number or type of responses. As discussed in a later chapter, we tend to think based on the types of questions we are asked.

If we are only asked questions for which there is the expectation of a single answer, that's all we'll get. On the other hand, if we pose questions that naturally generate a multiplicity of responses, then the collective creativity of the group is enhanced considerably.

30. Make It Strange: Rearrange. I'm sure you're reading this book right side up. Why? Well, because that's the way "you are supposed to read a book." But, what if you turned this book upside down and tried to read this page. Not only does your perspective change, but you also have to use skills you don't normally employ in order to make sense of the information on this page. You're forced to do something a little unusual and a little uncomfortable. In so doing, your mind makes some creative adjustments or innovative compensations in order for you to achieve an appropriate level of comprehension. When faced with a problem or challenge, try rearranging some of the elements in order to create new patterns or new thinking opportunities. Put the beginning at the end. Put the middle at the beginning. Put the bottom on the top or the top on the side. Put the outside on the inside or the inside just to the left of the top. Put the right on the left or the left halfway past the center or on top of the bottom half that is now on the inside. Rearrange.

31. Work Backwards. Imagine writing a press release for a brand new product long before you have even begun to design that product. Well, that's what the folks at Amazon do. When they conceive a new product, the team sits down and drafts a full and complete press release for that product as their initial step. What are the most compelling features of the new product? What are the most significant values of the new product to consumers? What is their primary audience and how will they target the new product to that audience? What benefits will customers get from the new product? Enormous time and energy is devoted to crafting a compelling press release long before (months or years) the product is ever ready for the marketplace. In short, product developers must travel into the future and imagine the day the product is released to the public. Then, they are tasked with moving backwards in time to conjure up the steps (in reverse order) that will be necessary to make that press release a reality. Backwards thinking offers a new reality. A study in 2004 conclusively proved that when participants were tasked with completing a project from back to front (rather than the more logical front to back), they achieved higher levels of creativity. The researchers noted that participants were forced to utilize abstract, high-level, and conceptual thinking rather than logical, concrete, and time-worn thinking.

32. Open-Ended Questions. Too often, when we're working on a project or some sort of intellectual challenge, we overly concentrate on solving a problem or finding a solution. We persevere, our attention is sharply focused on achieving some sort of solution, and we tend to lose sight of where we are going. The problem becomes all too consuming - taking up all our attention and all our mental efforts. We are determined to solve it "come hell or high water." What we often need is a mental pause - a redirection for our mental efforts that guide us into looking at our challenge from new angles and new perspectives. To that end, consider asking yourself - at regular intervals - one or more of the following open-ended questions:

➤ "What have I/we learned so far?"
➤ "Why is this information important?"
➤ "How does this information relate to any information I/ we have learned previously?"
➤ "How do I/we feel about my/our progress so far?"
➤ "How does this data apply to other situations?"
➤ "Where else could this be used?"
➤ "What do I/we think might happen next?"
➤ "How do I/we think this will turn out?"
➤ 'What new questions have I/we generated?"
➤ "Is there something I/we don't understand at this point?"
➤ "What are three new things I/we just learned?"

As you will note, these questions can be asked and answered individually, in small group discussions, or as part of the conversation of an entire department or division.

33. The Chaos Of Creativity. When working on a long-term project - this book, for example - my office often resembles the aftermath of a Category 5 hurricane. Piles of papers are strewn about the floor, the desk is a mish-mash of books, research articles, errant scraps of paper with notes and ideas scribbled upon them. A few coffee cups, and the detritus of several photocopied articles litter my desk. The five bookcases groan under the weight of hundreds of books in no particular order or sequence. A recliner and a love seat are festooned with random paperbacks, piles of printouts, and various materials I need in my research ventures. Let's be perfectly honest - this is not a pretty sight. It is chaotic, jumbled, and clearly messy. But, so is creativity.

There's a long-time maxim which postulates that "a cluttered desk is the sign of genius." I'm not sure how much I would agree with that statement, but I know that each morning when I climb the stairs with a cup of coffee in my hand I am entering my own domain - my creative sanctuary. I walk past books and the titles or illustrations on the front covers send my mind spinning with all sorts of creative permutations. I stroll by a stash of papers and the combination of those items with a stack of children's books and several photographs of towering redwood trees (for example) may give me a unique combination of ideas that set my mind soaring off into new dimensions and new possibilities. Maybe, once or twice a year, I am given to organizing my office just so I don't stumble over one too many piles or stacks of books I want to read in my search for new possibilities. Whenever I am bitten by the "cleaning bug" I find it difficult to locate materials simply because they are in an ordered location or filed in a drawer out of sight (and out of mind).

When I look at the chaos of my office, I am stimulated by the random arrangement of ideas - it is often that random combination of creative possibilities that gets my mind warmed up on a cold winter's day - ready to tackle the day's projects with a fresh vitality that would not be as clear with a straight and logical office space. I find that disorder is a germination for ideas...I see new combinations of words, thoughts, and patterns that might not surface if books were arranged in alphabetical order on the shelves or papers were neatly stuffed into clearly labeled file folders to be placed in clearly labeled file drawers. A chaotic and clearly random arrangement of materials is a stimulant for thought. It is the rocket fuel for intellectual journeys that begin my day with possibilities, rather than simply the continuation of yester-day's unfinished work.

I'm also aware that there is some anecdotal evidence that demon-strates that chaotic organizations - organizations that don't always move from Point A to Point B to Point C - are typically more creative than well-organized ones. Order and sequence often establish "guide-rails" to creative thought; chaos lets our minds wander in new places and new directions that would otherwise be undiscovered. It is a fertile field ripe for innovative growth and imaginative adventures. Put more chaos in your life (and business) and you may be injecting more creativity, too.

34. Create Analogies. I find that creating analogies is one of the best ways for me to break out of a creative funk. If I'm stuck on an issue or am having difficulty in finding a useful solution to an ongoing conundrum, I try to create a series of analogies to warm up my mental engines and take a look at something with a new and different perspective. For me, I like to draw analogies between an idea (or problem) and something in nature. These connections inspire me to move beyond common assumptions and into uncommon terri-tories. For example:

- ➤ My idea is like a pine tree because _____.
- ➤ My subject is like a cascade of fall leaves because _____.
- ➤ My thought is like a beaver dam because _____.
- ➤ My situation is like a deep winter snow because _____.
- ➤ My issue is like a chattering squirrel because _____.
- ➤ My project is like a soft summer breeze because _____.
- ➤ My manuscript is like a walk through a forest because _____.
- ➤ My invention is like a gurgling stream because _____.
- ➤ My challenge is like a wetlands trail because _____.
- ➤ My reconceptualization is like a family of field mice because _____.

35. What If. "What if...." is one of the most powerful idea generators I've ever used! It simply requires that you place the two words "What if" in front of questions or situations you might normally pose. The process of "what-iffing" stimulates the brain to think in very divergent and creative ways. It also moves you away from a tendency to look for single right answers.

For much of our lives we are predisposed to look for a single solution to a single problem. We have been "brainwashed" to think that for every problem there is one, and only one, way to solve that problem. Unfortunately, that's not the case. When we consider that there might be a multitude of potential responses to any problem we break out of the "one-problem, one-answer" syndrome and begin to look for a host of potential solutions (and a host of potential ideas).

Try 2-3 of the following "What if" questions. How many possible responses can you come up with for each one (Remember, you're not back in school - there are no right or wrong answers here)? Don't think about the *quality* of your responses (that will severely limit your creativity), just think about the *quantity* of responses you could generate for each selected query:

➤ What if cats would come when you called them?
➤ What if you were required to choose your life expectancy when you reached age 21?
➤ What if a small red circle appeared in the middle of everyone's forehead whenever they told a lie?
➤ What if every college student could be guaranteed a job immediately upon graduation?
➤ What if a car could be invented that would be immune to any type of accident?
➤ What if you had a watch that would predict what you would do over the next 24 hours?
➤ What if you could wash your clothes while still wearing them?

Asking "What if" questions is one of the most powerful creativity engines ever - it has the potential of producing a plethora of dynamic possibilities, helping us move outside our "mental comfort zones" and into new and exciting venues. In addition, it propels us into an imaginative frame of mind - a frame without assumptions and without limits.

Asking "What if" questions propels us in new directions (cognitively speaking). From a mental standpoint, it helps us move "outside the box" into dimensions that are typically not within our normal field of vision. Besides the fact that it's a fun mental activity, it's also one that can generate an undeniable quantity of possible responses (not right responses or wrong responses, just *possible* responses).

Let's play with a "What-if" question posed above: What if a small red circle appeared in the middle of everyone's forehead (and lasted for five minutes) whenever they told a lie? (I've organized my responses into three very arbitrary categories):

Politics
➤ Would political speeches be considerably briefer?
➤ Would presidential campaigns be much shorter?
➤ Would politicians pass a law that sessions of Congress could not be televised?
➤ Would new businesses start up guaranteeing "lie-proof" political speech-writing?

Dating
➤ What would happen on first dates?
➤ Would you be more inclined to talk about the weather than about yourself on a first date?
➤ Would the whispering of "sweet nothings" become more of an art form than an expectation?
➤ Would you rather talk with your date in a dark room than in a brightly lit restaurant?

Teenagers
➤ What would teenagers say to explain the "small dent" on the family car?
➤ What would teenagers say about why they needed a larger allowance?

➤ Would it be cool for teenagers to have a red dot on their foreheads?

➤ Would there be a competition between teenagers as to who could collect the most dots in a 24-hour period?

As you can see, the generation of just one "What if" question can produce a plethora of responses - responses all the way from the sublime to the ridiculousness. And, that's the important key to the success of this creativity strategy. "What-iffing" is non-judgmental - it doesn't make any distinction between so-called "good" responses and so-called "bad" responses. In fact, it makes no judgement whatsoever. It's beauty lies in the fact that it frees up the mind to produce a wealth of responses that might be hiding in the dark recesses of our minds or lodged in cranial corners that haven't even been explored yet. In many ways, "what iffing" is brainstorming with yourself - opening up your mind for all possibilities and putting all those ideas on the table before you.

Asking lots of "What if" questions and supplying a range of responses to those queries will not guarantee that you'll be able to solve every problem or conundrum before you. What-iffing" is not a mental panacea. It's highly likely that a whole bunch of 'What if" questions and a whole bunch of responses to those "What if" questions won't always give you the innovative, creative, dynamic or the necessary answers you need for every single problem at work or issues at home.

But (and this is a BIG BUT), "What-iffing" will exercise your imagination and give your creativity a good workout. It will move your mind into new dimensions - dimensions previously unconsidered or unimaginable. It will break you of your overt dependence on practical, workable, and grounded ideas - the same ideas you have always turned to in the past. Most important, it will *free your mind* to look at ALL the implications and ALL the dimensions of an issue or problematic situation.

Many people reject the notion of "What-iffing" simply based on the idea that it is a waste of time. "We need to find the answer to this situation right away," they may say. "We don't have time for such frivolous thoughts or non-productive ideas," they may say. Perhaps not. However, "What-iffing" opens up new possibilities, it gets the brain cells unstruck from "same old, same old" ideas. It twists and turns and tosses possibilities into the mental soup of our brains so that new ideas and new possibilities can emerge.

The value of "What-iffing" is further substantiated by some compelling research underscoring the importance of generating lots of ideas as opposed to a continued focus on coming up with a perfect solution or the "right answer." The author presents convincing data and persuasive anecdotes that demonstrate why a shift from quality to quantity "works because it forces us to push aside perfectionism and act in the real world...." And, as she concludes, "It's not 'quantity or quality' [that is important]. It's: 'quantity breeds quality.'"

11.
It's All in the Questions

It is not the answer that enlightens, but the question.
—Eugene Jonesco

1.

Allow me to take you back in time - to a time in either middle school or high school. Imagine, if you will, an American history class. The teacher ("Miss Boring") is leading the class in a discussion of The Underground Railroad.

"Who can tell me what the Underground Railroad was?" Miss Boring asks the class.

No response.

"Doesn't anybody remember what we talked about two days ago?" she inquires.

Still no response.

"Once again, what was the Underground Railroad?" she asks.

By this time, most of the eyes are at "half-mast" as students are struggling to stay awake, even though the period started a mere five minutes ago,

"Okay, Sarah, can you tell me a famous person associated with the Underground Railroad?"

"I dunno," Sarah replied.

"Jackson, what about you?"

"I can't remember," Jackson mumbles while texting his girlfriend.

"Ashton, can you tell us one significant fact related to the Underground Railroad?" Miss Boring asks.

The question catches Ashton unawares, as he is doodling in the margin of his history book. "I really don't know," he replies.

"Justine, how about you?"

"Harriett What's-her-name," she guesses.

"Well, almost," Miss Boring replies.

The painful and tortuous scenario continues until Miss Boring, frustrated at all the "non-answers," finally tells everyone that Harriett Tubman was one of the pivotal figures in the Underground Railroad movement. Some of the students dutifully write the name in their notebooks, while others force themselves to stay awake for the next round of (boring) questions.

This classroom scene might be more prevalent than we like to admit. It depicts a teacher asking inane questions, students with little or no involvement in the lesson, and a kind of verbal ping-pong in which the teacher keeps asking low-level questions of various students until one student "gets" the right answer or until the teacher is forced to "give" the answer to a class of uninterested and uninvolved students.

As you might imagine, little instruction is taking place. The only objective in this scene is to obtain an answer to a predetermined question. It's a guessing game between students and the teacher. Students try to deduce the answers imbedded in the teacher's head. If they get one, the game moves on to the next question; if they don't get it, the teacher keeps asking until someone does or until the teacher gives the correct answer.

Think back to your own classes in high school. Choose one course that was particularly onerous - a course you dreaded each time you walked in the classroom or each time the teacher stood up from behind his desk to give one of his "pitiful" lectures. You may indeed remember a class where most of the questioning was trivial, with an emphasis on memory and information retrieval. You were seldom afforded opportunities to think about what you were reading in the textbook and rarely were you invited to generate your own questions for discovery. For the most part, the teacher droned on and on and asked questions that were "limp" and focused on insignificant facts.

The minute hand on the clock in the front of the classroom couldn't move fast enough!

2.

Why do teachers ask questions? Actually, there are several reasons. One of the primary functions of questions is to tap into students' background knowledge about a topic. This is done to find out what students know before the lesson begins. Examples include, "Before we begin the lesson, why do you think plants are useful to humans?" or "Why do you think the Declaration of Independence is such a significant document?" These questions are critical because they give teachers insights into both the depth and breadth of background knowledge students bring to a lesson. This helps a teacher structure a lesson to fill in any gaps in students' knowledge base.

Teachers also ask questions in order to evaluate student progress or performance during a lesson. Samples of these questions include, "How would you summarize what we have discussed so far on the Trojan Wars?" and "Given what we have talked about, what would you consider as Joseph Priestly's most important discovery?" These are often called criterion checks and are a way of monitoring how well students are understanding a lesson. Typically, teachers stop every ten to fifteen minutes to ask questions about how well students comprehend the material.

You also know that questions are used to evaluate student understanding at the end of a lesson. Examples include, "What are the three types of rocks?" and "How is the diameter of a circle related to its radius?" Unfortunately, these may be the most overused function of questions. Yes, teachers need to know if students mastered the objectives of the lesson, but to always end a lesson with a barrage of short-term memory questions is a sure way to make lessons dull and boring. Just like that horrible class you recalled from high school.

Questions are a fact of life in every classroom at every educational level. So too, are most teachers aware of what constitutes "best practices." However, many teachers aren't always good monitors of their own performance. Let's take a look.

In one intriguing study, seasoned teachers were asked the following questions about the ideal and actual rates of student and teacher questions:

1. How many questions do you think you ask in a
    30-minute period?
2. How many questions would be desirable?
3. How many questions do your students ask?
4. How many student questions would be ideal?

What would your response be to those questions?

In the study, seasoned teachers estimated that they asked fifteen questions in a thirty-minute class period; they also thought that fifteen questions was the desired rate of teacher question-asking. Those same teachers also estimated that students in their classes were asking about ten questions, which was below their desired target of fifteen.

However, when these same teachers were observed by trained researchers, the data were very different from their original estimates. The results showed that these experienced teachers asked an average of 50.6 questions (during a single class); while students posed only 1.8 questions. To say that teachers were shocked by these findings would be an understatement. In fact, they refused to believe the data until they listened to an audiotape of their own classrooms and counted the number of teacher and student questions. The teachers were well aware of good classroom practices, but found it difficult to implement them in their own classrooms.

There is an old maxim that goes something like this: Teachers tend to teach as they were taught. That is to say, teachers tend to use the same techniques and strategies that were used on them when they were students. They often follow the behaviors and practices that were so much a part of their own education. If you've ever been in a new teacher's classroom, there is a better than average chance she is teaching in the same manner as did her teachers when she was taking that same course many years previously. As you might suspect, teachers use the models they had as students as their own personal models when they take the reins of a similar class. You and I probably did the same thing when we began working in our chosen professions. We followed what others did to ensure a comfortable entre into a new job.

Because most teachers had teachers who asked a plethora of questions in their classroom, that's what they do, too. This is evidence that many classroom teachers don't always do what they know to be good practice - they are often prone to do what their (former) teachers modeled. Even more compelling is the fact that they may not even be aware of those "violations."

3.

Let's dig a little deeper into the effect of questions on classroom instruction and student learning. To do so, we're going to examine some data out of the Advancing Educational Leadership (AEL) Academy where researchers generated a review of what teachers typically do in a classroom and what the corresponding research validates. These studies offer some significant insights as to how our creativity was unknowingly suppressed (via questioning practices) in our elementary and secondary classrooms.

The Academy's initial finding adds some punch to a classroom fact of life - a fact confirmed by generations of students. That is, teachers ask a plethora of questions! Even research conducted more than a half-century ago showed that teachers asked between one and four questions per minute. A more current summary of research on questioning concluded that teachers typically ask between one and three questions per minute. In the AEL study, 95 experienced teachers were asked to videotape themselves in a classroom episode where questioning was the primary instructional strategy; the average number of questions asked in 15 minutes was 43 (that works out to between two to three questions per minute.)

Let's put that data into perspective. Once again, take yourself back to a middle school or high school course - say, a history course. Let's assume the course meets every day and that each meeting is one-hour in length. According to the data above, you would be asked about 172 questions during a single class, roughly 860 questions per week, and approximately 3,440 questions over the course of a month (These, of course, are all averages). As we saw in the vignette that opened this chapter, as well as data shared in the previous chapter, most of the questions asked in that class would be those focused on regurgitating right answers (predetermined answers printed in the Teacher's Manual or in a curriculum guide).

> **Implications:** With more than 150 questions asked during a single class period there is little time for students to process the information and arrive at any type of creative response. The primary objective of this rapid-fire delivery of classroom questions is to "get the right answer" - so that the instruction can move on to the next "right answer" query. And, of course, the aim is to have students come up with the answers previously determined - and subsequently printed in that Teacher's Manual - by the folks who wrote it. Creative responses are sublimated by a desire to "get" lots of right answers to lots of questions. The secret message is that if students are giving lots of answers to lots of questions then they must be learning lots of stuff. Well, maybe!

Think back to that "dreaded" class you took in high school. I suspect that it overflowed with lots of factual information - lots of data you had to cram into your head, memorize for a test, or scribble in your notebook. It should come as no surprise, then, that the second conclusion that emerged from the AEL research review was that a large proportion of the questions teachers ask focus almost exclusively on memory or recall. That is, they were designed to test whether students could remember basic facts about a subject ("Bruce, in what year did Abraham Lincoln sign the Emancipation Proclamation?"; "Ami, can you tell me what a tympanic membrane is?"). If, as the researchers point out, a staccato of one to three questions are posed during each minute of class time, then the kinds of questions that are asked would typically be those that require the least amount of thinking.

> **Implications:** A seemingly non-stop barrage of low-level questions over the course of an instructional unit sends a very distinctive message to students. Over time (and tens

of thousands of factual questions) students come to the conclusion that education is merely collecting information or memorizing lots of facts. Additional research, in combination with my own anecdotal observations, confirms an immutable fact of classroom life: that is, **students tend to read and think based on the kinds of questions they anticipate receiving from a teacher**. That is to say, when a significant number of questions are factual in nature, students naturally get the message that memorizing stuff is much more important than analyzing stuff.

A third conclusion drawn from the AEL data demonstrates something we all know intuitively. That is, in most classrooms, questions are typically answered by a minority of students. In short, not everyone participates equally in the processing or answering of questions. For the most part, a select coterie of students are always the ones who raise their hands and, consequently, always the ones who answer the questions. Sometimes identified as "target students," these are individuals who dominate classroom discussions. For the most part, they are also the ones who can be counted on (by the teacher) to come up with the most correct answers to the machine-gun barrage of factual queries. One study presented evidence that these target students respond to questions more than three times as often as their classmates. Equally compelling is the finding that approximately 25 percent of students in any classroom never participate at all.

Implications: It is apparent that significant numbers of students are given little opportunity to actively engage in the dynamics of classroom instruction. In fact, many students have learned how to "hide" in a classroom environment - thus ensuring that they seldom, if ever, have to answers any questions at all. They are afforded a unique opportunity to be passive observers in the exchange of information that typically takes place in a classroom.[13]

---

13 Imagine a typical classroom set up: Several rows of desks in orderly rows. Stand in front of that imaginary classroom facing all those desks (just as a teacher would). Now draw an imaginary "T" straight down the middle two columns of desks and across the two rows of desks in the back of the room. Interestingly, almost all classroom questions are directed to students in the "T." As a student, if you want to "hide" from the teacher, take a desk that is in the front two quadrants of the room - at the corners. Trust me, you will become virtually "invisible."

In short, they are not engaged - either intellectually or creatively.

Listen in to many classrooms (at all levels), and you'll hear teachers assaulting students with a constant and never-ending bombardment of questions. If you will, imagine being in a meeting with your supervisor throwing out a nonstop array of questions; over 100 questions during the hour-long meeting. With so many questions coming at you and your colleagues, there would hardly be sufficient time to think about any single question, much less all the questions collectively. Your brain can only process so much information at a time.

Or, let's look at that meeting another way: the more questions asked, the less thinking occurs. If the only intent is to respond with a series of "right answers," then creativity is effectively quashed. Someone controls the discussion by asking multiple of low-level questions to the exclusion of higher-level queries. Indeed, the same thing happens in elementary and secondary classrooms all the time.

But, here is one of the most startling pieces of research data on classroom questioning: believe it or not, teachers typically wait less than one second for students to respond to a question! Yes, you read that right: less than one second! In practice, many teachers often conclude that students don't know the answer to a question if they don't respond quickly. In other words, if a student can't come up with a quick response to a factual question then they, most likely, don't know the answer. Mental contemplation and intellectual consideration are sacrificed at the expense of rapid-fire questions and rapid-fire responses. Students learn that answering a question quickly is rewarded and that taking time to ponder a potential response is systematically inhibited. Creative responses are discouraged; factual responses earn "brownie points" by maintaining the (rapid) pace of the lesson.

Prevailing research and teacher observations also reveals another, equally intriguing practice that takes place in classrooms every day. That is, if and when a student manages to get a response in (to one of those fact-based questions), most teachers tend to ask another question within an average time span of nine-tenths of a second! That is to say, the space between an answer and another question occurs in less time than it takes to blink your eyes three times.[14]

Think about that (please, take your time)!

On the surface, it seems as though the primary objective of many classroom teachers is to ask as many low-level questions as possible in the shortest amount of time available. Under pressure from a mandated curriculum pudgy with a surfeit of facts, teachers must often resort to practices that defy logic, "best practices," and common sense. They are often forced to cram as much substance into a lesson as possible, without the benefit of "think time."

> **Implications:** The rapid-fire pace of questions in most classrooms results in students who are not engaged and not thinking deeply about the content. The machine gun barrages of questions and machine gun responses to those questions creates an environment where speed is a priority and thinking is often an afterthought. Students are processing information superficially with little time given over to reflection, contemplation, and deliberation. Creativity takes a back seat to a rampage of questions and a riot of responses.

Let's take a break here and look in on another classroom. We'll make this one a tenth grade Biology class. The teacher (Mr. Darwin) is working on a lesson about invertebrates.

Mr. Darwin: "Marion, what exactly is an invertebrate?"
Marion: "It's an animal that really, really, soft."
Mr. Darwin: "O.K., a soft animal." "Jason, can you give us an example of an invertebrate?"
Jason: "I dunno."
Mr. Darwin: "Well, insects, arachnids, and molluscs are example of invertebrates. Can anyone tell us the biggest difference between invertebrates and verte-brates? Damian?"
Damian: "They don't have a lot of bones."

14 On average, most people blink their eyes [once] in one-third of a second.

Mr. Darwin: "Well, that's sorta right. Frankie, what do you think?"

Frankie: "I was just going to say the same thing."

Mr. Darwin: "Justin, what would you say?"

Justin: "I would say that they have that bone thing in their back."

Mr. Darwin: "And, what is that 'bone thing' called? Tamara?"

Tamara: "I think it's called a spine."

Mr. Darwin: "Well, that's almost right. It's called a vertebral column."

Another interesting point that surfaced in the AEL research was the tendency of many teachers to accept any type of response to a question. In the words of the authors, "Teachers often accept incorrect answers without probing; they frequently answer their own questions; most are reluctant to provide feedback to students who give less than correct answers; and even fewer are willing to stick with that student - and provide prompts - to help a student complete a response to a question asked." In short, many teachers are willing to accept any type of response, or even a non-response ("I dunno.") for the convenience of moving on to the next question in their repertoire. The authors further note a bank of studies showing that nearly half of student answers are at a different cognitive level than the teacher's question, yet teachers generally accept these answers as sufficient without probing or prompting correct responses.

Implications: The "rush" to get as many questions into a class period as possible leaves little time for teachers to engage students in any meaningful sort of dialogue about the implications or ramifications of their responses. In short, teachers subvert critical and creative thinking opportunities for the sake of convenience; and students are frequently denied an opportunity to process new information in meaningful contexts - all to "cover" an overweight curriculum full of facts, but frequently absent of engagement.

Finally, the AEL authors underscore the dearth of questions posed by students themselves. They note that in classrooms where teachers shower students with two to three questions every minute, there is little time for student queries. They cite research demonstrating that at both the elementary and secondary levels, students ask less than five percent of the questions posed over the course of an instructional day. Entertaining student questions, the authors contend, means that there is less time to "cover the material." That may get the instruction "off track." Yet, many educators have written persuasively about how student-generated questions are essential to learning.

> **Implications:** Creative thinking means time and opportunity to ask questions and seek answers. When students are denied this chance to explore, analyze, weigh, inspect, probe, scrutinize, and consider how information can be used, they are being denied an important part of intellectual inquiry. In essence, they become divorced from the reality of education; that true learning is more about the process and less about the products.

All our knowledge results from questions, which is another way of saying that question-asking is our most important intellectual tool.
—**Neil Postman**

4.

For a moment, let's go back in time to 1956, when educator Benjamin Bloom developed a taxonomy popularly known as Bloom's Taxonomy. This classification system was designed to assist teachers in recognizing the quality of questions available to them, no matter the grade level or subject area. The system (revised in 2001) contains six levels, arranged in hierarchical form - moving from the lowest to highest level of cognition - or from the least complex of thinking skills to the most complex. Let's examine them briefly.

1. **Remembering** - This is the lowest level of questions and requires students to recall information. Knowledge questions usually require students to identify information in basically the same form it was presented. Some examples of knowledge questions include: 1) "What is the biggest city in Japan?", 2) "Who wrote War and Peace?", and 3) "How many ounces in a pound?"

2. **Comprehending** - Simply stated, comprehension is the way in which ideas are organized into categories. Comprehension questions are those that ask students to take several bits of information and put them into a category or grouping. Examples of comprehending questions include: 1) "How would you illustrate the water cycle?", 2) "What is the main idea of this story?", and 3) "How could you put these blocks together to form a triangle?"

3. **Applying** - At this level of questioning, teachers ask students to take information they already know and apply it to a new situation. Some examples of applying questions include: 1) "How would you use your knowledge of latitude and longitude to locate Iceland?", 2) "What happens when you multiply each of these numbers by nine?", and 3) "If you had eight inches of water in your basement and a hose, how would you use the hose to get the water out?"

4. **Analyzing** - An analyzing question is one that asks a student to break down something into its component parts. To analyze requires students to identify reasons, causes, or motives and reach conclusions or generalizations. Some examples of analysis questions include: 1) "What are some of the factors that cause rust?", 2) "Why did the United States go to war with England?", and 3) "Why do you think the author wrote this book?"

5. **Evaluating** - Evaluating requires an individual to make a judgment about something. We are asked to judge the value of an idea, a candidate, a work of art, or a solution to a problem. Typically, evaluation questions do not

have single right answers. Some examples of evaluating questions include: 1) "What do you think about
your work so far?", 2) "Why do you think the pioneers left
the Oregon Trail?", and 3) "Why do you think Benjamin
Franklin is so famous?"

6. **Creating** - Creating questions challenge students
to engage in creative and original thinking. These
questions invite students to produce original ideas and
solve problems. Some examples of creating questions
include: 1) "How would you assemble these items to
create a windmill?", 2) "What would you need to do to
construct a tower one foot tall using only four blocks?",
and 3) "How could you put these words together to form
a complete sentence?"

As you will note, the six levels of questions move from those that
rely on simple recall (Remembering) to those that offer students opportunities for multiple responses and dynamic engagement (Creating).
In short, it's a scale that moves from least complex to most complex.
By the same token, it's also a scale that moves from least involvement
to greatest involvement.

5.

O.K., What does all this mean? Several things, actually! It means
teachers can ask their students several different kinds of questions.
However, if teachers only focus on one type of question (say "remembering" questions), their students might not be exposed to higher levels
of thinking important in a thorough understanding of a topic. If, for
example, teachers ask predominantly "remembering" questions, then
their students might think that learning (a specific topic) is nothing
more than the ability to memorize (or remember) a select number of
facts.

Second, teachers find that this taxonomy helps them craft a wide
range of questions - from low-level thinking questions to high-level
thinking questions. If variety is the spice of life, teachers can then

sprinkle a variety of question types throughout every lesson, regardless of the topic or the grade level they teach. However, a significant study completed more than forty years ago confirmed that most teachers spend only about twenty percent of their questioning time on queries that require thinking at higher levels. And, yet, additional studies have conclusively shown that the use of those higher-level questions in classrooms has a positive impact on the development of creativity.

But, there's something I need to interject at this point. That is, this taxonomy is not grade-specific. That is, it does not begin at the lower grades (kindergarten, first, second) with "remembering" and "comprehending" questions and move upward to the higher grades (tenth, eleventh, twelfth) with "evaluating" and "creating" questions. The six levels of questions are appropriate for all grade levels. For example, many people mistakenly think primary-level students (kindergarten through grade 2) cannot "handle" higher-level thinking questions (applying, analyzing, evaluating, creating). Nothing could be further from the truth! If you've ever been around a group of four-year-olds, for example, you know they can come up with some of the most penetrating questions known to human-kind ("How come birds can fly, but cats can't?, "Why is the sky sometimes blue and sometimes orange?", and "Why do we always have to go to Aunt Betty's for Thanksgiving?"). Challenging all students through higher-order questioning is one of the best ways teachers can stimulate learning, foster intellectual discoveries, and enhance creativity - regardless of grade (preschool to college), age, or subject matter.

Now, let's take a moment and look at one of the most critical conclusions from this enormous bank of research on the use of questions in any classroom. And, that is, students will approach any subject as a knowledge-based topic if they are presented with an overabundance of knowledge-level questions throughout a lesson. Think about some of the history or science courses you may have taken in school. If all you did in those classes was to respond to lots of fact-based ("Remembering") questions from your teacher, then it is likely that you pictured those classes as nothing more than "fact factories." On the other hand, if you were subjected to an array of higher level thinking questions (e.g. "Analyzing," "Creating") then you would have pictured those courses as creatively challenging and intellectually intensive.

The implications for all of us are critical: as students, we often receive few models to emulate, and few opportunities to engage in, creative thinking. Little wonder then, that by the time we graduate from high school, we will have had limited exposure to creative questions and the resultant thinking necessary to respond to those questions. We will have graduated with a head full of factual information (which earned us that high school diploma), but little practice in utilizing or expanding the native creative powers we enjoyed before we entered school twelve years previously. Our "creative education" will have been sublimated at the expense of our "practical education."

But...

There's a cautionary note to inject here. Lest we infer that teachers are to blame for our creative demise, we need to keep in mind that they are the purveyors of a heavyweight curriculum gorged with a plethora of facts, and mandated by federal, state, and local initiatives beyond their control. Those initiatives are often based on an antiquated belief that the more facts that can be crammed into individual student heads, the more "educated" they will be. In many subject areas, the prevailing belief is: more curriculum = more education.

As a result, classroom teachers are under intense pressure to "cover" a curriculum in a limited amount of time. To ensure that all the information in that curriculum is addressed, the speed and intensity of its presentation must be increased to ensure that the entire "package" is delivered within the mandated 180 school days. And, the most practical way to deliver that information is via a rapid-fire, low-level questioning protocol. In short, creative thinking is sublimated in favor of efficiency and convenience.

Truth be told, the models of creative thinking are frequently bypassed in an effort to inject increasing amounts of knowledge into students' heads. There's certainly nothing wrong with that knowledge - unless we are denied opportunities to manipulate it in dynamic and innovative ways.

Suffice it to say, questions are powerful learning tools. The questions we have been asked throughout our educational experiences (and the questions we were allowed to ask on our own) are precursors to a creative life. Denying inquisitive thought by inadvertently "controlling" the types of queries we were exposed to, in concert with offering relatively few opportunities to question the world in which we live, can have serious repercussions in fostering a creative mind and a creative perspective.

Any questions?

12.
How to Sizzle: 36 - 43

36. Go Higher. Remember that the types of questions we ask kids determines, in large measure, how they think. Ask lots of fact-based questions ("What is the state capital of Iowa?" "What is the chemical symbol for salt?" "What is the Pythagorean Theorem?) and children will tend to think primarily at a factual level. In any conversation with your children, focus more on higher-level thinking questions that promote creative thinking skills. For example, ask more questions that begin with the word "Why," than with the word "What." Most important, higher level questions also serve as models for the kinds of questions kids can ask themselves...and that eventually leads to more creative thinking.

37. More Questions From Kids. Typically educators ask most (if not all) of the questions in any educational endeavor. Recall that kids are frequently bombarded with up to 400 questions every school day. In short, students often get the message that teachers are in control of the thinking that takes place in a classroom. That can be a critical deterrent to creative thought. Instead, provide sufficient opportunities for kids to ask their own self-initiated questions. Teach them the different levels of questions and encourage them to use higher-level (Analyzing, Synthesizing, Evaluating, Creating) in every class discussion. Every lesson (no matter the grade level or subject area) can benefit tremendously from the addition of student-generated queries. I've seen students from Kindergarten to graduate-level become more engaged with the addition of opportunities to ask (and pursue the answers to) their own self-initiated questions. The results are transformative.

38. How To Conclude A Lesson. Don't end a teaching session, or department meeting, or conference presentation with the typical query, "Does anyone have any questions?" You'll always get a sea of blank expressions and non-responses. Assume participants have questions. Instead, at the end of a presentation, invite individuals to pair up and record two questions they have about the just-completed lesson or meeting. During the next lesson/presentation, weave the answers to those questions into any follow-up discussions or presentations. Now the lesson/meeting revolves around their queries - an important motivational tactic as well as a stimulant to creative thinking.

39. Reverse Roles. Convincing research has shown that most teachers ask far too many questions of their students and that most "instructional time" is devoted to asking (and answering) questions. As a college professor, I was aware of all that research and decided one day to reverse a common assumption (teachers ask the questions; students respond to the questions). I gave one of my classes a short lecture on higher-level cognitive questions. Then, for each of the next several days I presented a brief lecture on a specific topic related to the course. Then, I divided the class into several small groups and tasked each group with developing 5-6 higher-level questions about the lecture. The class reconvened and students were given the opportunity to ask me the questions and to engage me in a conversation about specific aspects of the topic (a reversal of roles). WOW! The result was some of the most stimulating and engaging classroom conversations ever! It also forced me to think about my subject matter in entirely new ways since students were also encouraged to evaluate my responses. On end-of-the-semester evaluations students consistently remarked that this activity was one of the most memorable and most educational.

40. Connections. Sometimes, when we are working on a challenging problem, we become locked in to old habits. As a result, it becomes more difficult to discover solutions because our mind is trapped in familiar ways of thinking. Here's one way to break free.

Ask a friend or colleague to give you a completely random set of eight words - words that come from several diverse fields and that apparently have no connection to each other. Then, try to divide the words into as many different categories or classifications as you can (each category must have a minimum of two items). For example, I recently asked my wife to give me eight random words. Here's what she shared: **valance, trip, book, snow, sheets, rug, tired, painting**. Here are just a few categories I came up with: things in the living room, things with the letter e, white things, things viewed vertically, things viewed horizontally, things manufactured in a foreign country, and things that go in a washing machine. Take this idea one step further and select eight random words from a project, document, or challenge that you are currently working on. See what kinds of different groupings you can put them in. You will discover, as I do, that you will be able to see that project with an entirely new set of eyes. You'll ask questions and see connections that were previously invisible. Best of all, you'll create novel arrangements that may offer some truly unique solutions.

41. Get Bored. Want to get really creative? Get bored. I frequently generate some of my best ideas when I'm doing something really boring or inane: Taking clean clothes out of the dryer and folding them. Walking through an antiques store with my wife. Any activity that involves a vacuum cleaner. Watching a Victorian romance via the BBC. Painting the bedroom (again). Boredom frees up your mind. It can now pursue other things and take off in other directions. According to Ozan Varol in his book *Think Like a Rocket Scientist*, "without boredom, our creativity muscles begin to atrophy from disuse." He goes on to advocate for the power of boredom to give us "...time to think - if we don't pause, understand, and deliberate - we can't find wisdom or form new ideas." In support of that idea, two British researchers poured through several years of research and came up with a startling conclusion; that is, that boredom should "be recognized as a legitimate human emotion that can be central to learning and creativity." By getting lost and mindlessly wandering, we are establishing a seedbed for innovative queries and opening up the door to creative possibilities. Watch carefully - you never know what might walk in.

42. A Questioning Environment. As you recall from earlier in the book, children enter school filled with a plethora of questions. However, by the time they graduate from high school or college, their willingness to ask questions has diminished significantly - often to the point of extinction. Fostering a creative climate in the workplace is often dependent on how much curiosity is embraced. We know, for example, that curiosity is dependent on the generation of questions and creativity frequently emanates from our constant search for answers to those questions. Thus, it is important for business leaders to establish an environment where curiosity is embraced and celebrated. Leaders who govern with a "My way or the highway" philosophy tamp down curiosity and the desire to ask questions. As a result, creativity is diminished (and often snuffed out). Group meetings, annual retreats, and monthly discussions should all be predicated on the idea that questions are encouraged, celebrated, and natural. Leaders who pose higher-level questions serve as positive role models. They send a powerful signal that knowledge isn't stagnant, and that progress can only come about when everyone is encouraged to pose divergent questions - both comfortable and otherwise - and supported in all those contributions.

43. Divergent Questions. *Divergent Questions* is a creative strategy I often use to re-charge my creative batteries. I keep a list of "question stems" like those below – each one written on a separate index card. These are kept in a recipe box on my desk. I add more question stems periodically (I encourage you to start with the ones below and, over time, add your own). When I've been to the "mental well" too many times and I need to charge up my mind, I pull a random card from the deck and fill in the blanks. The result – lots of great new ideas.

Here's a list to get you started:

1. List all the words to describe _____.
2. What are all the possible solutions for _____?
3. List as many _____ as you can think of.
4. How would _____ view this?
5. What would _____ mean from the standpoint of _____?

6. How would a _____ describe _____?
7. How would you feel if you were _____?
8. What would _____ do?
9. You are a _____. Describe your feelings.
10. How is _____ like _____?
11. I only know about _____. Explain _____ to _____.
12. What ideas from _____ are like _____?
13. What _____ is most like a _____?
14. What would happen if there were more _____?
15. Suppose _____ happened, what would be the results?
16. Imagine if _____ and _____ were reversed. What would happen?

A few years ago I began writing a children's book on rainforests, but I couldn't come up with a unique way to approach the topic. I thought about looking at rainforests from a number of different viewpoints and used my stack of *Divergent Questions* cards to give myself several self-imposed writing tasks. Here are some of the possibilities I generated:

➤ Make a list of all the words you can think of to describe a rainforest.
➤ How would a macaw describe a rainforest? How would an anaconda snake describe that same rainforest?
➤ How would you feel if you were a piece of driftwood floating on the surface of the Amazon River?
➤ How are river currents like ocean waves?
➤ You are a sloth. Describe your feelings about moving through the trees.
➤ What do you think would happen if there were fewer tarantulas in the world?
➤ Suppose all the rainforests were eliminated, what do you think might happen?
➤ Imagine that you had to live on a hut in the rainforest for the next year. What habits would you need to change?

You will note that all my questions were higher level (applying, analyzing, evaluating, creating). My intent was to open up my mind to an infinite array of writing possibilities. I've found that the use of *Divergent Question* cards helps me generate a plethora of new ideas that frequently lead me into newfound (and often unexpected) directions. The result of the "rainforest exercise" above was my children's book *A is for Anaconda: A Rainforest Alphabet* - a book honored as a *National Best Books Award Finalist* in 2009.

13.
Rewards and
Punishments

*Rewards and punishments are the lowest
form of education.*
—ZHUANGZI

1.

It's been more than sixty years, yet I can still see that chart hanging in my sixth grade classroom as though it were yesterday. It's impression is still seared into my memory - a forever reminder of my elementary education.

Mrs. Wilson was a stickler for spelling. She would often say that good spelling was the sign of a good scholar. If you couldn't spell (at least according to Mrs. Wilson), you were doomed to a life of scholastic failure, occupational heartbreak, and intellectual destitution (among myriad other tragedies). To make her point, she posted a large piece of white cardboard on the wall just behind her desk. All her students' names were written in neat alphabetical order down the left hand side. Across the top were listed all the Fridays of the academic year (Fridays being the day when we would take our weekly spelling test - twenty words to memorize and spell accurately). A series of blocks followed each student's name - boxes into which Mrs. Wilson would paste stars of certain colors. Get all twenty words correct on the weekly spelling test and you would get a gold star, nineteen words correct = a silver star, eighteen words correct = a red star, and seventeen words correct = a green star. Less than seventeen words correct meant there would be no star after one's name for that week.

So there, for public display was a record of our spelling prowess (or lack thereof). Anyone who entered the room (as well as every student in that room) quickly knew who the good spellers were and who the bad spellers were. The "Haves" and the "Have Nots" were clearly advertised for anyone to see. It was an intellectual hierarchy that seemingly foretold each student's academic future.

I will never forget Parent/Teacher Night in late November when my parents walked into that classroom and there - in full exhibition - was a blaring record of their son's spelling proficiency (or lack thereof). My best friend, Kevin, had a parade of twelve gold stars after his name (his parents were beaming). I, on the other hand, had two blue stars and one red star after my name (my parents were considerably less than proud). The damnable image of that spelling chart (and its repercussions) have stayed with me ever since. Trust me when I tell you that the "Spell Check" feature on my word processing program is, most likely, the greatest invention in all of recorded history (Although a good key lime pie comes in a close second.)!

But, this is not a collection of spelling vignettes; rather it's a chapter about behavioral reinforcements and other rewards and punishments handed out to students on a daily basis. It's also about how those "incentives" affect our creative sprit...often in a negative way.

2.

There is a common psychological concept, known as "locus of control," that helps define who we are and how we approach tasks - whether those tasks are academic, social, occupational, or personal. By definition, locus of control refers to an individual's belief system in regards to the causes of her or his experiences and the conditions or factors to which an individual attributes success or failure. Two terms are used to describe one's locus of control: External and Internal. By in large, "external individuals" feel they are strongly influenced by others (parents, teachers, peers). An individual with an external predisposition might say something like, "Of course, I failed the exam, the teacher was a flaming idiot!" "Internal individuals" feel they are primarily responsible for the events that happen to them. An Internal person would be most likely to express the following: "I put a lot of time and effort into that report and I'm really proud of how it turned out."

It's important to note that you and I aren't exclusively "Internal" or exclusively "External." That is to say, we're not at one extreme or the other. Rather we need to view the concept of locus of control as a continuum. That is, people aren't 100 percent external or 100 percent internal; they fall somewhere along a locus of control continuum , with a predisposition to one side or the other. Here's what it looks like:

External...Internal

(Outcomes outside your	(Outcomes within your
control—determined by	control—determined solely
the fate of other people.)	by your actions or beliefs.)

It's equally important to note that our locus of control vacillates over the course of our lives. There are times in our lives when we may lean towards an Internal locus of control (e.g. winning an award or contest, finding the love of our life) and other times when we may be more predisposed to an External view of life (e.g. personal tragedy, end of a relationship). Suffice it to say, however, that, for the most part, we all fall within a very narrow band on that continuum.

Now, just for a moment, I'd like you to step inside the mind of one of your children (or any other child who you know quite well). Below are some statements. I'd like to invite you to put a "T" (for True) in front of those statements with which you agree (remember, you are answering these statements as though you were a particular child). For those statements that you disagree with, place a "F" (for False) in front of each one.[15] As an alternate strategy, you may want to read these statements to a child and ask her if each statement is true or false (for her). You can them mark each statement appropriately. Of course, if your child has the requisite reading skills, she may want to take this survey independently on her own.

---

15 It's important to know that there are no "right" or "wrong" answers.

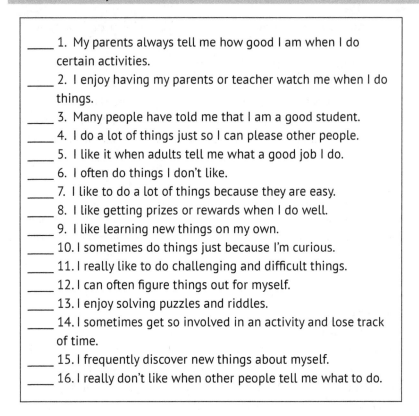

_____ 1. My parents always tell me how good I am when I do certain activities.

_____ 2. I enjoy having my parents or teacher watch me when I do things.

_____ 3. Many people have told me that I am a good student.

_____ 4. I do a lot of things just so I can please other people.

_____ 5. I like it when adults tell me what a good job I do.

_____ 6. I often do things I don't like.

_____ 7. I like to do a lot of things because they are easy.

_____ 8. I like getting prizes or rewards when I do well.

_____ 9. I like learning new things on my own.

_____ 10. I sometimes do things just because I'm curious.

_____ 11. I really like to do challenging and difficult things.

_____ 12. I can often figure things out for myself.

_____ 13. I enjoy solving puzzles and riddles.

_____ 14. I sometimes get so involved in an activity and lose track of time.

_____ 15. I frequently discover new things about myself.

_____ 16. I really don't like when other people tell me what to do.

When the survey is completed, add up the number of statements that were marked with a "T." If there are more true statements for numbers 1-8 than there are for statements 9-16, then the child (or you) is, most likely, externally motivated. On the other hand, if there are more true statements for numbers 9-16 than there are for statements 1-8, then that child (or you) is, very likely, internally motivated.[16]

A person with an external locus of control often attributes her success to luck or fate. As a result, they are often less likely to put in the effort to learn. "Externals" often feel as though they are not in control of their lives. On the other hand, people with an internal locus of control place their successes (or failures) in life squarely on their own shoulders. They take personal responsibility for the learning process. As you might suspect, students who are more internally motivated often demonstrate higher levels of academic achievement.

16 NOTE: This is an informal assessment of one's locus of control. There are several on-line scales you can use to gauge your individual locus of control. To locate one, just Google "Locus of Control Quiz."

On the other hand, external students frequently exhibit lower levels of academic achievement.

In any discussion of locus of control, it's critical to understand that an internal locus is not necessarily "good," and that an external locus of control is "bad." There is a whole panoply of psychological variables to be considered in addition to just locus of control. Suffice to say, however, that locus of control has a profound and lasting effect on how our children learn and how they view themselves as part of the learning process.

3.

There is an accepted belief that if classroom teachers can help students achieve a more internal locus of control, they can assist them in achieving higher levels of scholastic achievement. One of the most common ways teachers do this is through the use of positive reinforcement. The two "classics" of positive reinforcement are <u>praise</u> and <u>encouragement</u>. But, we need to be cautious here, because, although they sound similar, they are not the same thing; nor do they have the same effect on students. First, let's clarify the two concepts with brief definition

> ➤ Praise: to express a favorable judgement.
> ➤ Encouragement: to inspire one to do better.

Look carefully at those two definitions and you'll notice something. That is, praise is something that is done to someone else. That is to say, praise is when one person says something positive to another person ("You are doing a good job in math today, Jason," "You did your homework which is what I expect you to do every day."). On the other hand, encouragement is when one person moves another towards some type of favorable outcome ("What else will you need to do to continue your success in the chess tournament?" "How do you feel about your work so far?").

But here is the most important and most significant difference between these two concepts: praise and encouragement are at either end of the locus of control continuum. Praise tends to foster an external locus of control, while encouragement tends to foster an internal locus of control. This is not to say we (parents, teachers, scout leaders, day care workers) should eliminate all praise and concentrate solely on encouragement. Rather, we need to emphasize more encouragement than praise to help children achieve a more internal locus of control.

But, a word of caution is in order. Many of us tend to fall into a perilous trap: false and excessive praise. For example, teachers want to be friendly with their students, they want to let them know that they support all their academic efforts, and they want students to have good and positive experiences in the classroom. So, they hand out lots of praise...lots and lots of praise for anything and everything.

And so do we as parents.

The problem comes about when we praise children for minimal effort and achievement ("Oh, wow, Sonya, you got problem number 27 correct. What an absolutely terrific job!" "Oh, Steven, you remembered to feed the dog tonight. What an incredibly wonderful event. Let's have some chocolate cake!"). The message to the child is clear: I can get some recognition and commendation with very little work. In other words, less than my best work is good enough. What happens is that kids quickly get a message that minimal effort is perfectly acceptable (Because even some minimal effort will get some kind of praise.). In short, excessive praise not only fosters an emphasis on external controls, it "un-motivates" children.

At this point, you probably suspect a strong correlation between encouragement, locus of control and creativity. You might infer that more encouragement than praise leads to a more internal locus of control which, in turn leads to higher levels of creativity. By the same token, you might also assume that more praise than encouragement leads to a more external locus of control which results in lowered levels of creative output.

And, you'd be right!

Consider a research study in which elementary students were invited to work on a task requiring high levels of creativity. Individuals who were praised for their performance went on to do lower-quality work on a follow-up (and similar) task. By comparison, students who received more neutral comments evidenced higher quality work. Those results were confirmed by a classic classroom study which showed that elementary school students whose teachers frequently used praise showed less task persistence than their peers. This may be because praise sets up unrealistic expectations of continued success, which leads students to avoid difficult tasks in order not to risk the possibility of failure.

In another well-known experiment, children were given a single cognitive task to do and, after they completed it, were praised for their performance. Half of them were told something like, "Wow! You did really well - *you must be very smart!*" The other half were told, "Wow! You did really well - *you must have worked really hard!*" Even the lead researcher was surprised by the magnitude of the effects she saw. When students were offered follow-up tests to take, and told that one was easy and the other one was hard, the children who had been acknowledged for their effort eagerly embraced the more challenging test. Those who had been acknowledged for their intelligence were far more likely to choose the easy exam.

This eventually translated into performance during the third round of the project, when everyone was given another easy test. In this part of the research study, it was discovered that kids who had eagerly attacked the difficult problems showed improvement, while kids who had stuck to a task they could do well on actually performed worse.

Think about how grown-ups talk to children. "You're such a good boy!" we say. "Look at you - you're so smart!" Or "You're so pretty." The subtle message we are sending is that good qualities are something you *are*, not something you *learn* or *develop*.[17] That message is driven home by both parents and teachers, particularly in environments overflowing with an excess of praise and a dearth of encouragement. The comments expressed by adults have a significant, and often permanent, effect on how those individuals are willing to

---

17 Later in this book, we'll talk about two mindsets: The Fixed mindset ("I'm just not creative.") and the Growth mindset ("I have the capacity to improve my creativity."). Observe how praise ("You are an excellent student.") underscores a fixed mindset [A child's "fate" is determined by others.]. Note how encouragement ("What else could you have done to get a better grade?") supports a growth mindset [Children always have room to improve.].

grow their creative powers or even believe themselves to be creative in the first place.

4.

There's another common practice teachers and parents use in their attempts to motivate children: tangible rewards. These include things like stickers, smiley faces, coupons, patches, gold stars, and the like as motivational tools. The practice of providing these "motivators" has been a consistent one in education. But, as you might expect, there are some controversies surrounding the use of tangible rewards.

In his pivotal book, *Punished by Rewards*, author Alfie Kohn laments the overuse of rewards when he writes:

> "The core of pop behaviorism is "Do this and you'll get that." The wisdom of this technique is very rarely held up for inspection; all that is open to question is what exactly people will receive and under what circumstances it will be promised and delivered. We take for granted that this is the logical way to raise children, teach students, and manage employees. We promise bubble gum to a five-year-old if he keeps quiet in the supermarket. We dangle an A before a teenager to get her to study harder. We hold out the possibility of a Hawaiian vacation for a salesman who sells enough of the company's product.
>
> What concerns me is the practice of using these things *as* rewards. To take what people want or need and offer it on a contingent basis in order to control how they act - this is where the trouble lies. Our attention is properly focused, in other words, not on "that" (the thing desired) but on the requirement that one must *do this in order to get* that."

Think about how many times you've given a reward to someone. You promise your son a "surprise" if he mows the lawn. You tell your husband that you'll cook him a special dinner if he puts up a shelf unit in the bathroom. When each task is completed, you quietly applaud and tell them how proud you are of their newfound behaviors. And, you attempt to reinforce those behaviors by offering them something they might treasure: the latest video game for your son and a steak dinner (medium rare) for your husband.

But, what happens? In your desire to celebrate their "good behavior" with a reward, you exert a form of external control. In short, external control is when one person tries to control the behavior of another. Your "control" was in the form of a reward (video game, steak dinner) and their future behavior will be dependent on their anticipation of subsequent rewards. Or, as Kohn might put it, "If you do that, then I will give you this."

In short, you are using bribery and coercion (the rewards) to get what you want. You are fostering an external locus of control.

What are the implications of these rewards (for good behavior, for good performance)? First of all, there is a tendency for children (or husbands) to work for the rewards, rather than for the learning that might occur. In essence, they work for the external benefits, rather than for any internal growth. They develop a mindset that the reward is much more important than any learning that may occur. They are being manipulated and controlled and, as a result, the more rewards that are handed out, the more rewards come to be expected.

Here's another example: A team of young gymnasts are participating in a competitive gymnastics event. Let's say they all do well and the team gets second place overall. The instructor announces that she's going to give the team an ice-cream and cake party. That's a celebration because it was unexpected and wasn't a condition of the event. However, if the instructor says, "If you do well at the competition tomorrow, I'll give you all an ice-cream and cake party," that's a reward, because she tried to influence their behavior or performance with an external premium.

But, let's raise that thinking up a notch (or two). If we are dependent on rewards for our motivation, then we lock ourselves into a clearly defined way of thinking. We look for "right answers," because getting the right answer will also get us a reward. We engage in "safe" activities, because "safe" activities ensure a greater chance of getting some sort of external reward ("Just play on the jungle gym and you won't get hurt like you would in the woods."). And, we eschew creative thinking because (as we'll discover in the next chapter), creative thinking seldom results in any rewards.

More often, it results in condemnation.

Two carefully designed research studies clinch the case against the use of rewards. In the first, young creative writers who merely spent five minutes *thinking* about the rewards their work could bring (such as money and public recognition) wrote less creative poetry than others who hadn't been reflecting on these reasons for pursuing their craft. The quality of the first group's writing was also lower than the work that they themselves had done a little while earlier. In the second study, the researcher involved children and adults in tasks such as making collages and inventing stories. Some subjects were promised rewards - real ones this time - and others weren't. Again, rewards killed creativity, and this was true regardless of the type of task, the type of reward, the timing of the reward, or the age of the people involved. Engaging in novel problem-solving tasks is actually enhanced when there are no rewards, than when there are. That may seem counterintuitive, but the research is convincingly clear - rewards depress creativity.

We frequently use rewards and praise as "carrots" in the learning process - both at home and in school. Part of the problem is that rewards are typically based on artificial criteria established by adults, not children ("You will get this if you do that."). Even more interesting is the strong correlation between an internal locus of control and a positive creative outlook. Consequently, it behooves us (as teachers and parents) to emphasize practices that enhance personal responsibility, self-determination, and, ultimately, innovative thinking. Rewards won't do that!

5.

Let's wave a magic wand and turn you into a third grade teacher (Are you ready for a classroom of twenty-four rambunctious eight-year-olds?). During the course of the day, you are trying to squeeze in lessons on reading, mathematics, science, social studies, language arts, physical education, and art. Some of your students excel in certain subjects, while others struggle in others. In short, your classroom is not unlike tens of thousands of other third grade classrooms throughout the country.

And, just like in those other classrooms, you have some students you particularly enjoy working with and other students who, to be polite, you wish were absent (a lot). In brief, you have your favorites and you also have individuals you'd rather be elsewhere.

So, do you have a tendency to like the creative students and dislike the non-creative students? That was a question psychologists Erik Westby and V.L Dawson asked a few years back and they came up with some surprising answers. These researchers wanted to know if elementary teachers had a preference for creative students based on several measures of creativity.

To study this question, they identified a random sample of elementary teachers in the Albany, NY area. The teachers ranged in age from 25 to 70, who also indicated wide variations in number of years taught. In the first part of the study, the teachers were given a check list consisting of twenty statements. Ten of those statements, determined through previous research, focused on characteristics typical of creative children (e.g. independent, determined, individualistic); the other ten statements detailed characteristics of children with low levels of creativity (e.g. dependable, good-natured, practical).

The teachers were then asked to rate their favorite student on each of these twenty characteristics using a nine-point scale ranging from *least descriptive* (1) to *most descriptive* (9). The teachers were also asked to rate their least favorite student in the same manner. The results, though surprising for you and me, were not unexpected. They supported a large bank of other research studies, conducted over four decades, that teachers prefer traits that seem to run counter to creativity. These traits included personality characteristics such as conformity and unquestioning acceptance of authority. In other words, teachers tend to prefer students who are compliant, agreeable, and well-mannered. They tend not to enjoy creative students - those who frequently exhibit counter-productive behavioral patterns.

The results supported a discovery made by the well-known creativity expert Paul Torrance. He found that the reason why teachers tend to dislike creative students is that creative people often exhibit traits that are often referred to as *obnoxious*. Torrance described creative people as not having the time to be courteous, as refusing to take no for an answer, and as being negativistic and critical of others. Other researchers subsequently validated Torrance's conclusions in identifying characteristics of more traditional (i.e. teacher-directed) classrooms. These included adjectives such as *logical, peaceable, good-natured, moderate, tolerant,* and *reliable,* among others. Students who violated those precepts (e.g. creative students) were viewed less favorably than those who embraced them.

Westby and Dawson also wanted to address a strange contradiction that surfaced quite frequently when teachers talked about creativity. As reported, while teachers tend to de-value creative traits in their students, they also report that they value creativity in the classroom. In fact, a significant majority of teachers embrace the promotion of creative thinking in the classroom. Yet, they also decry the personalities of creative students. In response to this contradiction, it has been suggested that teachers, in declaring creativity as an important goal of education, may be giving the "right answer", but not necessarily the "real answer" when asked about their liking for creative students. Another possibility that has been explored in dozens of other research studies is that teachers' concepts of creativity may differ from those delineated by psychologists.

Westby and Dawson state that we need some clarification of the reasons for the conflict between research findings regarding teachers' preferences and teachers' self-reports. This is simply because teachers' expectations of students have a significant impact on students' grades and performance. As the authors point out, "If teachers' concepts of creativity are different from those generally accepted, it seems unlikely that they will recognize and nurture those students with creative potential."

Subsequently, the researchers gathered together another group of elementary teachers who were presented with a list of the twenty creative characteristics used in the first part of the study. For example, the teachers were asked, "How characteristic is each of the following of a creative eight-year-old child." Teachers rated each of the statements on a nine-point scale ranging from *behavior extremely uncharacteristic of a creative child* (1) to *behavior extremely characteristic of a creative child* (9).

What was most telling in this second study were the characteristics teachers rated as least typical of creative children. These included: "makes up the rules as he or she goes along," "is impulsive," "is a nonconformist," "is emotional," "tends not to know own limitations and tries to do what others think is impossible," and "likes to be alone when creating something new."

The researchers conclude that teachers often have a negative view of the characteristics associated with creativity. They suggest, then, that schools may provide an inhospitable environment for creative endeavors. They also posit:

"First, teachers' unwelcoming attitudes may alienate children from formal education. It has also been clearly demonstrated that children's performance is affected by teachers' attitudes towards them. A second possible outcome is that teachers' dislike of behaviors associated with creativity leads to the extinction of those behaviors. Thus, potentially creative students might learn to conform so as to improve the teacher-student relationship. This attempt to appease the teacher and do better in the classroom could cause children to suppress the very characteristics that make them creative."

What becomes clear is that teachers sometimes devalue creativity even while embracing the presence of creative students in their classrooms. By the same token, teachers may have an interpretation of creativity that is quite dissimilar from that of psychologists. This seems to suggest that while creativity is embraced, it may not be practiced by classroom teachers. The overriding conclusion is that teacher beliefs and teacher practices may be in conflict. As a result, kids who exhibit creative approaches to learning may be unconsciously rebuffed by their teachers. The result may be children denied creative expressions.

✍ ✍ ✍

Does our education influence our inherent creativity? Does the curriculum (and concurrent evaluation methods) have an impact on our imagination and inventiveness? Do the questions posed in any classroom (preschool, elementary, middle school, high school, college) affect our embrace of innovation? Is our locus of control an influential determinant of how creative we may envision ourselves (as both children as well as adults)? Are teacher rewards and teacher perceptions significant (in terms of creative inclinations) throughout our educational career?

"Yes!"

But, guess what? Your creative tendencies are subsequently assailed even after you leave school and get a job. Except that in the workplace the condemnations are even more severe...and more numerous.

Let's take a look.

14.
How to Sizzle: 44 - 52

44. Watch The Comparisons. In her book *Mindset: The New Psychology of Success*, author Carol Dweck cautions parents to be careful about the comments they make about others - especially when their children are listening. Remarks such as, "She thinks she's a real know-it-all," "He's probably the smartest person I know," and "She's as dumb as a rock" send a subtle signal to children: people are gauged by what they are, not by what they can do. With those kinds of comments, we assign labels to people - labels that are difficult to dismiss or change. We are saying to children that others are the sum of their parts, rather than a work in progress. As a result, children get the idea that they, too, are judged, not by what they can do, but rather by what they have done. As you might imagine, this has a profound effect on their sense of personal creativity. In short, they get the impression that they are either creative or not creative; a belief that one is either born creative or not (a significant construct we'll discuss in more detail in Chapter 14). Instead of saying, "You know Matt Jones just down the street? He sure is smart!" try something like, "You know Matt Jones down the street? He sure does like to learn lots of new things about space travel."

45. Be Curious. Albert Einstein famously said, "I have no special talents. I am only passionately curious." He also went on to say, "The important thing is not to stop questioning. Curiosity has its own reason for existing." For Einstein, curiosity was the engine that drove his creativity. Curiosity is the catalyst for questioning and questioning is what propels us to seek out the unfamiliar and the unknown. Curiosity is the fuel necessary for creativity to prosper and succeed. For, without questions, knowledge becomes stagnant and immovable - it becomes a classic case of "same old, same old." It does not move forward, nor does it have sufficient power to poke and peek and prod what may lie just below the surface or just slightly out of reach. One research study in 2017 tested the link between curiosity and creative problem-solving. What the researchers discovered, not surprisingly, was that general curiosity had a significant impact on the quality and originality of creative performance outcomes, even after accounting for differences in personality among the participants. The implication was that constant questioning (active curiosity) creates a constant state of mental activity that moves us beyond a tendency for us to rely on what we already know. In other words, we often assume that our knowledge about a work-related topic is *above average* and we are, therefore, not incentivized to move beyond that "box." Questions, on the other hand, stimulate us to look beyond, to look in new places, and to look past "comfortable" knowledge. In short, the more curious we are, the more creative we can become.

46. Eliminate Tangible Rewards. Get rid of the gold stars, achievement certificates, smelly stickers, and other "incentives" from your classroom. Such tokens send a wrong message to children - that education is all about getting awards, rather than learning something that is lasting and meaningful. These tangible rewards punish much more than they promote. And, take it from a former "bad speller" (who seldom got any gold stars), it is an occurrence that is remembered for a very long time. Put more of the emphasis on "internal evaluation," rather than external rewards and students will become more self-confident in their academic achievements.

47. Reduce Competition. Don't put a chart in the front of the classroom that reveals everyone's academic prowess (or lack thereof). Invite students to do some self-assessment. "What are some concepts you find challenging?" and "What might be another way we could address this issue?" are all appropriate questions to drop into every lesson. In so doing, you are beginning to create an "invitational classroom" - one in which students have an active role in the teaching/ learning process. They become less teacher-dependent and more student-independent - a strong measure of a successful learning environment.

48. Personal Affirmation. Psychologists point out that as humans, we often act, feel, and perform in accordance with what we imagine to be true about ourselves. In short, what we imagine to be true, becomes, in fact, true. The key is to keep that picture firmly fixed in our mind over an extended period of time. The longer we hold that picture, the more it becomes a part of who we are and how we act. Thus, you may want to do what I do - I frequently give myself an affirmation (a positive statement) that I am, indeed, a creative person ("Hey, Tony, did you know how creative you are?"). In talking with myself, I may use general statements ("I am always creative when writing.") or specific statements ("I am really creative when I write suggestions on how readers can also be creative in both their personal and professional lives."). To take this one step further, you may also want to write your own affirmations using a combination of first, second, and third persons. For example, "1) I, Tony, am a creative children's author. 2) Hey, Tony, did you know that your creativity is an inspiration for me. 3) Tony is one of the most creative people in our neighborhood." Here's another sequence: "1) My name is Muna and I am a creative doll maker. 2) Hi, Muna, glad to meet you. I hear that you are a very innovative doll maker. 3) Once upon a time, a woman named Muna made some of the most creative kachina dolls ever seen in northern Arizona." These statements may appear self-serving on the surface, but they will instill a basic reality in your brain: we become what we think we can become.

49. Something Different. We are creatures of habit. We get into routines simply because they're comfortable and safe. We prepare a Thanksgiving turkey the same way every year. We read the same mystery authors over and over. We look at the same news sources every day. For the most part, these are simple habits we get into and seldom get out of. They make our lives easier because we don't have to stretch - mentally speaking - rather we get things done and are satisfied with the results without...well, without really thinking. Yet, psychologists tell us that we can awaken significant parts of our brains by occasionally doing something different. Learning a new language, trying an unfamiliar ethnic food for dinner one night, watching a new TV program that you would normally not watch, or buying a new sweater in a color you don't normally wear are all small, yet significant ways, of stimulating parts of our brain that have been less than active. This unexpected mental stimulation often sparks new ideas simply because you're seeing new things with new eyes. Doing it on a regular basis (every other day, for example) will generate new expectations and new discoveries. Anyone for some *khorkhog* (Mongolian barbeque) for dinner tonight?

50. Eschew Goals. When you have a goal, you have a destination...a pre-planned conclusion. You create a series of steps and procedures that will help you in reaching (or achieving) your goal. Inevitably, you create a route that is comfortable, mundane, and predictable. In short, you're trapped by your logic. You set yourself out on a linear path that gets you from "Point A" to "Point B" efficiently and logically. But, what if you gave yourself permission to stray off that path – take a look at some sites along the way, stop every now and again for some refreshment, take a snooze, stop and chat with some strangers looking at a glorious sunset, or any one of a hundred different diversions? Do you think you might discover something you've never seen before, encounter people you've never met before, or find something you weren't looking for in the first place? Am I suggesting that you eliminate goals from your life? Of course not. But be careful, goals can sometimes be restrictive and hampering. They give you a target to aim for, but sometimes at the expense of missing the (new, exciting, dynamic, eye-popping, magnificent) views along the way. In your travels (physical and mental) stop every so often and investigate a new road or experience. You might be surprised at what you discover.

51. Improve Yourself. One of the most significant strengths of creative people is a desire and a commitment to self-improvement. It's not about having a particular skill or talent – it's about making that skill or talent better. Being creative has nothing to do with resting on our laurels. Your laurels will only get you so far. A significant majority of people who continuously generate creative products (Picasso, Edison, Michelangelo, Jeff Bezos) are those who spend considerable time at self-improvement. Having talent is one thing; having the desire to expand and improve that talent quite another. As you might imagine, this involves considerable time and effort devoted to improving what you have. Never become satisfied with the status-quo; instead, devote part of your day (at work or at home) to expanding your education, improving your talent, and exploring new dimensions. Self-improvement is the frosting on the cake – a commitment that you are a constant work-in-progress, rather than a finished product.

52. Punishment Reward. Heber City, Utah sits just 45 miles southeast of Salt Lake City. It receives an annual snowfall of approximately 70 inches per year. In February 2021, the city made multiple attempts to get people to move their cars off municipal roads and streets so that snow plows would be able to remove the accumulated snow. People refused to do so and, as a result, the local police department found itself issuing scores of citations. It is likely that the police department then decided to ask itself a most creative question: What if we turned this "negative" into a "positive?" And so, they announced on Facebook that they would toss a parking ticket for anyone who brought in five non-perishable, non-expired food items - all of which would be donated to local food banks. The response was overwhelming. The city received tons of donations and even had people without citations calling in to donate food. According to a spokeswoman for the police department, it was a more than successful way of helping out folks who were dealing with some of the economic repercussions of the COVID-19 pandemic. So, can large entities, such as municipal governments, infuse creativity into their daily operations? You bet!

PART FOUR

Heigh-Ho, It's Off to Work We Go

15.
"What a Stupid Idea!"

The brain is a wonderful organ. It starts the moment you get up and doesn't stop until you get into the office.
—ROBERT FROST

1.

The morning sun is streaming through large picture glass windows. Seven people are seated around a long table in the boardroom of a major corporation. In the center of the table is a strange contraption bristling with wires, metal connections, screws, bolts, a few bells, and numerous (unknown) parts. One distinguished gentleman - a Mr. Alexander Graham Bell - in a black suit and starched white shirt is sitting at one end of the table. Six other individuals in coats and ties are arrayed around the table staring at the unusual machine before them. The year is 1876.

> **PERSON #1** (Management): So, Mr. Bell, tell us a little about this contraption of yours.
>
> **ALEXANDER GRAHAM BELL**: It's called a telephone. It's designed to transmit sound, allowing people to talk to each other over great distances.
>
> **PERSON #2** (Research & Development): Why would people want to talk over long distances? If they want to communicate, they can always use the telegraph. *It's just not practical.*
>
> **PERSON #3** (Maintenance): And look at all those wires. Do we have to string those wires from one city to another? *It'll never fly. It's too complicated.*

PERSON #4 (Marketing): Why do we need a talking devise when we have the telegraph. It certainly sends messages without any problems. We've done all right so far with the telegraph. *Why rock the boat?*

ALEXANDER GRAHAM BELL: Just imagine one of these devices in every home. People could talk to their neighbors without leaving the house. They could place an order with the local grocer without going out in the rain. They could send birthday wishes to a grandchild without leaving the comfort of their home.

PERSON #5 (I.T.): Who would want one of those things in their home? Where would you put it? It seems so big and bulky. *It'll be more trouble than it's worth.*

PERSON #6 (Accounting): *We've done all right so far.* Why should we invest in this telephone thing?

ALEXANDER GRAHAM BELL: People want to communicate with each other. Think of all the advantages that businesses would have with an improved communication tool.

PERSON #1: *It's all right in theory, but....*

PERSON #2: *Do you realize the paperwork it will create?*

PERSON #3: Something like that has to be expensive to manufacture. And, I'm afraid, *it's just not in the budget.*

ALEXANDER GRAHAM BELL: This is revolutionary, to be sure. It will be a significant influence on the history of this country, not to mention the history of the Industrial Revolution. The implications are far-reaching.

PERSON #4: Maybe so, *but it's not for us.*

PERSON #5: I know this for certain, *people don't want change.*

PERSON #6: I'll tell you what, Mr. Bell, *we'll get back to you on this.*

Fortunately, the scenario above is a work of fiction...or is it? Please go back and re-read the script and observe the italicized phrases. Do they sound familiar? They should - they're phrases and reactions used almost every day in corporate America; phrases and reactions that are frequently tossed out whenever a new idea or innovation is proposed. They are often a knee-jerk reaction to change. "If it ain't broke, why fix it?" is an all too common retort to new ideas.

These are corporate put-downs.

2.

Let's say you've got a great new idea, an idea that will transform your department into a dynamic new entity within the company. Profits will soar, people will be happy, and, of course, you'll get a substantial raise. You bring this new idea to the weekly department meeting and announce it to all your colleagues. There is stunned silence. But, finally, from somewhere in the back of the room, somebody raises their voice and says something like, "That's got to be the most ridiculous idea I've ever heard! I'll never work!"

You've effectively been shot down. You've been hit between the eyes with a verbal bullet and your idea, for all intents and purposes, has been killed on the spot. It's dead in the water, it bit the dust, it's dead as a doornail, it gave up the ghost, it's belly up, it bought the farm, it's counting worms, it died with its boots on, and it kicked the bucket (use your own idiom). In short, it's history!

It probably wouldn't surprise you to know that we (children and adults) are assailed by these verbal put-downs regularly. At least one study has confirmed that, on average, children receive more than 25 negative statements per waking hour. These include statements from both parents and teachers such as, "Don't touch that," "I don't think that's such a good idea," and, perhaps, the most damning comment of all (in terms of creativity), "No, you can't do that!" Add to that the intensity of cyberbullying experienced by young people (In April 2019, the Cyberbullying Research Center reported that 37 percent of all students experienced cyberbullying in their lifetimes.) and we can quickly see that youngsters face a regular and sustained onslaught of negative comments. That negativity frequently carries over into our workplaces where negative criticism is not only condoned, but is often the *modus operandi* for an organization.

Some people are masters at tamping down new ideas. These are the naysayers - those folks who challenge every new idea as though it was a bad idea. They'll say "no" at the drop of a hat! In many cases, it's the result of our natural resistance to change. Change is something new and thus change is scary. Cro-Magnons may have been reluctant to hike over a mountain ridge because they didn't know what (or who) they'd meet on the other side. They had established a comfort zone on one side of the mountain and venturing into a new environment probably meant a new set of survival skills. "Let's play it safe," "Let's not take that chance," they may have said. "No" is safe, "yes" holds the possibility for unknown dangers, new fears, and lots of uncertainties.

Modern humans often have the same set of apprehensions - living their lives in fear. "Stay with what's comfortable; what's known," they say to themselves (and others). Consequently, they want to wrap others into that comfort zone - imposing their will on colleagues who may wish to venture outside that zone and see what's "on the other side of the mountain."

Why do some people feel compelled to say "no" to every new idea? Let's take a look at a few reasons. First, it's a control issue. For example, when you tell someone her idea is no good you exert a measure of control over her. Those we refer to as "control freaks" are the ones who often want to trample our energy and enthusiasm. It wasn't *their* idea, so it can be controlled by saying it was a *bad* idea. They maintain their control by rejecting our ideas.

Second, there is a region of the human brain known as the amygdala, which serves as an automatic alarm system whenever there is danger (or the possibility of danger). Many psychologists believe this is the brain's default position - that is, if something new and unusual appears in front of us we have a natural tendency to picture it as harmful or dangerous. As a result, we will either protect ourselves or flee from the potential danger. In evolutionary terms, this is how prehistoric humans survived a harsh and often unpredictable environment. In modern terms, this means that new ideas are often viewed as *dangerous* ideas. And, if an idea is dangerous, then it must be squelched.

Third, some people are comfortable being pessimistic. They see the glass as half-empty[18], they view the world as a negative environment,

---

18 I'm reminded of the quote from comedian George Carlin: "Some people see the glass half full. Others see it half empty. I see a glass that's twice as big as it needs to be."

they always see the "bad" in a situation, and they always want others to know of their dissatisfaction with the way things are. When someone shares a positive idea, they seek to counter it with a negative reaction. These folks are reactionaries rather than visionaries. They are most comfortable in maintaining the edges of "the box." As you might imagine, these are individuals who frequently solicit collegial approval. Thus, if someone doesn't tell them they're doing a good job (regularly), they certainly aren't going to celebrate the ideas of others.

Fourth, as we'll examine in somewhat more detail later on, some people are locked into a "fixed mindset." They are incapable of embracing new ideas just as they are incapable of embracing change. They resist change in themselves, just as much as they resist change in others or in an organization. For them, change is difficult to fathom - it's a intimidating proposition. It's a journey into new territory and for some that's both frightening and worrisome. They are content right where they are, so why do things differently? Why venture into the unknown when the "known" is very comfortable just as it is?

Fifth, and perhaps most important, naysayers get attention when they say something that goes against the grain. They are recognized (often for the wrong reasons) for a gibe, a put-down, a taunt, a sneer, or an insult. The spotlight is (temporarily) on them. They are the center of attention. Moreover, they get a reaction - sometimes a negative reaction - but for a moment, all eyes are on them. They've inserted their thoughts and (re)claimed their space.

People who live their lives without being
curious have made up their minds about
everything.
—ALBERT EINSTEIN

3.

In my research and in conversations with business leaders, CEOs, psychologists, and human resource experts I've collected a daunting array of creativity killers - phrases often used in meetings, conferences, gatherings, conventions, seminars, corporate retreats, and other places where new ideas might be shared. Take a look at this (abbreviated) list and see how many you've heard recently.[19]

1. "Are you sure that's realistic?"
2. "Be practical!"
3. "Because I said so."
4. "Can you save that for the next meeting?"
5. "Come on, get a grip!"
6. "Do you really have a screw loose?"
7. "Do you realize the paperwork it will create?"
8. "Do you really think we're made of money?"
9. "Don't be ridiculous (or "silly", or "stupid")."
10. "Don't fight city hall."
11. "Don't get me wrong...."
12. "Don't give up your day job."
13. "Don't rock the boat."
14. "Don't waste time thinking."
15. "Get a committee to look into that."
16. "Get a grip."
17. "Great idea, but not for us."
18. "Have you lost your marbles?"
19. "I don't want to hurt your feelings, but...."
20. "I'll get back to you."
21. "I'm the one who gets paid to think."
22. "If it ain't broke, why fix it?"
23. "It isn't your responsibility."
24. "It will be more trouble than it's worth."
25. "It'll never fly."
26. "It's all right in theory, but..."
27. "It's not in the budget."
28. "It's too far ahead of the times."
29. "Let's deal with that some other time."
30. "Let's not start anything new just yet."
31. "Let's stay focused here."
32. "Let's stay on topic."

---

19 Please note: This list is not meant to be comprehensive or exhaustive. It only serves to illustrate the wide variety of put-downs we are frequently subjected to. While you're at work, I invite you to listen carefully and add additional comments from your own place of employment.

33. "Let's stick with what works."
34. "No!"
35. "Obviously, you misread my request."
36. "Oh, crap, not another hair-brained idea!"
37. "People don't want change."
38. "Put it in writing."
39. "Say, what?"
40. "So, what you're really saying is...."
41. "That's a joke, right?"
42. "That's irrelevant."
43. "That's not in your job description."
44. "That's not on the agenda, let's save it for another time."
45. "The competition will eat us alive."
46. "The boss will never go for it."
47. "We haven't got the manpower."
48. "We tried that before."
49. "We've always done it this way."
50. "We've done all right so far."
51. "Well, there you go again."
52. "What the hell were you thinking?"
53. "What will people say?"
54. "Yeah, when pigs fly."
55. "Yeah, right!" (sarcastically)
56. "Yes, but..."
57. "You can't teach an old dog new tricks."
58. "You must be one brick shy of a load."
59. "You think that's good, listen to this."
60. "You're obviously not the sharpest knife in the drawer."
61. "You've got to be kidding."
62. "You've got to be s***ing me!'

Nonverbal Killers of Creative Ideas

1. ...condescending grins...
2. ...contemptuous looks...
3. ...dirty looks...
4. ...finger across the throat...

5.   ...finger down throat...
6.   ...frowning...
7.   ...giggling...
8.   ...laughter...
9.   ...patronizing glare...
10. ...one thumb down...
11. ...raised eyebrows...
12. ...rolling eyes...
13. ...shrugging...
14. ...silence...
15. ...smirking...
16. ...sneering...
17. ...staring...
18. ...supercilious stare...
19. ...suppressed laughter...
20. ...two thumbs down...

4.

I imagine that sometime during the late 1800s, brothers Orville and Wilber Wright asked themselves a most intriguing question: What if humans could fly through the air just like birds? To say that there would have been a lot of negativity in response to that question would be to state the obvious.

> *"Heavier-than-air flying machines*
> *are impossible."*
> — LORD KELVIN, BRITISH MATHEMATICIAN
> AND PHYSICIST, PRESIDENT OF THE BRITISH
> ROYAL SOCIETY, 1895.

> *"Flight by machines heavier than air is*
> *unpractical [sic] and insignificant, if not*
> *utterly impossible."*
> —SIMON NEWCOMB

"Every machine, or particular application,
seems a slight outrage against universal laws."
—HENRY DAVID THOREAU

"Everything that can be invented
has been invented."
—CHARLES H. DUELL, COMMISSIONER - U.S.
PATENT OFFICE, 1899

The death of several glider pilots in the late 1800s, unreliable methods of pilot control in those gliders, and the severe problem of banking an "air machine" while in flight certainly would have been delimiting (and, most certainly, negative) factors in the Wright Brothers passion for achieving manned flight. In fact, it often seemed as though their entire venture was filled with all sorts of negativity and overt criticisms (several newspapers, including their hometown newspaper in Dayton, Ohio even refused to print the story of their first flight at Kitty Hawk, NC simply because "it couldn't be done.").

Yet, the Wright Brothers persevered - they continued to look for all the positive aspects of their question. That positivity steeled them against all the forces that told them they wouldn't succeed. It girded them for the inevitable setbacks and, eventually, propelled them to aeronautical success.

Throughout history, there have been numerous (and famous) put-downs. Here are a few:

➤ Walt Disney was fired from the Kansas City Star in 1919 because, his editor said, he "lacked imagination and had no good ideas."
➤ "Groups with guitars are on their way out." - Decca Records, turning down the Beatles, 1962
➤ "There is no reason for any individual to have a computer in his home." - Ken Olsen, president of Digital Equipment, 1977
➤ "What use could the company make of an electric toy" - Western Union, rejecting rights to Alexander Graham Bell's telephone, 1878.

➤ "What? You would make a ship sail against the wind by lighting a fire under her decks? I have no time to listen to such nonsense? - Napoleon I of France, dismissing Robert Fulton's steam engine.

➤ "Sensible and responsible women do not want the right to vote." - Grover Cleveland, president of the United States, 1905.

➤ "The world capacity for computers is five." - Thomas Watson, Sr., founder of IBM, 1943.

➤ "Who the hell wants to hear actors talk?" - Harry Warner, president of Warner Brothers, 1927.

➤ "You ain't going nowhere, son. You ought to go back to driving a truck." - Jimmy Denny (the manager at the Grand Ole Opry) to Elvis Presley.

Obviously, we don't like to be told we're wrong. And, we don't like to be told that our ideas or thoughts aren't worth anything. Aside from the expected blow to our emotions, there's evidence to suggest that we suffer physiologically as well. For example, when a co-worker says that she doesn't think your idea is a good one, there is a sudden release of dozens of stress-producing hormones throughout your body. These chemicals have a decided impact on your brain sufficient to result in an impairment of logic and reasoning as well as your ability to communicate and use language.

Interestingly, a negative comment (or a series of negative comments from several different individuals) increases anxiety levels. Physiological research has convincingly demonstrated that a stream of negative comments can actually damage key structures that regulate your memory, feelings, and emotions. These, in turn, may cause long-term reactions that can negatively affect your sleep, your appetite, your sex life, and your daily functioning.

From an evolutionary standpoint, humans tend to prefer environments that exclude or significantly reduce stressful situations. Cro-Magnons and Neanderthals quickly learned how to avoid potential predators much larger than themselves. Modern day humans like to avoid major arguments and rush-hour traffic. When people tell us "That's a stupid idea," or "You're kidding me, right?"

stress chemicals surge through our body. Quite naturally, we want to avoid those situations.

As you well know, the easiest way to avoid those situations is to never suggest new or creative ideas in the first place. Knowing that there is a better than average chance your innovative idea (for example) for improving the profitability of your organization is going to be shot down by one or two individuals suggests that it might be a good idea to keep your mouth shut and not offer anything at all. Why subject ourselves to a rush of stress hormones, when it's just much safer, and much more pleasant, to say nothing at all?

So, how common are those negative comments? According to one report, it appears as though negative reactions to new ideas are on the rise. The researchers interviewed over 3,000 U.S. business leaders about behaviors in the workplace. The results showed that 53 percent of the respondents have seen an increase in "Criticism," 48 percent have seen an increase in "Dismissing Others' Ideas," and 36 percent have seen an increase in "Hostility" or "Disparaging Others."

What is causing this increase in workplace negativity? One thought is that we have "legitimized" criticism via the internet. For example, think about any product you have purchased on Amazon. Everything from rubber duckies to lingerie to chain saws is subject to a review. We can give a product a rating of one to five stars AND include comments about its performance or lack thereof. We can tell others exactly how we feel about a product, whether it's worth the money we spent for it, and whether others should purchase that product, too. And, we can do it anonymously without fear of retribution or rebuke.

So too, can we rate movies on *Rotten Tomatoes*, we can evaluate hotels on *Hotels.com*, we can weigh in on our vacation experiences on *Trip Advisor*, we can tell people what we think about a restaurant on *Yelp*, we can rank our doctors and dentists on *Healthgrades.com*, and, of course, we can tell everyone what we think of a business via *Facebook* and *Twitter* and other social media sites. All anonymously. The internet has legitimized denunciation and, as a result, we have become a nation of critics.

Am I suggesting that all that criticism is bad? Of course not. We sometimes need someone to stop us if were headed over a cliff (metaphorically speaking) or if something we're doing might lead to injury or the discomfort of others. There's a good reason why we stop at intersections with an eight-sided red sign on the street corner and why we turn off our cell phones when flying in a commercial aircraft. Sometimes inappropriate or unsafe behavior needs to be stopped. It's often for our own good.

But, there's a growing body of research to suggest that it's the proportion of negative criticism to positive encouragement that affects creative output. In one study of business teams, it was discovered that the single most significant factor in the difference between successful and non-successful teams was the ratio of positive comments ("That sounds like a terrific idea," or "Wow, I never looked at it that way.") to negative statements ("You're joking, right?" or "You've got to be kidding me.") that members of various teams made to each other.

The researchers discovered that the average ratio for the low performing teams was about one positive comment for every three negative comments; for the medium-performing teams that ratio was about two positive comments for each negative comment; and for the highest performing teams the ratio of positive comments to negative comments was approximately six to one. The data clearly does not suggest that negative comments should be eliminated from the workplace in order for creativity to flourish, but rather the data establishes a working model (ratio) that ensures and nurtures increased levels of creative output.

A subsequent review of this research substantiates these ratios and also notes that a little bit of criticism can be essential to the creative work of a team. The researchers suggest three reasons why: 1) criticism tends to grab someone's attention; 2) a little bit of criticism guards against complacency and self-satisfaction, and 3) an appropriate measure of criticism negates groupthink and blind conformity. The researchers were careful to note, however, that it's not the amount of criticism that is important, but rather its relationship to the amount of positive feedback that drives the success of any business venture.

The ratios reported above were substantiated by some compelling research conducted by John Gottman. Gottman sought to examine the likelihood of wedded couples getting divorced or remaining together. Interestingly, when his research data was analyzed, the single most important determinant was the ratio of positive comments to negative ones that partners make to one another. The results showed that the optimal ratio was strikingly similar to those above. That is, couples who stay together have a ratio of approximately five positive comments for every negative one. On the other hand, couples who ended up divorced had a ratio of 0.77 to 1 - or roughly three positive comments for every four negative ones. (O.K., guys, time to dial up those "This is the best meat loaf I've ever had! It's so much better than Mom's!" comments.)

The implications are twofold. First of all, the 'weight" of corporate put-downs often becomes unbearable. Imagine yourself subjected to these negative comments over the entire length of your professional career. Being continuously bombarded by a plethora of "That'll never work," "That's got to be the stupidest idea I've ever heard!" and "Let's stay focused here" tends to wear after a while. After months and years of hearing a constant parade of negative comments, we tend to lose our creative spirit and will. That constant barrage would certainly be a significant contributing factor as to why we tend to score the lowest on creativity tests in middle age. (Who scores the highest on those tests? Five year olds!).

Second, creativity thrives when is promoted and supported in an environment that is significantly more positive than negative. In those workplaces where the naysayers, critics, and detractors predominate, creativity withers and dies. More importantly, people with ideas are effectively told not to suggest or promote creative solutions because they know those suggestions will be met with a bombardment of critical reviews, a dearth of supportive comments, or just plain silence. Is it any wonder then that the Society for Human Resource Management reports that most employee suggestion programs are vastly underutilized?

When the positive/negative ratio is out of whack, the opportunities for positive change and innovation are significantly reduced. Creativity becomes a footnote - rather than a mantra - for the organization. Suffice it to say, creativity put-downs are immediate killers of both individual initiative as well as corporate long-range goals. They are also a precursor to an entrenched belief that often throttles our creative spirit and puts the brakes on any innovative ideas long before they ever reach the conference table or board room.

It's a fear we have all experienced; and one we all dread.

16.
How to Sizzle: 53 - 60

53. Crush Corporate Put-Downs. Duplicate several quotes from the list of "corporate put-downs" as presented in this chapter. Share those statements with your staff along with reasons why these comments depress creative suggestions from anybody and everybody. Invite employees to add to the list. What have they heard in the workplace? What are some common expressions on the production line or in the boardroom? What is often shared in the lunchroom? Post the "put-downs" and challenge employees to conduct meetings or discussions without the use of any of these derogatory comments.

54. Recognize That Everyone Has Creative Possibilities. If you have a financial challenge to address, don't limit your meetings to just financial people. Bring in the marketers, administrative assistants, technicians, custodians, sales people, lawyers, and representatives from every other department. A diversity of minds ensures a diversity of ideas. When everyone's thoughts are solicited, the chances for a solution are increased exponentially. This is the *modus operandi* at Dreamworks Animation - everyone from top to bottom is encouraged to present ideas on new films and current projects. You may well discover that some of the most innovative ideas come from those not directly connected to a project. They are often able to see things with a different set of eyes. As the former chair of an academic department, I got one of our most innovative ideas from the administrative assistant in a completely different department. She saw something I was too blind to see.

55. Hire Diversity. Don't hire new staff because they "fit" into the culture or thinking of the organization. You don't want everybody thinking the same. Hire folks who have a diversity of experiences and a diversity of opinions. Hire those who challenge the status quo, who think far outside the box, who ruffle some feathers every now and again, and who chart their own courses. In his book *Think Again*, author Adam Grant makes a strong case for diversity when he states, "The ideal members of a challenge network are disagreeable, because they're fearless about questioning the way thinks have always been done and holding us accountable for thinking again. They give the critical feedback we might not want to hear, but need to hear." In short, don't hire "comfortable" employees, hire those who make waves (There's a lot of energy in waves.).

56. Celebrating People. According to Robert Half, the world's largest specialized staffing firm, one of the top three drivers for creative and marketing people is an overall feeling of appreciation for their work. This means that if business leaders want to create an environment where creativity is both valued and promoted they also need to create an environment in which success is lauded...not occasionally, but regularly. It is also an environment in which every staff member feels appreciated, and one where they are celebrated for their contributions to the company's mission. It's a corporate culture that puts a premium on letting employees know how critical their contributions are in helping the organization reach its goals. Creativity is promoted when employees have an opportunity, and a place, to "show off" completed projects (i.e. a bulletin board, company landing page, "Wall of Fame," periodic newsletter, press releases). Corporate creativity is also promoted when employees are recognized for going above and beyond their job descriptions: retreats, premium parking spaces, announcements in the local newspaper, plaques in the company lunchroom, awards dinners. An overall feeling of appreciation (along with an attendant and instant recognition) for one's work can significantly increase the creativity quotient for any organization.

57. Different Folks, Different Strokes. I'm stuck. I'm writing a book and my mind shuts down. No, it's not "writer's block," it's just that ideas are not flowing as rapidly as I would like. I'm losing steam and my mental energies are on "Pause." I need a kick in the seat of my pants...mentally speaking. So, I turn my manuscript over to an architect in Newcastle, England, an eleven-year-old girl with cerebral palsy, a violin player with the Los Angeles Philharmonic Orchestra, or an Olympic distance runner preparing to compete in the 10,000 meter run. How would they handle this concept? What would they say about this particular section of the book? What ideas could they offer that would help me break out of my funk? What suggestions would they proffer? By "asking" folks from several different walks of life for their advice I can assure myself of some new perspectives and new visions. What would a computer technician, stonemason, or pediatric oncologist say about the rhythm and flow of Chapter Nine in *From Fizzle to Sizzle*? I want to listen to the ideas of different folks. How would they approach this challenge?

58. Break Away. During the COVID-19 pandemic, my wife and I confined ourselves to our house rarely venturing out save for an occasional trip to the grocery store or a doctor appointment (true social distancing). Our lives were on autopilot – each day was the same routine as the day before...and the day before that...and the day before that. We were stuck in a routine. We also discovered that our respective "creativity quotients" were significantly reduced (My wife is a professional artist.). So, we made a pact that every four days or so we would go out for a mini-adventure. This might include a drive to a town we'd never visited before, a venture to a previously unknown site overlooking the Susquehanna River, a walk along a new trail in a state park, or a picnic beside a stream exactly 30 minutes from our house. Our brains were no longer on autopilot – they had to solve some new challenges (where to park, what food to bring, how to dress for the weather, what routes to take, etc.). In essence, we were challenging our "comfortable" ways of thinking and forcing our minds to creatively develop solutions to brand new events. We were escaping the status quo and re-igniting the creative fires. We put ourselves in unfamiliar places full of discovery and exploration. So, if you're working on a long-term project give yourself a mini-vacation every now and again. Your brain will thank you (profusely) for it!

59. Be A Cut-Up. You're working on a project...slowly, patiently, pedantically. It's taking forever, time is moving so slowly, and the work seems to take forever. You're slowing down - ideas seem to be frozen in time. The project keeps stalling - occasionally gaining some traction, but, more often than not the progress is slow...very very slow. Try this: print out significant pages of the project, take a pair of scissors and cut random words out of the pages. Don't look at the words, just select them haphazardly, and cut them out. Try for a pre-established goal - for example, 15 words cut from each page or a perhaps a grand total of 50 words in all. Move the words around on your desk; arrange them in various ways and different configurations. Scatter them into different locations on your work space. Create new sentences, weird sentences, incomprehensible sentences. Forget logic, look for possibilities. What you will soon discover is that you have freed your mind of the most logical way to approach the project and are now looking at it through creative eyes. You are escaping the artificial "box" that has constrained your thinking and are moving into another dimension that has no barriers, no restrictions. What you will discover are new possibilities and new patterns of expression. Your mind has been given a unique opportunity to pursue what it wants, rather than what it must. If you would like a graphic representation of this process, take a look at the paintings of Salvador Dali, Max Ernst, and Joan Miró.

60. 47 Uses. Too often, we think logically. Our education and experiences have taught us that logical thinking is planned, systematic, and dependable. That's true, but too much logical thinking crushes our creative instinct and frequently prevents the generation of unique and signature ideas. We often sacrifice creativity for efficiency.

One of the best ways to break yourself from this creative yoke is to create alternative uses for common objects. For example, let's assume you are wearing a pair of socks. What are some other alternate uses for socks? Here are a few I came up with: A cover for your golf clubs, hand warmers on a cold morning walk, keep your dog's legs warm when you take him outside, a protective "bag" to carry eggs. Use them to dry the dishes or to create a surrealistic mural on your living room wall (dip them into paint and paint away). You also have a set of puppets to tell a story to your child - draw a face on each one and create your own story characters. Cut the end off each one and slide the ends over your ears in the winter: inexpensive ear warmers. Or, slip an old one over your hand to clean off the side-view mirrors on your car.

So, here's your challenge. Identify a common object at home or at your place of work (e.g. pencil, file folder, computer mouse, broom, screwdriver, lamp, bottle, shoelace, etc.). See if you can conjure at least 47 different uses for that item (Why 47? Well, I was born in 1947, so I just like that number. If you want, pick your own number [or birthdate]). Generate as many possibilities as you can within a designated period (e.g. five minutes, ten minutes). You, like me, will most likely discover that you have set your mind on fire - breaking it out of its more familiar thinking (logical) patterns and setting it free to examine new ideas and new possibilities.

If you're the competitive type, do this activity with a friend or colleague. Who can come up with the most alternative uses (for a piece of copper wire, a coffee filter, or this book, for example, in five minutes)? You will be amazed at what transpires.

17.
Fear of Failure

Only those who dare to fail greatly can ever achieve greatly.
—ROBERT KENNEDY

1.

Imagine you are in charge of the Human Resources Department for your company or organization. In looking over the applications for one of the top-level positions currently open, you come across a resume with a most remarkable admission. The applicant has indicated that he has had 5,126 failures (and just one success) in his professional career.

Would you hire him?

In the late 1970s, Englishman James Dyson was completely frustrated with the performance of his home vacuum cleaner. The dust bag pores kept getting clogged causing the cleaner to lose suction the longer it was in operation. Bags were constantly replaced time and time again. Dyson thought there must be a better way.

He began experimenting with several different types of suction. Relying on his wife's salary as an art teacher and after about five years of trial and error he came up with a cyclone technology based on something he had seen at a local sawmill. After 5,126 various prototypes he invented the "G-Force Cleaner" in 1983. Unfortunately, English manufacturers and distributors were not ready for this innovative tool. That's because, at the time, replacement vacuum bags were a $127,000,000 market in England.

So Dyson began selling this innovative vacuum cleaner in Japan. Then, in 1993 he set up his own manufacturing company in Malmesbury, Wiltshire, along with a research center and factory. This crazy new tool, however, did not "sell like hotcakes." It wasn't until several years later when a new TV ad campaign emphasized that, unlike all his rivals, Dyson's vacuum cleaner did not require the constant purchase of replacement bags that sales really took off. The company's slogan - "Say goodbye to the bag" - was just the incentive the public needed to see the advantages of Dyson's machine over those of his competitors. The elimination of the need for replacement bags struck the public more than the machine's suction efficiency. As a result, the Dyson Dual Cyclone became the fastest-selling vacuum cleaner ever made in England. It also became the market leader (by value) in the U.S.

In an interview in *Fast Company*, Dyson underscored the significance of failure in one's life. "I made 5,127 prototypes of my vacuum before I got it right," he said. "There were 5,126 failures. But I learned from each one. That's how I came up with a solution. So, I don't mind failure. I've always thought that schoolchildren should be marked by the number of failures they've had. The child who tries strange things and experiences lots of failures to get there is probably more creative."

Dyson's company now has more than sixty consumer products on the market. In 2018, those products generated more than $6 billion in sales (an increase of 25.6% over 2017 revenues). Not too shabby for a guy with 5,126 failures on his resume!

2.

Atychiphobia is not a word that pops up in many conversations around the water cooler at work or at the picnic table during the neighborhood block party every summer. Yet fear of failure is a common condition that frequently stops creativity in its tracks and prevents us from moving forward in our lives. Although we all experience failure in our lives, we all don't react to it in the same way. Some of us embrace the concept of failure as a way of re-focusing and re-shaping our thinking. Others react to it by curling up into a little ball (an armadillo threatened by a large hungry feline comes to mind) and shutting themselves off from the rest of the world. There is considerable evidence to support the notion that some people embrace failure while others shun it at every conceivable opportunity. To some failure is good, to others it is bad.

An interesting body of research has underscored the notion that there are some people who embrace challenges and disappointments as opportunities to re-focus their thinking. These are folks with a "growth mindset." Then, there are other people who see failure as... well...as a complete failure. They believe that they never had the talent or skill anyway, and they probably never will. These are folks with a "fixed mindset." These individuals embrace the belief that you are either born with talent or you're not. In short, you're either in one group of the other.

The psychologist Carol Dweck has studied these kinds of mental sets extensively and provides clinical evidence that most people intentionally place themselves in one of those two groups. Dweck said that the group to which you have assigned yourself frequently determines how to react to any intellectual challenges. If you experience failure and give up then you have conveniently assigned yourself to the "fixed" group; if you experience failure and use that as a learning opportunity or stepping stone to improve, then you have placed yourself into the "growth" group.

The implications of her research is that failure is an inevitable condition of our daily lives (we missed the left turn on our way to a friend's house, we forgot to pay the electric bill on time and are assessed a penalty, we make a New Year's resolution to lose twenty pounds and six months later we are still at the same weight). It's how we approach that failure that determines whether we are fixed in our thinking or ready for some growth. And, as you might imagine, people who believe they are members of the "growth" group tend to generate more creative ideas than do those who self-assign themselves to the "fixed" group

To illustrate, consider Thomas Alva Edison. In the latter part of the 19th century, Edison was attempting to improve the light bulb.[20] For more than two years, he experimented with a host of potential

---

20 There is a common myth that Edison invented the light bulb. Not so! The first electric light was developed by the English chemist and inventor Humphry Davy in 1802 - fully seven decades in advance of Edison's work on improving the already established device. And, in all fairness, it was Edison and his team of technicians who came up with the concept of the incandescent light bulb in 1879. However, since Edison was the boss, the resulting patent was, of course, issued in his name.

filaments – bamboo shoots, animal hair, spider webs, carbon and copper. 400 times, 600 times, a thousand times he tried to discover an element that would sustain light. Sometime during this long and arduous process, a reporter was sent to interview him. During the interview, the reporter asked Edison, "It seems as though you've tried and tried to invent the incandescent light bulb and continue to fail each time. Why is that?" Edison looked the reporter square in the eye and said, "I have not failed. I've just found 10,000 ways that won't work."

Edison knew that his interpretation of failure was a critical part of the discovery process. He believed that each unsuccessful attempt was moving him closer to his ultimate goal. In studies of creative people, psychologists have discovered that one of the most distinguishing features separating creative people from non-creative people is that creative people always make lots of mistakes and continue to work through them, while non-creative people make a mistake and stop. Most people consider success and failure as opposites; in reality, they are both part of the same process.

Former rocket scientist Ozan Varol (who certainly saw his share of technological failures) clarifies the importance of this construct:

"If we don't acknowledge we failed - if we avoid a true reckoning - we can't learn anything. In fact, failure can make things worse if we get the wrong messages from it. When we attribute our failures to external factors - the regulators, the customers, the competitors - we have no reason to change course. We throw good money after bad, double down on the same strategy, and hope the wind blows in a better direction."

3.

You and I and almost every other person on the planet had an epiphany around the time we were two years old. We were all engaged in a task that almost everyone older than two could do with relative ease. But, when we tried to do it we failed. Or, to use more common vernacular, we flunked...and we flunked miserably. We were all trying to learn how to walk - upright on our two feet.

Up until that point in our lives, we had gotten around the house by crawling on our hands and knees. It was not a very efficient form of locomotion, but it was a practical one. Our bodies had not developed the strength or balance to stand on both feet without falling over. But, we saw that everyone else in the family was walking on two feet, so it seemed only logical that we should, too. And, so we tried to stand up. And we fell down - not once or twice, but many times. Day after day, and week after week, we would try to stand up and we would always fall down.

Our parents may have even placed us at the end of the living room couch and using that piece of furniture as a crutch, we would slap our hands on the cushions and slowly work our way down to the other end. But, inevitably something happened when we reached the terminus of the couch. We took one more (unsupported) step and...fell down. This walking thing was hard; every time we tried it we failed.

But, we kept trying. And through sheer determination and persistence (and lots of encouragement from Aunt Betty and Uncle Joe) we learned to walk. Tentative steps at first, then wobbly steps, then steps with more assurance and confidence. After a couple of weeks we were officially WALKERS! We had used our failures as learning opportunities. We pushed through all the times our butts made contact with the living room floor and learned how to walk on our own. We had turned failure into success. Our "growth" mindset was firmly in place.

But, then we grew up and something happened. It's as though an invisible switch was flipped in our head and we discarded failure as a learning tool and saw it as something to be avoided. For many of us, this may have come about as a result of enduring lots of criticism during our formative years. Because we experienced humiliation or shame throughout our childhoods ("Why can't you be an 'A' student like your brother?") we carry those feelings into adulthood and avoid tasks that might have unsuccessful results. By avoiding any chance of failure we believe we will also avoid any chance of being ridiculed or denounced.

As a result, we often tag ourselves with a conclusive and definitive label that frequently achieves a sense of permanency - "I have failed a lot, thus I must be a failure." What we often forget is that failures are an inevitability of everyday living; they are not a life sentence. Self-designating ourselves as a "Failure" is similar to giving ourselves the sobriquet "I'm just not creative." Over time, it becomes a mental block that is difficult to dislodge and difficult to override. It becomes a mantra we embrace whenever faced with any type of creative challenge.

It's a box!

In his book *Failing Forward*, John C. Maxwell makes a case for how we view failure in our lives. It is his contention that our perception of failure is one of the most critical factors that signals the difference between average people and achieving people. Failure is inevitable, but it is when we turn those inevitabilities into a label ("I'm a failure") that failure becomes a detriment to creativity, rather than as it should be - an incentive.

Maxwell makes a convincing case that we, all too often, make a judgement of failure in negative terms. He is equally careful to point out that our personal perceptions have evolved through a lifetime of negative events *and the reactions and opinions others have had about those events* (emphasis added). As a result, we have developed a host of misconceptions. Maxwell puts forth a list of seven false statements we tend to embrace. That is, most people believe that failure is: 1) avoidable, 2) an event, 3) an objective, 4) the enemy, 5) irreversible, 6) a stigma, and 7) final. His contention is that failure is "none of the above."

Psychologist Guy Winch has spent considerable time studying the mysteries surrounding fear of failure. Not too long ago he published a provocative paper that has major implications on why this concept derails many of our creative efforts. Winch states that although most of us hate to fail, for some of us failing presents an overwhelming psychological threat that our motivation to avoid failure often exceeds our motivation to succeed. This fear, according to Winch, causes us to unconsciously sabotage our chance of success. As others have contended, humans often will do more to avoid pain than they will to gain pleasure.

Winch states that for many people it is not the actual failure that elicits the fear, but rather that a fear of failure is essentially a fear of shame. By his definition, a fear of failure means we are motivated to avoid failing, not because we can't manage the basic emotions of disappointment and frustration, but more because failing induces feelings of embarrassment, humiliation, or remorse. Failing is seen as a weakness - quite often a public display of several weaknesses. And when those weaknesses are revealed to others, our self-worth suffers mightily. We are seen as less than adequate in the eyes of our colleagues and associates. As a result, our self-esteem deteriorates, our identity is diminished, and our egos wilt. The message is clear: don't take a chance with a new or innovative idea. You might fail. And, if you fail, you will be seen as less than adequate. And, if you're seen as less than adequate, you will *feel* less than adequate. And, that's not a good feeling.

> *People succeed when they realize that their*
> *failures are the preparation for their victories.*
> —RALPH WALDO EMERSON

4.

Here are some folks for whom failure was just part of the creative process: Stephen King, John Grisham, Herman Melville, and Joseph Heller. What do you think they all had in common? At one time in their lives they all experienced failure! Each of them had book ideas rejected, not once or twice, but many times in their professional writing careers.

Stephen King's first novel - *Carrie* - was rejected by thirty different publishers. He now commands multi-million dollar advances from his publisher, even before a single word is written. John Grisham's first book - *A Time to Kill* - was rejected by twenty-eight different publishers. He now has a net worth of $350 million. *Moby Dick* was initially rejected by multiple publishers. It's now a classic reading requirement in hundreds of high schools. Joseph Heller titled his WWII novel *Catch-22* after the initial 22 rejections he received for it. *Gone with the Wind* by Margaret Mitchell was rejected 38 times; *Watership Down* by Richard Adams was rejected 26 times; and *Twilight* by Stephanie Meyer was rejected 14 times. These writers, all of whom experienced a lot of failure early in their careers, saw those failures as necessary stepping stones to commercial success and financial independence. Not too shabby!

Oh, the book you are now holding in your hands...began its life as a failure - a multiple failure.

Several years ago, as the result of a lifelong fascination with the concept of creativity, I put together a proposal for a book about some strategies and techniques people could use to add more creativity to their lives. At that point in my writing career, I had authored well over 100 books and, thus, felt I had the "chops" to write a book about the strategies I and many others have used to approach personal and professional challenges in a more creative manner.

I signed on with a well-known literary agent - an individual who had shepherded hundreds of books through the labyrinth of publishing to publication. The fact that this individual took me on as a client was sufficient to tell me that I had a product that was destined for greatness. You can well imagine my despair and consternation when a steady stream of rejections (over twenty) came back over the course of a year from a who's who of publishing houses that the book "just wasn't right for us."

Eventually, the agent and I parted ways, most amicably I might add. He still liked the concept, but he agreed that the market just wasn't ready for another creativity book. But, I was not to be dismayed.

I dug in deeper and discovered that there were tens of thousands of creativity books in publication. Indeed, it could be said that the market was saturated with creativity books (as I am writing this chapter two new books on creativity in the workplace were released just this week). It soon became apparent that being more creative was an all-consuming interest of the American reading public. But, as I read many of those books, I sensed that something was missing. I conjured several questions...several unanswered questions that began to tickle the edges of my brain. Yes, there were lots of books on creativity, but why? Why do people feel the need to purchase so many creative tomes? Why is it that they feel so "non-creative" in the first place? What was it that made people feel that they weren't innovative or inventive? What were the forces that crushed their creative spirit sufficient that they felt the need to purchase an array of those "How You Can Be More Creative and Save the World" books available in your local bookstore? These were questions that, as far as I could tell, had never been asked before.

This book - a book that literally rose from the ashes of its predecessor - is my answer to those queries.

5.

You may be familiar with Sara Blakely, the woman who founded Spanx. Her first product, a comfortable girdle, was invented because she wanted to wear pantyhose (with no feet) underneath her fitted pants. Her prototype was crude and had several design problems. But, she persevered and kept coming up with better and better designs. However, her efforts at getting the new product manufactured also met with lots of "Thanks, but no thanks." Manufacturers thought the idea was silly and distributors constantly told her that no one would buy such a radical departure from typical women's undergarments (Almost all of those manufacturers were men, by the way.).

But, Sara persisted. In the book *Getting There: A Book of Mentors* she wrote: "Most doors were slammed in my face. I saw my business card ripped up at least once a week, and I even had a few police escorts out of buildings." She received a lot of "no's", but she had also developed an immunity to all those negative reactions. She had embraced the "growth" mindset and would not be deterred in her efforts at getting her products off the ground and into the shopping carts of potential customers. She shrugged off failures like rainwater - knowing each one was further incentive to press on.

And, press on she did. In 2012 *Forbes* named her the youngest self-made female billionaire in history.[21]

Blakeley attributed that tenacity to her father. Every week, as they sat around the dinner table, her father would ask both her and her brother the same question: "What did you guys fail at this week?" According to Blakeley, her father "...knew that many people become paralyzed by the fear of failure. They're constantly afraid of what people will think if they don't do a great job and, as a result, take no

---

21 In 2012, Blakely was also named to Time Magazine's "Time 100" annual list of the 100 most influential people in the world.

risks. His attitude taught me to define failure as not trying something I want to do instead of not achieving the right outcome." In short, Sara Blakeley's philosophy is that failure is a learning opportunity, not an epitaph.

Part of the issue is that throughout our lives we were never taught how to fail or, more importantly ever given permission to fail. We have been constantly told that winners are those who achieve - those who reach the highest pinnacle of success. In sports, we are told that winning the championship (or even just the game) is the true measure of success. In the classroom, we are told that getting an 'A' was the epitome of academic achievement. At work, we are told that increasing sales or production is the path to excellent performance evaluations and raises. Drop a touchdown pass and you're a loser; do poorly on a test and you're academically incompetent; show a decline in quarterly sales figures and you're out of a job. The message is clear: the ultimate goal in life is to be successful at every turn. No failures allowed!

And so, psychologists list fear of failure as one of the biggest stumbling blocks to our creative intents. If you are afraid of making mistakes, you tend to play it safe. As a result, your innate creativity withers and dies. In the business world, companies want to be seen as innovative and "cutting edge." But, those same companies are composed of legions of employees adverse to trying new ideas because new ideas can fail and when they fail they could be out of a job. Workers would rather play it safe than take a chance. Playing it safe tethers us to reality and logic and ensures that the status quo will be maintained. Why live in fear (of failure) when it is much easier and less demanding to stick to the familiar. The unfamiliar - the creative - has so many more risks and so many more potential dangers. We mentally resort to, "Thank you, but I'm fine just as I am."

A work culture where experimentation and failure are valued or even celebrated is a rarity. Laurence Lehman Ortega, affiliate professor in strategy and business policy at HEC Paris Executive Education, believes that the culture of experimentation in the workplace is unusual as only success is celebrated. "It's a learned behavior pattern," he says. "As children we're told that we need to succeed and are rewarded only when we do so. Managers in firms are only recognized and incentivized on their success and as a result are reluctant to take risks. Very few companies such as Google actively incentivize managers if they admit early on that they've failed or reward the time spent on failed exploration projects."

The successful executive is faster to recognize the bad decisions and adjust, where as failing executives often dig in and try to convince people that they were right.
—WALT BETTINGER, CEO OF CHARLES SCHWAB

6.

Tom Peters, coauthor of *In Search of Excellence*, emphasizes that there's nothing more useless than someone who comes to the end of the day and congratulates himself, saying, "Well, I made it through the day without screwing up." People who fear failure expend every effort to ensure that they don't screw up. By avoiding the inevitable pain that goes along with screwing up, we also avoid the inevitable shame linked with all those mistakes. That avoidance puts a severe damper on our ability (and certainly our inclination) to generate new and original ideas. What results is a mindset of fear that severely impedes our creative spirit.

But, let's take that idea one step further and agree that failure is painful and putting our failures out for public display may only deepen the pain. But, when we deny or avoid the inevitable failures that go along with any professional enterprise we only make things worse than they are. We discount the learning and growth that should result from that acknowledgement. In a business environment, this has critical ramifications, since an executive's behavior is often the standard or benchmark people use for their own model of behavior. If a business leader is unable or unwilling to acknowledge their failures - in other words, they do not make any mistakes - then it is likely that employees will be inclined to do the same. However, creativity is never about perfection...it is more about effort and desire. No one does anything perfectly the first, or second, or even third time they attempt it. Hiccups, bumps, and bruises (e.g.

mistakes) are inevitable with any new venture or innovative design. If a leader doesn't accept that inevitability, her staff will infer that mistakes are bad and will eschew creative enterprises or endeavors - avoiding risks at all costs. The result: institutional stagnation.

Consider this dynamic exercise developed by creativity researcher Bob McKim. He gathered an audience of adults together and provided each person with a drawing instrument (pen or pencil) and a blank sheet of paper. He then invited each of the participants to turn to their neighbor and spend thirty seconds drawing a portrait of that individual. As you might imagine, almost everyone was immediately uncomfortable; they offered apologies, made lots of excuses, and downplayed any artistic talent. Snickers, guffaws, and laughter filled the room during the entire thirty-second exercise.

At the end of the thirty seconds, McKim asked each person to show her or his drawing to the individual who served as the model. The results were to be expected. Almost everyone made excuses for their lack of artistic talent. They were embarrassed by the caricatures they created. They feigned smiles as they timidly presented their illustrations. They wondered (often aloud) what their partners would think about their apparent lack of artistic creativity.

Children, as McKim discovered, had just the opposite reaction to this exercise. They enthusiastically embraced it. They smiled, they laughed, and they demonstrated a sincere sense of accomplishment and authorship when sharing their sketches. They were proud of their creativity. The adults - not so much!

As children, we have little fear of failure. Over time, however, it often become part of our personality. Being yelled at when we miss a winning free throw, being berated when we get more than four words incorrect on the weekly spelling test, and being dismissed every time we come up with a new idea furthers the development of a fear of failing. That fear hampers our creative impulses. And, if we are afraid of making mistakes we will also be afraid to invent, create, and innovate.

That's true of ourselves as it is of any commercial enterprise. Southwest Airlines, known for its innovative business models thrives on a simple motto: "Risk more. Fail Faster." Sochiro Honda, founder of Honda , once said, "Success is 99 percent failure." And, Tom Watson, the founder of IBM stated that the way to accelerate your success is to double your failure rate. Quite obviously, the intent is not to focus on the mistakes. They're not the goal after all. They are inevitable consequences of a creative mind; so the object is to get through them quickly in our search for an innovation or new idea. Fear of those inevitable mistakes puts the brakes on our creativity and dims our desire to do something new, something different.

To illustrate this concept further, let's look at the sports page of the daily newspaper. Here is where we expect failure and even reward failure. For example, we say that a professional baseball player who has a .300 (or better) batting average is having a good season. That means that that player has gotten three hits for every ten times he's been at bat. But, let's look at that statistic from the other side: The player has made an out seven out of the ten times he has been up to bat. Examine that statistic in educational terms and you'll note that the player received a 30 percent on his annual batting exam (over the span of 162 games).

30 percent, and he's considered to have a good year![22]

Remember the story about James Dyson? Here's an insightful quote from his interview in *Fast Company*: "We're all taught to do things the right way. But if you want to discover something that other people haven't, you need to do things the wrong way. Initiate a failure by doing something that's very silly, unthinkable, naughty, dangerous. Watching why that fails can take you on a completely different path. It's exciting, actually." It's abundantly clear that Dyson has absolutely no fear of failure. Indeed, he embraces it.[23]

A life spent in making mistakes is not only
more honorable, but more useful than a life
spent doing nothing.
—GEORGE BERNARD SHAW

---

22 I'm fairly certain that if college students obtained 30 percent on all their assignments and exams they would not be having a good year. I'm equally certain they would be in serious danger of not graduating. When baseball players get 30 percent they get a substantial pay raise; when college students get 30 percent they get a very special letter from the Dean!

23 As a writer of children's books, I'm often invited to elementary schools as a visiting author. I frequently receive stacks of 'Thank You" letters from students after each visit. Once, after a visit to a school in Lexington, SC, I received the following letter: "Dear Mr. Fredericks: Thank you for coming to our school. I enjoyed your visit very much. I like many of your books, but the rest are just not that good. Good luck with your future. Sincerely, Danny McDade." That letter hangs over my computer. It is a constant reminder of the power of failure. It is also my creative inspiration.

18.
How to Sizzle: 61 - 69

61. Embrace Failure. Ted Williams was, arguably, the best hitter in major league baseball. After nineteen seasons with the Boston Red Sox, he retired with a lifetime batting average of .344. In 1941 he posted a batting average of .406, becoming the last major league player to bat over .400 in a season. A .400 average means he had four hits for every ten at-bats. It also means that he failed to get a hit six out of ten times he was at bat. In other words, the greatest hitter in professional baseball failed more often than he succeeded. But, as Williams himself once said, "There's only one way to become a hitter. Go up to the plate...."

62. A Search For Ignorance. There's an old saying that goes like this: "Ignorance is bliss." If that brief statement is true, then I'm probably one of the happiest people on the planet! I celebrate my ignorance; in fact, what I don't know could easily fill a hundred museums, a thousand libraries, and a million books (except for this one). There are vast realms of knowledge that are beyond my grasp; there are entire universes of information that will never pass before my eyes; and there are whole worlds of unfathomable concepts and principles that will never ignite a single brain cell in my head. I absolutely enjoy my ignorance.

Ignorance - or a realization that there is "stuff" out there that we will never read or comprehend - is a fuel that powers our creativity. I am not ashamed of my ignorance; indeed, I use that lack of knowledge to discover. I constantly bombard my brain with a plethora of unanswered (and, sometimes, unanswerable) questions. I frequently ask questions that begin with "Why?" Not necessarily because I want to discover all the answers, but simply because I want to continue asking questions about the unknown. For me, the fact that there is an "unknown" provides reason and motivation to generate a vast array of questions in search of a few answers.

Yes, I'm "stupid" about some things...and I celebrate that. It gives me reason and rationale for discovering new intellectual territories. Lewis and Clark did not set out across the vastness of the American West because they knew everything about the topography, the geology, the cultures, or the flora and fauna of that region. What would have been the point of the journey? They set out because there was a vast "unknown" out there and they (and President Thomas Jefferson) wanted to learn about that "unknown." "What do we not know that we can know?" may well have been a question they asked themselves on May 16, 1804 in St. Charles, Missouri as they set out to explore the "unknowns" of the Louisiana Purchase. They were quite ignorant when they began, but came back more than two years later with many fascinating answers.

Celebrate your "not-knowing" - it's a potent fuel that powers your creative instincts and excites your intellectual journeys. It provides you with determination and purpose to discover what you don't know (or, at least, some of what you don't know). And, who knows, you may discover some new territories as you trek through the wilderness of your ignorance.

63. Have An Accident. Not too long ago, I was working on two book manuscripts (two completely different subjects) simultaneously. Without thinking, I cut four paragraphs from one manuscript and pasted them into the other document. It wasn't until a few days later that I noted the error. I swore at myself, but then took a closer look. Some of the sentences from the first document actually made better sense inside the second document. They truly made the second document much better. I got rid of everything else and left them there.

As modern-day humans, we are told that accidents are bad; they should be avoided at all costs. We spill a cup of coffee, our pen leaks on an important document, or the cat decides that the almost completed manuscript on the floor next to the desk would make a great litter box. Mistakes are inevitable. We have a tendency to view those regular errors as bad, as something to be avoided. But, what if we looked at mistakes as new opportunities to think? What if we looked at them in a positive way, rather than a negative way? What if we embraced accidents as a learning opportunity? Charles Goodyear discovered vulcanized rubber as the result of an accident. The wonder drug, penicillin, was discovered quite by accident in 1928. The microwave oven was discovered accidentally by Percy Spencer in 1946. Thomas Adams accidentally discovered chewing gum in 1870. Accidents often give us a new opportunity to examine a project in a different - and, yes, unexpected - way. Rid yourself of the preconceived notion that all accidents are bad. Pause and look at them as a window into the undiscovered or an opportunity for the unexpected.

64. Out On A Limb. Creativity is all about going out on a limb. Not taking the safe route, but rather taking a route that's never been taken before. It is venturing out into the unknown and the unfamiliar. It's being comfortable with a ideas, not because it's the right idea or a safe idea, but just because it's an idea that has never been proffered before. As one philosopher put it, "Creativity is not for the cautious." It's not for those who want to play it safe; it's for those who want to take a chance, a risk, or an adventure into uncharted waters and unknown territories. It's for those who feel comfortable about being in uncomfortable situations. It's for those willing to make waves...and surf those waves all the way to the beach. A willingness to put your neck on the line is much more preferable (and much more creative) than sticking your head in the sand.

65. Do The Impossible. Several years ago, I began writing an adult nonfiction book about horseshoe crabs - one of the most enigmatic and mysterious seashore creatures you'll ever discover on the Eastern seaboard. Colleagues emphatically told me it couldn't be done and that no one would be interested in a relatively unknown critter ("Who wants to read a book about an ancient crab...a very ugly ancient crab?"). Undeterred, I went on to write *Horseshoe Crab: Biography of a Survivor* - a paean to a critter that's been around since long before the dinosaurs. It's also a creature whose blood has saved the lives of tens of millions of humans (including most readers of this book). After the book was published, one reviewer ceremoniously wrote, "An entertaining guide to a creature that is 445 million years old and still having sex on the beach." *Horseshoe Crab* is also a book that has generated an abundance of 5-star reviews. So, when someone tells me "It can't be done," that's all the incentive I need to go out and try get it done. Am I successful every time? No! But, I've challenged the status quo and generated some terrific ideas in the process. Creative people attempt the unimaginable; non-creative people accept "business as usual."

66. Six Words. Describe your life in just six words. No more, no less. Write about your oldest child using just six words. Express affection for your partner using just six words. Describe your most current project at work with just six words. Explain your philosophy of life in just six words. By confining your thinking to just six words you are creating an artificial barrier that forces you to think a little differently, a little more creatively. Whenever I start working on a new book I create the theme of the book in just six words. If I need more than six words, then my theme is too complicated or obtuse. My goal is to explain a book (to a stranger in an elevator) in just six words so that she will understand it completely. For this book my six words were: **Life's creative impediments; how to regenerate**. Define your current project in just six words - you'll begin to see it with new eyes.

67. Don't Finish. Here's a mental trick I use to really get my creative neurons fired up and spinning in a hundred different directions. When I'm working on a manuscript, I'll often stop in the middle of a paragraph or middle of a sentence. I'll save my work and attend to other chores and duties. The next day, when I return to my document, I frequently discover that my mind has, subconsciously, been preparing all kinds of possible extensions of the unfinished work. In short, it has been sparking some new ideas. In essence, when something is left incomplete, you give your brain creative license to try and resolve or finish the project. You are not starting with a "blank slate" (or blank computer screen), rather you are stimulating your thought processes to finish the unfinished. The human brain wants things completed (a school of psychology known as "gestalt") and will do anything it can to be sure they are finished. So, when writing a report, stop in mid-sentence and finish up the next day. When building a birdhouse with your son, stop in the middle of cutting a board, finish up the next day. When writing a message to your lover, stop in the middle of a paragraph and finish it off the next day. Leave things unfinished (and pick them up later) and you'll fire up some critical brain cells...cells that will generate all sorts of creative responses.

68. Resist Perfection. Creativity is never about achieving perfection. It's about embracing possibilities – neither good or bad – looking at things with new eyes and new vision. In and of itself, creativity doesn't change a product from mediocre to incredible; it merely illustrates different ways of seeing the same thing. Using creativity as a way to achieve a perfect product or perfect project is often a lesson in frustration. Perfection is never the goal; it is, quite often, a barrier to achievement. When kids begin putting together a sand castle at the beach, they aren't trying to create the perfect sand castle, they're simply creating a sand castle – one that may have several flaws, imperfections, or design errors. That doesn't make it right or wrong, it simply makes it one version of a sand castle. In short, when people embrace their creativity (like kids), they also embrace the concept of imperfection. Their emphasis is on the process of creation, not the finality of the product. Take a lesson from children: be comfortable with the imperfections in life (and in a project). Far better to create imperfect products than to create nothing at all. For example, the first time I wrote this paragraph it had two misspelled words, a dangling modifier, a split infinitive, and far too many commas. After some creative editing, it seems all right now.

69. Crap. If you're a writer, one of the classic books you should have in your library is *Writing Down the Bones: Freeing the Writer Within* by Natalie Goldberg. Goldberg, an accomplished author herself, offers sage advice and insightful perspectives on what it takes to be a successful writer (She does not equate success with placements on the New York Times Bestseller List or mountains of books in every metropolitan bookstore in the country). Her writing is down-to-earth and impactful and often goes against the grain of what most writing instruction books do. Her admonitions for the creative life are to subtract rules, rather than add more rules to an already overburdened process.

One of the finest pieces of advice in the book - and one I have taken, quite literally, to heart - ever since the book's publication in 1986, is "Give yourself permission to write crap." It is, in so many ways, a piece of advice that says as much about creativity as it does about writing. When people learn that I have written well over 150 published books, they are frequently amazed. But, what I frequently don't tell them is that I have probably written well over 550 books worth of crap.

When I begin writing a book, I start with a first draft (or "Sloppy Copy"). My task is, through a long series of revisions, edits, and modifications, to create something that is both readable and accessible. Does that happen all the time? Absolutely no. I know that I will write a lot of imperfect paragraphs, disconnected thoughts, run-on sentences, misspelled words, bland descriptions, and weird thoughts. I'm perfectly O.K. with that. Not everything that comes out of my computer will be Pulitzer Prize perfect. A lot of it will be just what it is: crap!

One of the challenges I face every morning; indeed, one of the challenges writers of every stripe face when seated in front of their computer, is to get ideas out of my head and onto a screen. Will all of those ideas be perfect? No! Will all of those ideas be ready for readers to read? No! Will everything that appears on the monitor be fit for publication? No! A lot of it will be crappy, but I'm getting it out, I'm getting it down.

We often have this belief when faced with a creative challenge: the key is to generate a really good idea that will save the day (and ensure my continued employment). As a result, we focus on "the perfect idea" or "the best solution." That thought perhaps does more to curtail creativity than anything else. While it may be a focal point for a professional project or personal task, it narrows our vision and sublimates our creative fires. We try and conjure a single "really good idea" without the necessity of generating lots of crappy ones along the way. Being comfortable in producing unworkable, impractical, worthless, and sophomoric ideas is a necessary part of the creative process.

Give yourself permission to create crappy ideas; it will lubricate your mind to produce lots of ideas. And, one of those ideas may be just what you're looking for.

19.
Corporate Killers

*Creativity requires the courage to let
go of certainties.*
— ERICH FROMM

1.

For a moment, imagine you are the head coach of one of the two teams playing in the Super Bowl. On the week before the "Big Game," the press has an extensive array of interviews and press conferences lined up. Everybody gets interviewed this week - from the mega-rich quarterback to the guy who stacks towels in the locker room. But, all those reporters are most interested in the views, opinions, and predictions of the two head coaches. And, you're one of them!

It's the Wednesday before the game and the interview room is packed side to side and front to back with hundreds of reporters from around the world. You and your opposing coach are up on the dais with a platoon of microphones in front of you. One of the reporters stands up and throws the first question your way, "This is obviously the biggest game in the history of sports. Over a hundred million viewers from all over the world will be watching. It's the most valuable sports event in the world - generating over $600 million in revenue. Advertising costs alone will well exceed $5 billion. This game is bigger than big! What are you feeling right now?"

"Well, Jake. I'm not so sure we're the #1 team today. The Bobcats have a much bigger offensive line, their quarterback is at the top of his game, their defense is second to none, and their coaching staff has some of the most respected guys in the business. They're a sound organization with a ton of talent and a ton of respect. We may not be #1, but we'll certainly give it our best."

The whole room is instantly silent. Rows of seasoned sports reporters are sitting with their jaws agape and their eyes bulging. Everyone is staring at you as though you were some kind of six-headed phosphorescent space alien from Venus. "He really didn't say what I thought he said," everyone is saying to themselves. Others are mouthing, "He must be one of the dumbest coaches on the planet...or in the universe." Still others are thinking, "I really think he needs his head checked. This guy's a flaming idiot. He just told everyone in the world that the Bandits are the #2 team in the country. Not #1, but #2."

But, that's just what happened in 1962. And it set the business world on its ear!

For years, Avis had lagged behind Hertz, the rental car industry's market leader. They turned to their ad agency, Doyle Dane Bernbach and asked them for an entirely new ad campaign that would clearly distinguish them from their perpetual rivals. The agency came up with a unique and distinctive way to promote the company's dedication to customer service. "When you're only No. 2, you try harder" was the new slogan.

The reaction was immediate and unprecedented. In less than a year, Avis went from losing $3.2 million to earning $1.2 million. This was the first time the company had been profitable in over a decade. People rushed to rent Avis cars at the airport in unprecedented numbers. Avis's campaign had captured the imagination (and wallets) of the American public as had few advertising efforts. Over the course of the next four years the market-share percentage gap between the two companies shrunk from 61-29 percent to 49-36 percent. Hertz executives worried that by 1968 Hertz would be relegated to the No. 2 position as a result of this dramatic and "outside-the-lines" campaign. Although the ads never mentioned Hertz by name, the implications were clear. "Avis can't afford to have dirty cars." "Avis can't afford to give you lousy customer service." and "Avis can't afford to have you wait in long lines."

Avis bucked the status quo. Traditionally advertising (in the 1960s) touted the popularity, brand recognition, and brand strength to the buying public. "Never reveal your weaknesses, always tout your strengths" seemed to be the mantra of advertising executives. Demonstrate confidence and downplay any sign of weakness was almost the rule of law in those days. But, Avis sought to upset the apple cart with their "smaller-is-better" approach and the result was transformational.

How good was the "We try harder" campaign? It was so effective that Avis kept it in place for fifty years before finally retiring it in 2012.[24]

2.

Many business leaders subscribe to a belief that in order to stay competitive in an ever-changing world, they must embrace creativity and innovation as primary goals of an organization. A creative environment engenders new ideas, products, and approaches that can solve problems and offer goods and services that meet the immediate needs of a sometimes fickle buying public. To support that perception, IBM conducted a Global CEO Study several years ago. 1,541 chief executives, general managers, and public-sector leaders across thirty-three industries and sixty countries around the globe were surveyed. Approximately 60 percent of those executives cited creativity as the most important leadership attribute needed for future success.

Yet, in spite of an overwhelming embrace of creativity as a significant factor in the success of a business or organization, many companies have practices and principles in place that actually crush the creative spirit of their employees and seriously hamper the generation of new ideas and dynamic change. Indeed, there is a plethora of tales in which well-respected firms actively work against creative expression on an almost daily basis. In short, far too many businesses "talk the talk, but don't walk the walk."

In his seminal book, *Where Good Ideas Come From: The Natural History of Innovation* Steven Johnson makes a compelling case, not just for the generation of creative ideas, but also for the habitats that stimulate, foster, and enhance creativity in the first place. It is his

---

24 Interestingly, many marketing experts today recommend that a multi-channel advertising campaign last for no longer than three months.

contention that specific types of environments are necessary in order for creativity to prosper. These environments, according to Johnson, may encompass diverse locations including the office, nature, the home, or through an interaction with media. He caps his thesis with a most profound thought, "On a basic level, it is true that ideas happen *inside* minds, but those minds are invariably connected to external networks [physical environments] that shape the flow of information and inspiration out of which great ideas are fashioned."

Michael Roberto, Director of the Center for Program Innovation at Bryant University, describes several organizational mindsets that tend to inhibit creative expression in the workplace. Roberto describes these as "a collection of explicit and implicit beliefs that shape how people analyze and evaluate, make decisions, and take action with regard to imaginative, original ideas." These mindsets include:

1. The Linear Mindset: Many business leaders envision creativity as a linear process - one that moves from problem identification to analysis to idea formulation to execution to solution. By rule, creativity is frequently discontinuous.

2. The Benchmarking Mindset: It is not unusual for many businesses to copy or reproduce the solutions proffered by their competitors. "If it worked for someone else, it must work for us," is a common misconception.

3. The Prediction Mindset: Predicting what will come next and relying on experts to foretell the future impedes creativity. Managers often become overconfident that "experts" have "inside information" on what will happen next.

4. The Structural Mindset: Redrawing and redesigning the organizational chart is often seen as a way of improving performance and stimulating creativity. It rarely does!

5. The Focus Mindset: Establishing rigid time, place, and setting parameters for "creative work" seldom work. Creative thinkers oscillate between periods of focus and un-focus. Creativity seldom happens in confining circumstances.

6. The Naysayer Mindset: As we saw in Chapter 9, an organization that allows or even encourages naysayers causes many good ideas to wither and die. More important, it significantly reduces the number of good ideas in the first place.

Roberto postulates that these mindsets need to be completely eradicated before the creative process can thrive in any organization or business enterprise. He strongly suggests that if these beliefs aren't eliminated from the corporate mindset then "...the production of fresh and original ideas from all sectors of the organization is seriously jeopardized."

3.

They may be quiet and walk on cats paws, or they may be loud and ham-handed. They are the practices, processes, and procedures integrated into the daily workings of tens of thousands of businesses that unknowingly mitigate against creative thought or expression. In many cases, they are so ingrained in the workings of a company that they are taken for granted as inimitable to the operational philosophy. They create friction, impede progress, stifle innovation, and curtail free expression. They are emotional and psychological depressants.

In an article posted on *Money Watch*, Margaret Hefferman writes, "Every conversation I've had with business leaders recently has revolved around creativity. Fundamentally they all come down to the same thing: Why aren't my people more creative? In their frustration, many business leaders ultimately decide they're surrounded by lousy people and blame them. Such thinking is almost always wrongheaded. Most people are infinitely more creative than their jobs allow them to be - it's one of the principle reasons people leave their jobs to start their own businesses."

Let's take a look at the three most common corporate crushers.

A. Brainstorming

It probably wouldn't surprise you to learn that many organizations, when faced with a challenge or problem, brainstorm it to death. "Let's all get together in the Conference Room and we'll throw a bunch of ideas up on the whiteboard and we should have this thing hammered out by lunchtime." The prevalent thinking is that a bunch of people tossing random ideas at one another will eventually discover an idea (or a combination of ideas combined into a super solution) that works.

There is a persistent practice that the only way to solve complex problems within an organization is via brainstorming. Indeed, brainstorming seems to be the default answer to any organizational issue. As a result, some problems are brainstormed to death. Other creative endeavors are eschewed in favor of a strategy that been around for several decades. "If it's been around for that long," the thinking goes, "then it must be good."

Unfortunately, the prevalence of brainstorming as a problem-solving strategy masks its reality. Nicholas Kohn and his colleagues at Texas A&M University looked into the real effects of brainstorming on creative thinking and found that, rather than leading to a wealth of new ideas, brainstorming can narrow the focus of a group to just one, non-optimal idea. Kohn's group found that in brainstorming sessions, it was common for members of the group to become fixated with the ideas of others unconsciously, and for the group to eventually coalesce and conform to a single idea in the group rather than exploring a range of ideas.

Although well-entrenched in corporate America, many experts have underscored brainstorming's lack of effectiveness as a creative endeavor. For example, in any group situation, no matter the organization, there is a perceived hierarchy. That is, some people in the group are perceived to have more "power" than other members of the group. Junior members of an organization are perceived to have less power and less influence that the older more established members. This power differential may result in some members generating a disproportionate amount of ideas than other members, based solely on their standing in the group. "The more extrovert and assured members of the group assert their ideas first and then those less confident agree, even if they might have equally sound ideas."

True to form, brainstorming sessions also have finite limits: a one-hour meeting, a single and well-used meeting room, or a designated time of the week or month. In other words, artificial constraints are placed on the potential generation of ideas. As we know, ideas come at odd times and in odd places - not always during a regularly scheduled department meeting in Room 103 at 3:30 on Tuesday afternoons.[25] R. Keith Sawyer, a professor of education, psychology, and business at Washington University in St. Louis writes, "Brainstorming often focuses on the generation of lots of ideas in a closed environment within a designated time frame. In short, it violates what we know about the generation of creative thoughts - simply that creativity is not a linear process: it's adding ideas, subtracting ideas, combining ideas together, divorcing ideas, allowing ideas to simmer (or boil) over time, and slicing ideas up and putting them back together in new patterns or configurations."

Brainstorming also gives us permission to throw out a vast array of ideas - everything from incredibly bad to unbelievably good. For the most part, all the ideas put forth are considered equal. Even the unworkable ideas are put forth, tossed up on the whiteboard, and incorporated into the conversation with the same degree of fervor and compassion as the good ones. One of the basic ideas behind brainstorming is that the emphasis is on generating a vast quantity of ideas, rather than the looking at the quality of those ideas. In essence, every idea is treated equally. We suspend any critical responses for fear of derailing the production process. Bad ideas are given a cache of acceptability that frequently inhibits the embrace of positive problem-solving.

You may work for an organization that suggests several problems "for consideration by the team." A member of management might toss out an "issue" or two at various times of the month. A group of people is assembled to brainstorm for possible solutions. And, unsurprisingly, a solution seldom creeps out from all the ideas tossed about. That's simply because nobody within the brainstorming group

---

25 Ever get a brilliant idea in the shower. Yeah, me too! Why is that? Harvard researcher Shelley Carson postulates that a shower offers us a mental distraction. If you are stuck on a problem, an interruption can force an "incubation period," she says. "In other words, a distraction [like a warm shower] may provide the break you need to disengage from a fixation on the ineffective solution." Pass the soap, please!

"owns" the problem. The problem is artificial - it has been proposed by someone outside the circle of "problem-solvers" who are tasked with producing a solution without an investment of ownership.

As you might imagine, this violates one of the essential components of effective problem-solving. That is, we can best solve our problems when we <u>own</u> those problems; without the ownership element, the problem belongs to someone else. Without the emotional investment there can be little creative investment. Problems that are "given" to us get little more than superficial treatment; problems that emanate from our own minds are those in which we have a personal stake...and a desire to solve. For example, as a teenager, did you ever engage all your relatives in a brainstorming session to come up with solutions to your out-of-control love life?

I didn't think so!

We also assume that a brainstorming session will, or should, produce a feasible answer to a problem within the assigned time limit. Yet, in *Where Good Ideas Come From*, Johnson writes, "... brainstorming is...finite in both time and space: a group gathers for an hour in a room, or for a daylong corporate retreat, they toss out a bunch of crazy ideas, and then the meeting disperses. Sometimes a useful connection emerges, but too often the relevant hunches aren't in synch with one another. One employee has a promising hunch in one office, and two months later, another employees comes up with the missing piece that turns that hunch into a genuine insight. Brainstorming might bring those two fragments together, but the odds are against it."

Part of that problem is a lack of incubation time. As humans, we are an impatient species. We often expect instant gratification and are frustrated when we have to wait in a line at the grocery store, pause at an unbearably long traffic signal, or try to get sleepy kids out of bed and off to school. In most brainstorming sessions, the implied goal is that we arrive at a solution or a collection of potential solutions within a designated time frame ("We only have an hour for this meeting, so I want you guys to generate a lot of potential ideas in the 60 minutes we have."). The result is often a superficial hodgepodge of disconnected and disjointed ideas generated within the constraints of time, but without the advantage of percolation. We know that good ideas don't always spring up organically; often they need to simmer and stew for a while in order to reach their full flavor and intellectual potential. Let's take a look at that time factor.

B. Insufficient Time

For college students majoring in business, creativity is a concept they know will permeate many aspects of their courses as well as their eventual success in the corporate world. But, their conception of the term often is in conflict with the reality of what people need in order to be successful creatively. To assess that disconnect, I asked a former colleague - a professor in the Business Department at York College of Pennsylvania - if I could assess his students regarding their perceptions of creativity. As part of a two-question survey, I asked the twenty-four freshmen in his "Introduction to Business" course to each define one of three words: "Smart," "Intelligent," or "Creative."

Eleven students randomly drew index cards with the word "Creative" printed at the top. Each individual was then asked to provide her/his own personal definition, rather than a definition that might appear in a textbook or dictionary. Here are their responses. See if you notice a trend:

- ➤ "Somebody who can turn an idea of almost nothing into something."
- ➤ "Lots of artistic ability and good ideas."
- ➤ "Innovating/creating something from nothing."
- ➤ "When someone is creative they are able to create something out of nothing and use that to inspire others."
- ➤ "The ability to design, organize, or create something."
- ➤ "Being able to do things in a different way."
- ➤ "The ability to design, organize, or create something that was previously not there."
- ➤ "Being able to think outside the box and create something from nothing."
- ➤ "Creative means unorthodox, being original, and not doing things that are expected of you."

➤ "To be able to analyze a situation and come up with a solution that is unique or non-traditional."

➤ "Somebody able to create big ideas from very little."

While, admittedly, not a scientific survey, this assessment of how future business leaders view creativity early in their professional lives is revealing in the sense that it underscores a persistent belief (or myth) that creative ideas spring from minimal resources, or no resources at all. It perpetuates a belief that people with high levels of creativity are able to create something out of nothing. The rest of us, on the other hand, can't come up with a creative idea - even with all the resources in the world.

Chief among those resources - and the one that may have the most impact - is time...unrestrained time. Creativity doesn't happen within a frame of minutes or hours - it's an ebb and flow of thoughts over an unrestricted period of time. Telling workers they must solve a problem "...in the next thirty days or our competitors will eat us alive" is disingenuous at best, and counterproductive (to the creative process) at worst.

To illustrate, let's take a look at some interesting survey results. iStock by Getty Images is an online photo and video service. They polled 400 "creatives" and discovered that 60 percent of them had "great ideas" in the preceding year, but didn't have the time necessary to follow through with those ideas. 70 percent of the respondents indicated they needed more "creative time" for their work. Equally interesting was that 63 percent said they're so busy doing mundane tasks that there was no time left over for "creative reflection and inspiration." Approximately 25 percent of the people in the survey revealed that they spend only about two hours a day on creative work. However, the most damning evidence was that nearly 50 percent of the respondents believed that creativity where they work has stalled or dropped off significantly. Ellen Desmarais, general manager at iStock, put it this way: "Rising pressure from increasing workloads, ever-tighter deadlines, and constrained budgets are wearing creatives down."

Not enough time! Sound familiar?

We're all under pressure to do more things in shorter allotments of time. Our boss tells us to "get that report in by the end of the week," an editor tells a writer to "submit your manuscript by the designated due date...or else," and a supervisor lambasts an employee, "Are you kidding me? I told you to get that done by the end of the day." We've all experienced time constraints on our work, but there's increasing evidence to support the notion that when we're asked to generate creative ideas we react particularly badly to a work environment that is rushed or hurried.

Consider, for instance, a long-term study called "Creativity Under the Gun." Researchers examined daily diary entries from more than 9,000 people "working on projects that required high levels of creativity." They measured individuals' ability to innovate under different levels of time pressure. The results indicated that most people were least productive when they were constantly required to fight the clock. Interestingly, when laboring under extreme time pressure, most people generated fewer fresh ideas, not just on the day of the deadline, but for two days afterward.

"Organizations routinely kill creativity with fake deadlines or impossibly tight ones," wrote the head researcher in an article appearing in the Harvard Business Review. "The former create distrust, and the latter cause burnout." She added that companies typically (and unwittingly) dampen creativity by giving employees little slack in their schedules for the kind of creative problem-solving that can often result in breakout ideas and dynamic innovations. "It can be slow going to explore new concepts, put together unique solutions, and wander through the maze" of untried and novel possibilities. Without sufficient time to do that, it is as though we are operating inside a rigid enclosure with no room for (mental) expansion.

Google, for example, has set a unique precedent for the business world, as it allows its employees to spend 20 percent of their working time tackling whatever they want. They have established a trust that their employees will be able to produce new ideas and new products when they are offered the most precious resource any company can give: time. In one penetrating article the point was made that "Asking employees to work...within an unrealistically short time frame might sound like a budget-conscious company's dream, but it's sure to burn out employees very quickly and leave them resenting you, hating their jobs, and fresh out of new ideas."

C. Not Taking Risks

Let's take a trip to your local park or playground. I'd like to invite you to take a seat on the bench nearest a concentration of playground equipment: slides, swings, jungle gyms, seesaws, merry-go-rounds, sand boxes, trapeze rings, and a maze or two. Sit quietly and listen to some of the sounds - most of which are coming from the mouths of parents: "Don't climb up there, you're going to get hurt," "No, you can't go all the way to the top. It's too dangerous," and "How many times have I told you not to push your sister so hard. She could get injured."

Now, let's take a trip to England and sit near one of the playgrounds in the suburbs of London. Look around and you'll see something quite different (Yes, you'll still hear parents shouting at their children). But here, the playground equipment is a little more edgy, a little more "dangerous." You'll see taller climbing poles, higher slides, and faster merry-go-rounds. This new equipment is in response to playground environments that are viewed as being just a little too safe. "Playgrounds [in England] are being toughened up because a generation of children is failing to learn how to handle risk," according to a recent article.

Apparently, Britain's embrace of a risk-averse culture goes far beyond the creation of safe playgrounds. A nonprofit organization is so concerned about England's low tolerance for risk that it has established a special commission to examine what it perceives to be a critical issue in the overall health of the country. "It is forgotten that risk can be a good thing," the group writes in an overview of its mission. "People often make an active choice to take a risk because they see a potential opportunity to reap rewards. Risk is the essence of many creative projects and can be about daring to do something new or different, or taking a chance, in the hope of securing benefits."

We know that taking risks is essential in our overall growth and development. We all took some risks when we learned how to walk. By the same token, we took a risk when we got our driver's license and took the family car out for a spin,[26] and many of us took a risk when we joined up with another individual and said that we would spend the rest of our life with this person ("Till death do us part."). I think we can all agree that taking risks is an essential element in our learning curve. Yet, what we practice in

26 My first spin in the family car was directly through the (closed) garage door. Suffice it to say, there were two "not so happy campers" waiting for me as I slunk into the house.

the corporate world is often altogether different. It's similar to the way parents "monitor" their children on a playground - "Don't do that or you might get hurt." Minimize the risk and you can minimize the potential hurt. But what results is often stunted creative expression. Innovation is all about taking a chance; all about venturing into unfamiliar territories with the possibility of discovering something new or something different. That's not possible without some risk-taking.

"Playing it safe" or "same old, same old" is the way many companies minimize loss by limiting risk-taking. When you don't take a risk, you systematically avoid making mistakes. And, lots of mistakes cost lots of money. It's much easier and less risky to do things the way they've always been done in the past. "It was proven successful then, surely it must be equally successful now. Why change?" This certainly makes sense from a logical standpoint, but it places unnatural hurdles in the way of creative progress. It restricts the generation and implementation of creative ideas - new ideas essential to progress. When we adhere to the same routines and standards used in the past, we prevent innovation, we restrict creativity In short, if employees are forced to stay within existing mental boundaries, they will be less inclined to move beyond those practices...and less inclined to exercise their creative powers.

When companies kill creativity they de-value risk-taking as an opportunity for employees to try something new. Often those new ideas fail, but even those failures offer unique opportunities to see what doesn't work, what can be learned from those failures, and how those failures might influence the development of future ideas. "If you punish employees that don't immediately deliver amazing results through their innovations, then you will teach staff members to be afraid of creativity, and stifle future voices that could improve your company. Instead, encourage people to learn from their mistakes, and reward them for being open about their failures and mistakes to ensure that future issues aren't swept under the carpet."

An aversion to risk-taking also has another consequence: a tendency to micro-manage an organization. A close and careful monitoring of every aspect of a company, in logic, keeps a "handle" on what is happening and how well it is happening. But it also has a negative impact on creative advancement. Creativity involves the freedom to move into uncharted territories and unfamiliar vistas. When workers feel that someone is "looking over their shoulder," they are less inclined to venture into unknown spheres or expanses. They are less inclined to come up with a new craft, a new direction, or a new map that opens up creative vistas. They feel constrained, not only in what they do, but, more importantly in what they could do. Their creative spirit is manacled and their sails sufficiently trimmed that they seldom venture outside their safe harbor and into uncharted seas.

4.

In his classic tome *Out of Our Minds: Learning to be Creative*, Sir Ken Robinson includes a section entitled "The Roles and Principles of Creative Leadership." I'm going to take some creative license and turn his principles on their head. That is, I'm going to reverse what he has stipulated as essential to any organization and, instead, share how those factors, when not implemented, can have a most negative impact on the "creativity quotient" of an organization.

For example, his first principle is stated thusly: "Everybody has creative potential." The obverse of that principle - and the one often exhibited in numerous commercial enterprises - becomes: "Only a select few are recognized for their creative potential." In short, employees are either part of the "Creative Class" or part of the "Noncreative Class." We'll address this practice in more detail in a later chapter. Suffice it to say, that when the inherent creativity of EVERYBODY is not recognized, celebrated, and invited, any business enterprise will suffer concomitantly.

Robinson's sixth principle ("Creativity takes time.") often takes the form of "We just don't have the time to be creative." It's difficult to put a monetary value on creativity. We can do that with time and products, but assigning dollars and cents to innovation is virtually impossible. Besides creativity is not bound by the constraints of workplace time (9:00 - 5:00) - it happens irrespective of the standard work day - often inviting itself to a social gathering on the weekend, slipping past the front door and up the stairs in the middle of the night, or catching up to a family car trip at the Grand Canyon or through the Florida Everglades. Creativity is not governed by schedules or calendars - it can be, and should be, unrestrained.

Following, then, are nine principles that effectively quash the creative potential of any organization (2nd column) be it a school, a small business, a nonprofit organization, a college classroom, a major corporation, or a local charity.

IN PRINCIPLE	IN PRACTICE
1. Everybody has creative potential.	Only a select few are recognized for their creative potential.
2. Innovation is the child of imagination.	Innovation is discouraged at every turn.
3. We can all learn to be more creative.	Only a few people are capable of learning to be more creative.
4. Creativity thrives on diversity.	We must all think alike for any progress to occur.
5. Creativity loves collaboration.	Collaboration is frequently discouraged.
6. Creativity takes time.	We just don't have the time to be creative.
7. Creative cultures are supple.	'It's my way or the highway!"
8. Creative cultures are inquiring.	We have all the answers we'll ever need.
9. Creative cultures need creative spaces.	Everybody works better when they stay in their own office.

A successful business is seldom static. It moves forward; it moves ahead. And, as we've seen, it also embraces a creative philosophy that celebrates innovative thinking as an essential component of the organization, rather than as an afterthought. The conscious awareness of the import of creative ideas on "the bottom line" often means changing the status quo and reducing or eliminating "corporate killers" from the workplace. Admittedly, when some practices have been in place for a long time, that's difficult to do. But, if ignored or downplayed, they do have the potential to seriously and negatively impact forward progress. And, that's never a good thing.

How does your workplace embrace creativity?

20.
How to Sizzle: 70 - 78

70. Redefine Brainstorming. If you have a challenge, invite employees to brainstorm for all the potential solutions to a problem ahead of the meeting. Have them jot their ideas on the white board or duplicate them as handouts before the meeting begins. Now, devote meeting time to looking at all the possibilities, irrespective of who generated them or their perceived practicality. Not only will the quantity of ideas increase; so too, will the quality of the interactions between those ideas escalate appreciably. There will also be less emphasis on who generated the most ideas or who offered the "best" ideas. As a result, the focus is less about the origins of the ideas and more about the value of the ideas.

71. For Your Desk. Consider duplicating some of the following quotes and posting them on your desk:

➤ "An idea that is not dangerous is unworthy of being called an idea at all." - Oscar Wilde

➤ "Instead of worrying about what you cannot control, shift your energy to what you can create." - Roy T. Bennett

➤ "Creativity is an import-export business." - Ethan Zuckerman

➤ "We have to continually be jumping off cliffs and developing our wings on the way down." - Kurt Vonnegut

➤ "I want to involve creativity more in technology and business. It is obvious that for us to be successful, a

healthy relationship with creativity is needed." - Harper
Reed

➤ "Great minds discuss ideas. Average minds discuss events. Small minds discuss people." - Henry Buckle

➤ "You can't use up creativity. The more you use, the more you have." - Maya Angelou

➤ "Imagination is everything. It is the preview of life's coming attractions." - Albert Einstein

➤ "Learn the rules like a pro, so you can break them like an artist." - Pablo Picasso

72. Reduce Micro-Managing. The "My way or the highway" model of corporate management does more to depress the natural creativity of employees than almost any other tactic. It take away a sense of personal ownership in the organization. Employees feel a sense of disenfranchisement - they are less committed to the goals of the organization and more tied to the edicts or philosophy of the boss. In essence, the company becomes a "one-man operation." If you set yourself up as the paragon of thinking in your business, then employees will have no incentive to think or innovate on their own. Their creative spirit will wither and die.

73. Picture-Storming. This chapter pointed out some of the dangers of traditional brainstorming sessions. Here's a different approach - one I use quite frequently since most of my work is done, not as a member of a group, but by myself. I get a pack of 5 x 8 index cards, some cellophane tape, and a tall stack of old magazines. I take a pair of scissors and cut out as many pictures as I can. I don't look for any particular type of picture or photograph - my only restriction is that it must be less than 5 x 8 inches. I usually set a predetermined goal ahead of time; for example, 100 pictures. Afterwards I tape each picture to a card and then turn all the cards over. Then, I randomly select two cards (I can't see the pictures on the other side) and paper clip them together. Eventually, I'll wind up with 50 random pairs. I'll arbitrarily select one of the pairs, turn the cards over, and see if I can determine any similarities between the two pictures. For example, I recently turned over a picture of a Mountain Gorilla and an old-fashioned dial telephone. Here are some of the similarities I generated: both are endangered, they both make noise, they both are difficult to locate, they both have black circles, they both have a protruding "belly," and they both have carbon components. By focusing on similarities (rather than differences) I am exercising my mind to look at items in a more creative way. This activity, done every week or so helps me generate creative solutions to problems completely unrelated to gorillas or telephones. Try it and you, too, will begin generating creative responses to many of your problems.

74. Shut Up And Listen! Several recent research studies have shown conclusively that business leaders spend too much time talking and not enough time listening. Soliciting, encouraging, and listening to employee ideas has been proven to be a significant boost to morale as well as to the production of creative ideas. Innovative ideas (particularly from your employees) most often come about when your mouth is closed and your ears are open. Make this a regular active process, rather than a passive component (suggestion box) of the organization. Go out and solicit new ideas and new ways of thinking. Then, shut up and listen!

75. Vacation Time. My most creative time is usually not when I'm at my desk working on a book manuscript. It's often when I need to relieve myself or get myself a fresh cup of coffee. During the walk from my desk to the bathroom or kitchen, my time there, and the walk back to my desk I often generate some of my most creative thoughts. Why? Simply because I'm giving my mind a break...a mini-vacation from the mental challenges on my computer screen. My mind is less-focused and less-stressed. Now, it can wander anywhere and everywhere it wants to. I can dream, imagine, create, innovate, or just sail away to a tropical island. There are no artificial restrictions - this is recovery time. My mind is cleared and now it can play. And, play it does. I've learned that by un-focusing from time to time - by giving myself a mental sabbatical every so often - I can truly play with ideas. Your mind, too, needs breaks: make lots of coffee; go to the bathroom more often.

76. Take A Risk. A creative work environment is a work environment not afraid to take risks. Unfortunately, many business have become risk-adverse often to the point of punishing employees who take seemingly unnecessary risks. Given the financial dangers associated with risk-taking this stance is understandable. However, overprotection of "Well, it worked before, certainly it will work again" becomes self-defeating in the long run. A tendency to rest on our laurels is a tendency to stagnate and extinguish the full potential of the organization. Michael Hvisdos, founder and CEO of Inquizo, emphatically states that, "Encouraging and incentivizing risk taking will open up the organization's thinking and create more engagement. Since organizations with high levels of employee engagement outperform other businesses by 202 percent, upside for the business is huge!"

77. Read Biographies. One of the best ways to become more creative is to read the biographies of creative people. How did they solve problems in their field? How did they generate new ideas or innovative thoughts? How did they meet the challenges of their day or the conundrums of a project? How did they solve the puzzles related to their work? For me, the biographies of Leonardo daVinci, Galileo, Marie Curie, Picasso, Benjamin Franklin, Bill Gates, Albert Einstein, Ruth Bader Ginsburg, Mel Brooks, and Steve Jobs have given me more creative insights and more creative possibilities than I can "shake a stick at." Not only do the people profiled offer personal models of creative thinking; so too, do they provide insights into the workings of the creative mind. Keep a biography on your nightstand and you'll fall asleep each night with a whirlwind, an avalanche, and a tsunami of creative thoughts slipping into your dreams. The next morning: Watch out world!

78. Thinking In Similes. Highly creative people often use comparisons to help them define a problem and to think about possible solutions. They look at their problem, define it, and may even give it a name. Then they create one or more similes – ruminating about what their problem is like.

Here are some of the advantages of thinking in similes:

➤ Similes focus your mind on relationships (real or imaginary) of ideas, images and symbols.
➤ Similes make complex issues easier to understand. They take the all-too-familiar and put it into a new context – a new frame of mind.
➤ Similes force you to think divergently. The emphasis is never on "right answers," but rather relationships that lead to new ideas.
➤ Similes can turn old, stodgy facts into many new ideas.
➤ Similes allow you to see a larger picture.

Creating similes is a relatively easy process. It's an effective way of generating new ideas and an equally effective way of breaking through a mental roadblock when you're stuck on how to get started or what to do with a new idea.

Here's how I do it: Every once in a while I'll get a stack of blank index cards (10-20). I'll find a book, magazine or newspaper and randomly open it up to one page. I'll locate 2-3 nouns and write each one on a separate index card. I'll turn to another page and repeat the process with another 2-3 nouns. I'll do this again and again (random pages, random nouns) until I have about 25-30 cards. These cards then go into a special box. The following week, I'll select a new book, magazine or newspaper and do the same thing all over again. I also carry a few blank index cards in my pocket whenever I'm on the road and find myself reading a local newspaper or browsing through a magazine in an airport.

My goal is to get about 100 cards (with about 100 nouns). Every once in a while, I'll sit down with the deck of cards and shuffle it thoroughly. Then I'll deal myself two cards at random. Using those two cards I'll try to create a simile. For example, I've just taken my current deck of cards and dealt myself the following two cards: "School" and "Human Body." I placed those words in a simile stem!

School is like a *human body*.

Now, I'll try to create a reason or rationale for that simile. Here's what I just came up with:

Simile: *School is like a human body.*
Explanation: *Teachers are the guts. The administration is the mouth. The kids are the blood. The photocopy machine is the reproductive system. And the secretaries and custodians are the skeleton that supports the body.*

Now, I'm not sure if that simile will ever develop into a New York Times bestselling book. That's not the point. The point is that I've flexed my mental muscles in some new directions and new ways of thinking. I've looked at something from new angles and new perspectives. Instead of "same old, same old," I can now begin to create writing possibilities and writing options that I wouldn't have seen otherwise.

I used this technique a few years ago while trying to generate some new ideas for an adult nonfiction book about clams (*The Secret Life of Clams: The Mysteries and Magic of Our Favorite Shellfish*). I dealt myself two cards – "Monsters" and "Games." I wrote those two words in a simile stem: *Monsters are like games*. Then, I began to generate a rationale for that simile (NOTE: It's not important, or even necessary, for the rationale to make sense. You just have to make a connection):

Simile: *Monsters are like games.*
Explanation: *They have a Monopoly® on their ability to destroy and/or annihilate human-made structures. Humans don't have a Clue® about how to keep them from all that destruction. They often play Hide and Seek with humans as they move from one location to another. Some monsters play "Tag"; others play "Catch" by throwing things around.*

From that single simile I came up with an opening for a chapter all about the commercial harvesting of clams (Chapter 9: It Came from Beneath the Sea). I opened the chapter with an overview of a classic movie monster - the gargantuan octopus in the 1955 film *It Came from Beneath the Sea* - and some of the "games" it played with humans (snaking a tentacle down San Francisco's Market Street, wrapping its arms around the Golden Gate Bridge, and darting away from an atomic submarine.). I compared its actions with those of my central figure - clams - and some of the similarities (and dissimilarities) between the movie creature and the real-life creature in both behavior and character.

Keep these tips in mind in order to make this strategy an effective one:

➤ Keep collecting word cards.

➤ Prune your collection every once in a while (for example, remove 20 percent of the cards every month or so and replace with an equal number).

➤ Start your day off with a self-created simile. You'll wake up your brain cells and get them "energized."

➤ Your similes don't have to make sense.

➤ You may not come up with a workable idea for every simile. Nevertheless, file each one away and come back to them at a later date. You may discover a previously created simile that will be just right for the moment.

PART FIVE

Everyday Beliefs

21.
"Here Be Dragons!"

*Nothing is more difficult than competing
with a myth.*
- FRANCOISE GIROUD

1.

In 1510, the Spanish author Garcia Ordóñez de Montalvo penned
a popular novel entitled *Las Sergas de Esplandián*. In it, he writes:

> Know that to the right of the Indies there is an island
> called California very close to the side of the Earthly Paradise;
> and its inhabitants were black women, without a single man,
> for they lived in the manner of the Amazons. They were
> beautiful and their bodies robust, with fiery courage and great
> strength. Their island is the most formidable in the world, with
> its steep cliffs and stony shores. Their weapons are all made of
> gold, as are the harnesses they use to tame their wild beasts,
> because there is no other metal on the island other than gold.

The mythical island of California propelled many explorers,
including Hernán Cortés, to send expeditions to find and claim this
mysterious land. One of those explorers, Francisco de Ulloa, followed
the coastline northward, eventually determining that the island was, in
fact, a peninsula. Soon thereafter (in 1541) California began to appear
on maps - correctly and accurately drawn as a part of the mainland.

For almost sixty years, what was then known as California, was
portrayed on a succession of European maps as a peninsula firmly
part of the North America continent. Then, something very strange
occurred. In 1622, cartographer Michiel Colijn of Amsterdam,

redrew California as an island (although he never set foot in California, he may have been significantly influenced by the early Spanish novel or perhaps he decided that for marketing purposes, maps of California as an island would sell much better). Subsequently, other cartographers copied Colihn's interpretation and began producing a succession of cartographic drawings prominently displaying California as a distinct island. This misperception of California as an island floating in the Pacific, continued throughout the 17th century and much of the 18th century. Modern day cartophiles, such as British author Edward Brooke-Hitching, surmise that this misinterpretation may have been fueled by journal entries recorded by Friar Antonio de le Ascensión during Sebastian Vizcaino's voyage up the California coast in 1602. For some unknown reason, Ascensión's notes identified California as a geographical landmass separated from the continent by the "mediterranean Sea of California."

In those days, cartography was an inexact science. Most mapmakers relied on adventurers, travelers, and explorers for accounts of new lands or distant ports for details necessary to illustrate those regions. The stories sailors and other adventurers brought back were often less than accurate, imbued with their own personal perceptions of what something looked like or how one landform (for example) compared with another. Google Earth and GPS were obviously nonexistent at the time and cartological instruments were rudimentary. There was certainly a lot of guesswork, conjecture, and supposition involved in the construction of early maps. They were imprecise at best and often reflected creative imaginations and nonexistent geography.

As a result, a succession of cartographers perpetuated the "California as an island" myth well into the 1700s. Eventually, the Jesuit Friar Eusebio Kino made several expeditions to and through what is now the American southwest. He realized that California was geologically and geographically connected to the mainland. He subsequently created a map that confirmed those observations. Additional expeditions by other explorers verified "the attachment." Finally, in 1747, Ferdinand VI of Spain decreed that "California is not an island." It was officially "reattached" to the continent.[27]

27 One of the most intractable and persistent myths is the belief that a major chunk of California will eventually break off the North American continent and float out into the Pacific Ocean during the next major earthquake along the San Andreas Fault. So, if you should be driving through the Mojave Desert towns of Palm Springs, Barstow, Lucerne Valley, or Twentynine Palms and just happen to see sailboats sitting in the front yards of the residents there, perhaps you might want to ask yourself, "Are they just being creative; or are they just being cautious?"

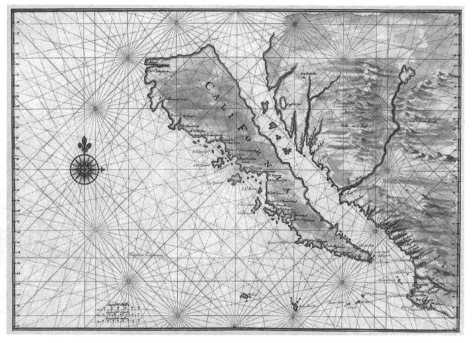

Island of California (drawn by Johannes Vingboons, Dutch cartographer, c. 1650)

2.

It is often said that once myths get started, they become difficult to dislodge from the public consciousness. When those myths are seemingly confirmed by learned people (in the form of maps, books, or articles) then they become fact. In modern terms, the proliferation and dissemination of 'Fake News" stories throughout the internet, eventually are accepted as fact - irrespective of their validity or truthfulness. Tabloids are notorious for initiating a rumor, myth, or falsehood, printing millions of copies of a supposedly factual article, and conning tens of thousands of readers into believing that something far-fetched and clearly unscientific is actually true (e.g. "Football Field Size Alligator Discovered in Minnesota Back Yard"; "Prehistoric Dinosaur Chickens Live in New York Subway"; and "Half-Man, Half-Woman has 43 Children."). Interestingly, many of these articles show journalistic creativity in full flower.

Myths are a tradition of every culture and civilization since the dawn of language. They bind human beings in a celebration of their history and heritage. They are part and parcel of the human experience, because they underscore the values and experiences a society cherishes as well as those we seek to share with each other. Myths are stories that command our attention and help us appreciate the values, ideas, and traditions we hold dear. By extension, myths are also stories of tradition and timelessness, tales that enchant, mystify, and excite through a marvelous weaving of characters, settings, and plots...tales that have stood the test of time.

The myths of our youth conjure all sorts of visions and possibilities - far away lands, magnificent adventures, enchanted princes, beautiful princesses, evil wizards and wicked witches, a few dragons and demons, a couple of castles and cottages, perhaps a mysterious forest or two, and certainly tales of mystery, intrigue, and adventure.

But, it's important to keep in mind that, by definition, a myth is simply a narrative that may or may not be grounded in truth. However, whatever truth may have existed early in the "life" of a myth, through repeated tellings by various storytellers over time, may have been diminished or significantly reduced over many decades or centuries of storytelling. Colloquially, the term "myth" is often a popular or common belief that often has no basis in fact. It is a story that seems real on the surface, but exists solely to try and explain something without proof.

Today, we also create and perpetuate myths. For example, here are some common science and history myths - narratives many people believe in spite of the fact that they have no basis in fact:

➤ Toilet flushes always spin in a different direction in the Southern Hemisphere.
➤ Lightning never strikes in the same place twice.
➤ Bananas grow on trees.
➤ Humans only use 10 percent of their brains.
➤ A mother bird will reject its baby if it's been touched by a human.
➤ Bats are blind.
➤ George Washington had wooden teeth.

➤ The Salem witch trials burned people at the stake.

➤ Thomas Edison invented the light bulb.

➤ Humans have five senses.

➤ The Great Wall of China is the only human-made object visible from space.

➤ Ostriches stick their heads in the sand to hide from enemies.

➤ The Declaration of Independence was signed on July 4, 1776.

➤ Christopher Columbus proved that the earth wasn't flat, but round.

Just like in ancient times, we continue to make up stories in an attempt to explain why certain events occur or to fill in gaps in our knowledge base. Ancient humans relied on myths to explain how the world worked. Modern humans create myths to explain mysterious events (the Salem witch trials), unusual circumstances (swirling water, lightning), or unfamiliar occurrences (a flat earth). Nowhere is this more true than in the topic of creativity. Often, it is a belief in one or more of these myths that become a severe impediment for our creative inclinations.

Let's take a look at some of the most persistent ones.

3.

You surely know the story. One day in 1666, Sir Isaac Newton was leisurely sitting under an apple tree. Suddenly, and without warning, an apple dislodged itself from an overhead branch and fell on his head. He leaped to his feet, shouted something quite profound ("Eureka!"), and immediately generated the concept of gravity.

The reality is quite different. True, Newton did see an apple fall from a tree (but, not on his head). The falling apple raised several intriguing questions in his mind, "Why is it that that apple should fall perpendicular to the ground? Why doesn't it fall sideways? Why doesn't it fall upwards? Why does it always fall towards the center of the earth? Is there some sort of 'drawing power' at work here?"

Those queries fired a twenty-year mental sojourn - a search for answers. It wasn't until 1687 that he published his groundbreaking book, *The Principia: Mathematical Principles of Natural Philosophy*, in which his theory of gravity was first presented to the world. The truth of the matter is that there was no sudden inspiration - but rather, the falling apple initiated two decades of research and contemplation that eventually resulted in one of the most accepted (and mythicized) scientific principles of all time.

One of the most persistent illusions about creativity is that it strikes when least expected (the epiphanous Eureka! myth). Like a bolt of lightning, creative thoughts come "out of the blue" and we have an immediate answer to a most perplexing challenge. We suddenly see the light (in cartoon form, a giant light bulb suddenly flashes over a hero's head). We enjoy these tales because of what they are: stories.

What we don't see is all the mental preparation that either preceded or followed this "flash" of inspiration. Thomas Edison is credited with the saying, "Genius is one percent inspiration and ninety-nine percent perspiration." To couch that quote in terms of creativity, Edison might say that it is one thing to have a good idea, quite another to put in the time and effort necessary to make that idea sensible or workable. Creative ideas are valuable, not necessarily for what they are, but rather for the effort put into them to make them workable.

The Eureka! myth is also the result of selective hindsight. What's missing from a story about an apple falling near an English scientist, Archimedes realizing he could calculate the volume of irregular-ly-shaped objects (in a bathtub, no less), Einstein's Theory of Relativity, or Tim Berners-Lee's invention of the World Wide Web is all the labor (mental and physical) that preceded these creative endeavors. We only see the results of those labors, but seldom the actual work that made them possible.

There's also another element embedded in the Eureka! myth. That is, you have to be in the right place at the right time in order for a creative idea to hit you. Known as "serendipity," it is a belief that creativity is random, uncontrollable, and unpredictable. In short, creativity happens in an instant - an instant over which we have no jurisdiction. Seldom do we see creativity as a long-term process of hard work, curious exploration, playful experimentation, and systematic investigation. Constantin Brancusi, one of the pioneers of modernist art, wrote: "Being creative is not being hit by a lightning bolt. It's having clear intent and passion."

All the hard work (and extended time) necessary for an innovative idea to surface wouldn't make for an "edge-of-your-seat" story. The myth is that creativity is a tweet. The reality is that creativity is a novel.

4.

Many people equate creativity with knowledge; that is, the smarter you are, the more creative you can become. Nothing could be further from the truth. Creativity guru Roger von Oech says, "...the real key to being creative lies in what you do with your knowledge." In short, society has put a premium on how much "stuff" we have crammed into our heads, and considerably less emphasis on what we are able to do with all that knowledge.

In actuality, creativity involves taking the knowledge you already have (either through formal or personal education) and manipulating it in new and unique ways. This presupposes that you have a body of knowledge to work with. In order to obtain that body of knowledge you need a certain level of intelligence. Psychologists often refer to this as the *threshold hypothesis* - an assumption that a certain level of IQ is a precondition for creative expression.

One interesting study examined the relationship between intelligence and creative potential in a sample of about three hundred individuals. What the researchers discovered was that an IQ score of around 100 was the necessary threshold for creative potential. To put that in more concrete terms, if you are reading and understanding this book then, by definition, you have the necessary threshold (or baseline) for creative expression. The study also revealed that even lower levels of IQ (around 85 points) served as the intellectual baseline for quantitative measures of creative potential. What was most revealing was this statement from the investigators: *"...we obtained evidence that once the intelligence threshold is met, personality factors become more predictive for creativity."* [emphasis added]

Creativity expert Tanner Christensen further solidifies a connection between intelligence and creativity. He states,

> "...intelligence matters, [since] it demonstrates your ability to gather knowledge and effectively use it. Creativity [on the other hand] is the ability to go beyond the intelligence frame and capitalize on seemingly random connections of concepts. [E]xpert creatives don't need to be more intelligent than the average person. They simple do three things more diligently than anyone else: they have more experiences, they think on their experiences more often, and when they start pursuing potential outcomes to problems or projects they simply work more with the ideas they come up with (whereas everyone else gives up after evaluating just one or two possible ideas, or by letting their inner critic prevent them from exploring more)."

Other researchers have acknowledged that knowledge is only a foundation - a starting point. Using that knowledge in dynamic ways is what creativity is all about. Highly creative people don't just sit on their knowledge (or rest on their laurels), they actively play with their knowledge. They religiously generate lots of new ideas - practical ideas, childish ideas, wild ideas, off-the-wall ideas, crazy ideas, foolish ideas, quiet ideas, loud ideas, obtuse ideas, weird ideas, and strange ideas. They also look for random connections between (often dissimilar) concepts. For creatives, creativity is, quite simply, playing with their mentality. It's not the level of intelligence that is important; it's what we do with our innate intelligence that is.

Creativity requires the courage to let go of certainties.
—Erich Fromm

5.

One of the major requirements of office secretaries throughout the 1900s was the ability to type error-free documents. Applicants for office positions were often administered a typing test that required both accuracy and speed. Points were deducted for errors. "How fast can you type?" became a familiar question in job interviews.

The introduction of electric typewriters in the mid 1950s put additional pressure on typists - not only were they expected to type faster, but were also expected to maintain error-free documents. Make too many mistakes and your advancements and pay raises may be severely limited or your career as a typist may be short-lived. Enter Bette Nesmith[28], a 27-year-old divorced mother who desperately needed to maintain her job in order to keep a roof over her head and food on the table. In fear of her job, she decided to do a little experimenting in her kitchen. She took a mixture of white tempera water-based paint and put it into a nail polish bottle. Whenever she made a typing error at work, she would brush over the error with the "paint" and it would magically disappear.

She kept her "invention" secret, but when she transferred to a new job, her small bottle of "Mistake Out" came with her. Other secretaries soon noticed it on her desk and wanted some for themselves. She began filling a few orders, until eventually an office supply dealer persuaded her to market the liquid correction fluid locally. She engaged her teenage son and his friends to fill the bottles and by the end of 1957 she was selling about a hundred bottles a month.

In 1958, a trade publication printed an announcement about this new product. Five hundred new orders came in immediately. Nesmith recruited her best friend along with several part-time workers to fill the bottles as the number of orders increased. She then enlisted her new husband and soon production increased to five thousand bottles per week. In 1964, Bette moved her small company into a modern production facility outside Dallas and began shipping about nine thousand bottles of *Liquid Paper* per week.

---

28 Those of a certain age (the author included) will remember a popular rock group of the 1960s - The Monkees. The Monkees had a hit TV show and a string of chart-topping songs ("Daydream Believer," "Last Train to Clarksville," and "I'm a Believer" among others). The group consisted of four musicians, including Michael Nesmith, the son of Bette Nesmith. Rock on!

As more bottles appeared on the desks of office secretaries everywhere, word of this dynamic product spread like the proverbial wildfire. Office supply stores couldn't keep up with the demand as, not only secretaries, but wordsmiths of all stripes made sure at least one bottle was on their desk.

In 1968, revenues topped $1 million. Soon after, headquarters for the company moved to a new and larger building. There, Bette and her associates were able to produce a staggering sixty bottles a minute. In 1979, Gillette purchased the company for $48 million. When Bette Nesmith passed away in 1980, she left an estate worth approximately $50 million. All with a little help from her friends.

An interesting story, to be sure. But, it flies in the face of another persistent myth surrounding creativity. That is, creative ideas are always the result of the work of a single individual. We love hearing stories about how one person, against all the odds, uses her brainpower to save humanity, make the world a safer place in which to live, eradicates a social, medical, or political menace for the betterment of all, and makes a fortune in the process. One person against the world. Makes for a compelling story (and a few Oscar®-worthy movies)! But, as Bette Nesmith proved, a creative idea also needs a support team to make it viable. The Lone Ranger concept certainly works well for a TV western (1949 - 1957), but seldom in real life.

Thomas Edison's work on the lightbulb is a case in point. He is given all the credit, but the fact is, the resulting product was the work of up to fourteen different engineers, machinists, and physicists working together. The association of Thomas Edison with the electric lightbulb may have been more the result of Edison's own public relations efforts in concert with his realization that the public loves a story about one person saving the universe (or, at least lighting the way).

We like to believe that creativity is the result of a determined, focused, and solo entrepreneur who, through a flash of inspiration (see Eureka! above) solves a problem for the betterment of humankind. It's a great plot line for a TV special, but it ignores a basic fact of life about the stories of most innovations: They rarely include the human networks that sustain (and make possible) radical new ideas or changes. In fact, history is frequently edited in order to recognize a sole genius or innovator. Phil McKinney, host of the nationally syndicated radio show, *Killer Innovations*, puts it this way:

> We have a saying in the innovation industry: 'There's no such thing as a truly new idea. Ideas are the result of building on the work of others.' Many of the creative ideas that led to creating great companies were the result of a team. Some examples: Microsoft, Intel, Google, Skype and many more.

6.

One of the more persistent myths is that a creative idea is a totally original idea. That is, to be creative one must be able to create ideas that have never been thought before...ideas that never existed before. The thinking is that each idea must be new, original, and fresh - a thought or an object that has never before existed in any shape or form. It is absolutely original.

We often believe that new ideas must be revolutionary, ground-breaking, and world-shattering. The truth is that most innovative ideas are not. In most cases, they are simply the combination of previous ideas into a new concept or format. Creativity often involves the ability to take existing knowledge and restructure it into a new format. It's about making connections with stuff that's already there. Steve Jobs, the founder of Apple, brought this all into perspective when he said:

> "Creativity is just connecting things. When you ask creative people how they did something, they feel a little guilty because they really didn't do it, they just saw something. It seemed obvious to them after a while. That's because they were able to connect experiences they've had and synthesize new things. And the reason they were able to do that was that they've had more experiences or that they have thought more about their experiences that other people."

One of the most-oft cited cases of creativity centers around Johannes Gutenberg who, in 1450, combined the wine press and the coin punch to create movable type and the printing press. Movable metal pieces allowed pages to be printed much more quickly than the standard wooden blocks used to press ink onto paper. His "combination of pre-existing technologies" created printing presses that could print thousands of pages a day. This revolution allowed books to be printed more quickly and more efficiently - allowing the middle class to obtain them as never before. The result was the rapid spread of knowledge across the European continent. That intellectual revolution came about due, in large measure, to the combination of two previous (and seemingly unconnected) ideas: a wine press and a coin punch.

Ancient Greeks were also aware of the power of creative combinations. For example, it was the Greeks who combined soft copper with soft tin to create hard bronze. At their most basic levels, Gutenberg's printing press and the creation of bronze were simply a combination of already existing ideas. History also records these interesting combinations of pre-existing concepts:

1.   copier + telephone = fax machine
2.   bell + clock = alarm clock
3.   trolley + suitcase = suitcase with wheels.
4.   igloo + hotel = ice palace
5.   mathematics + biology = laws of heredity
6.   fish + woman = mermaid

A wonderful harmony is created when we join
together the seemingly unconnected.
- HERACLITUS

Yet, we still believe that to be creative is to have the ability to create new ideas rather than to combine old ideas into new configurations. It's a persistent myth that frequently blocks us whenever we're faced with a personal challenge or work-related endeavor. To the contrary, however, creativity is not always a series of "brilliant new ideas," but often is the result of lots of lifetime experiences and diligence in working on combinations of those ideas (instead of giving up on them after one or two failures). The myth that every idea must be an idea never considered before (in the history of humankind) is a significant impediment in our ability to think creatively.

7.

Let's assume you're making preparations for a weekend party. Lots of your friends are coming over and you want to be sure you have some great food and their favorite beverages. So, you drive over to your local liquor store and ask one of the employees to suggest a good wine. She takes you over to a display area of new wines and points out two different possibilities:

1. *El Vino de Hoboken* (Hoboken, NJ): This Cabernet Sauvignon has been fermenting in industrial steel drums since Tuesday.
2. *Fleur Élégante* (Sonoma Valley, CA): This Cabernet has been fermenting for at least four years in fine old oaken casks.

Which one do you select?

Here's one of the most difficult things I do as a writer: I give my manuscripts fermentation time! After I've gone through a couple of drafts with a book idea, I put the manuscript in a desk drawer and let it sit. I don't disturb it, I don't re-read it, I just let it sit there...fermenting. It begins to mature; it begins to age. But, most important, I move on to other projects and allow that manuscript to exit from my consciousness.

While I work on new projects, the former one is receding from view and is becoming a distant memory. Perhaps five weeks go by, three months, a half-year. My thoughts have been elsewhere, my brain cells have been purged of its memory, and my mind has been cleansed. I resist all temptation to take it out and peruse it just for the fun of it. After all, would I disturb a fine wine aging in an oaken casket while it is still fermenting?

After extended time has passed, I retrieve that manuscript and read it through. I now have a different perspective and the realization that I'm looking at this product as though it was brand new. I begin to see some things I hadn't noticed before. I see some vocabulary that must be replaced, I see a description that's not particularly well-developed, and I see some facts that now sound silly. In short, I see the manuscript through new eyes. I know there will (and should) be changes and now I'm ready to address those needs with a fresh viewpoint and a new perspective. That "fermentation" has offered me something quite different than what I started with and the resultant editing is usually more intense and definitely more precise.

As discussed earlier, there is a persistent and complimentary belief that creative ideas spring from self-induced pressure. We often believe that if we are fighting a time constraint, our creativity will soar and our ideas will multiply. We envision our brains as though they were a tube of toothpaste. Squeeze them hard enough (and often enough) and some creative ideas will ooze forth. In reality, however, deadlines are often the death knell of creativity.

In one piece of research, investigators looked at a group of individuals working on a specified project within a pre-established time frame. They compared the work of those individuals to the work of another group who had no time constraints or deadlines. What they discovered was a kind of time-pressure hangover. That is, when we work under great pressure, our creativity goes down. Time pressure stifles our creativity because we can't deeply engage with the problem. The researchers concluded that creativity requires an incubation period - an opportunity for us to immerse ourselves in a challenge and allow new ideas to bubble up naturally. In short, although deadlines are the *sine qua non* of our work environments, they may be more harmful, than beneficial, to our creative output.

8.

Mara O'Shannon[29] was a Marketing major while a student at the University of Arizona.[30] Immediately after graduation, she obtained a job at a large manufacturing firm outside Atlanta. On her first day, as she was trying to decide what plants to put on her office windowsill

---

29 A fictitious individual.
30 Not a fictitious institution

and where to position the computer on her desk, her supervisor came in and calmly sat down on the plastic chair just inside the doorway.

"Mara," she began. "I would like to welcome you to our company. I think you're really going to enjoy working here. We have a lot of great employees, many who have been with us for several years. It's a great crew." The supervisor went on to tell Mara that she needed to read the Employee Handbook as soon as possible, see Human Resources to make sure all the proper forms were filled out, and secure any necessary supplies to get her office up and running.

Then, in a most serious tone she said, "Mara, I just want you to know how impressed we were when you applied for the position. It was very clear that you are a bright, energetic, and creative young lady and that your vision of Marketing was just what we needed to move forward. You were also one of three people brought on to help us with a most critical issue. And, that is that our customer base is slipping... and slipping dramatically. 82 percent of our customers are women in their 30s and with so many options out there, they don't stay long with any single company. Brand loyalty today is not what it used to be two decades ago. We need to broaden our base - perhaps more men, perhaps a younger population, perhaps we should be concentrating on the Canadian market. We just don't know and so we're looking to you to help us out...to help us with your creative spirit and your innovative ideas. We know you can do the job and we're counting on you to make a difference in broadening our appeal to more customers. I'm looking forward to seeing a big uptick in the next couple of months. Once again, welcome aboard."

Less than a year later, Mara was updating her profile on LinkedIn and posting her resume on Monster.com. She was actively looking for a new position with a new company.

A myth that slows down many businesses is the belief that if "I just hire a lot of creative people I can have one of the most dynamic and forward thinking businesses in the industry." Unfortunately, holding fast to that misconception has doomed many an entrepreneurial enterprise. Creative thinking does not rest solely on the people working for a business, but more so on the environment in which those people work.

In another chapter, we looked at some of the business practices that tend to depress creativity. These were "same old, same old" practices that have been in place for years, nay for decades, that have stymied and throttled creative thinking for both management and staff. One of those constraints involved the role of the work environment in hampering creative output. Teresa M. Amabile, a professor at Harvard Business School, points out that the social environment, including school, home and work, plays a big role in creativity. "Across all talent levels, people have peaks and valleys in their creative productivity - due, in part, to the supports and constraints operating on them at the time."

Amabile and her colleagues analyzed almost 12,000 daily journal entries from 238 people from seven different companies. The research team found that people were more creative when they viewed their work environment in a positive light, they felt they had their boss's and their co-workers' support, they perceived their projects as challenging, and they had autonomy to complete these projects. In short, creativity is about environmental conditions just as much as it is about the people who work in those conditions. Creativity cannot spring from a vacuum, it must be supported by an environment that offers employees challenges, support, and self-initiated motivation. When we subscribe to the idea that creativity is all about the individual, we sublimate the influence of the work environment in ensuring that creative endeavors flourish.

Many companies and organizations hold fast to the concept that creative individuals alone are the key to improving a company's bottom line. Just hire the right people, so the belief goes, and we'll be able to turn this company around and send profits into the stratosphere. Au contraire! Such a belief ignores one of the most basic of creativity tenets - creative ideas are generated in an environment - either produced by the "generator" or established by others - that is positive and supportive. When people are beat over the head with killer phrases, forced to endure insufficient resources, insufficient time, and insufficient support, and tied to dated organizational practices, creativity withers (and frequently dies). The environment in which we work is the "potting soil" that allows our creative "seeds" to germinate, sprout, and flourish.

9.

One of the elements of the creative process is our ability to dislodge or remove absolutes from our mind. In other words, to mentally let go of common myths and free our mind to examine things with fresh new eyes. I'll admit, that's sometimes difficult. We get used to common beliefs: doing things in certain ways, thinking about things in certain ways, and processing information in certain ways. Overwhelming and sustained belief in the myths of creativity may put us in a "mental comfort zone," but it's always counterproductive to progress. It's relying on the common without actively searching for the uncommon.

Then, again, perhaps we're just thinking like adults.

22.
How to Sizzle: 79 - 86

79. Argue With A Myth. Select one of the myths from this chapter. Imagine it to be a living person. Strike up an argument with that "person." Tell the "person" why she has been such a negative influence on your life, how she has messed up your thinking, how she has slowed down your production of new ideas, and why she is such a pain in the %&#@$. Shout at her, scream at her, break down her every counter argument. Let her know that you're now in charge. Next week argue with a new myth. Or, make up a list of your own myths about creativity. What do you believe and why do you believe that? How did that belief come about? Is that belief true all the time or only in certain situations? You may be surprised to discover that there are some things you hold fast to that are dragging down your own creative efforts. How can you get rid of them?

80. Journey Through New Fields. We frequently get comfortable...way too comfortable...in our chosen occupations. Architects see the world through the lens of an architect. Plumbers see the world as a leaky pipe. Teachers see the world as a classroom. Lawyers see the world as a courtroom. Move away from your "comfort zone" and look at the world with a new (and refreshing) lens. If you're an artist, watch a carpenter at work. If you're a dentist, read a book about archeology. If you're a computer programmer, visit a children's museum. If you're a seamstress, take time to talk with a physical therapist. If you're a psychologist, watch a professional mountain climber ascend Half Dome in Yosemite. If you're a videographer, have a cup of coffee with a blues guitarist. Like most people, you'll see the world a little differently and you'll also be able to generate new ideas a little more easily. New lenses give you new vision. Change your outlook and you'll change your perspective.

81. Steal It. Austin Kleon, author of *Steal Like an Artist*, makes a case for stealing ideas from others. He points out, quite emphatically, that there is no such thing as an original idea. All creative work builds on what has come before - something tagged "creative" is just the juxtaposition of two or more ideas that have never been combined before. He enthusiastically pens that "Nothing is completely original...every new idea is just a mashup or a remix of one or more previous ideas." The trick is to 1) collect as many different ideas as you possibly can, and 2) put them together in crazy, random, nonsensical, silly, ludicrous, cockeyed, harebrained, and cockamamie patterns or arrangements to create your own idea. In short, the more ideas you collect from various sources, the more possible combinations you'll be able to make. The trick is not to look for the best ideas (that prejudgment will stifle your creativity), but to look for all kinds of ideas from a wide variety of sources and resources. Creativity results when you put two or three of those ideas together in a unique and distinctive combination.

82. Invite Dissention. Ask employees to disagree with you. What's wrong with your ideas? Why are you not seeing "the whole picture?" What are your preconceived notions or prejudices? What's getting in the way? During staff meetings and department meetings offer time for employees to "let it out." Don't rely on a Suggestion Box (which are rarely used), but rather schedule regular time during each meeting to discuss some of the corporate barriers or decisions that may be counterproductive to the overall mission. Feel free to talk about some of the errors or unworkable decisions you have proffered. Feel comfortable in letting staff know that you are not a paragon of excellence and that you are comfortable in admitting your own mistakes. Rather than fostering a company of "yes men" encourage others to take exception to your plans or thinking. They may well see something you can't.

83. Another Mind. As a children's author, I'll often visit a park, a playground, or even a shopping mall. I'll search for a group of children and identify one (the one with the yellow t-shirt, for example). I'll give that child a fictitious name (Mitch) and then imagine how "Mitch" would view a book I'm working on. What would he say, what would he think, and what improvements would he offer? In an airport, while waiting for a flight, I'll randomly select someone (a teenager waiting for a cup of coffee, a harried businessperson sprinting up the concourse, a mother guiding five kids into a rest room). Again, the person gets a fictitious name and I imagine having a conversation with her or him about a current writing project (this book, for example). How would they suggest I handle Chapter 15? How would they describe this book to a friend? What else could be added to Chapter 4? Interestingly, there's some compelling research to suggest that we think more creatively when we are able to remove ourselves from a project or problem. By putting myself into the mind of someone else, I'm able to trick my brain into seeing a project (and potential solutions) in a new way. Take some time, on a regular basis, to people-watch and imagine how they might handle a situation or challenge. Seeing a problem with a different set of eyes may reveal different kinds of solutions – ones that YOU do not or cannot see.

84. Doubt What You Know. Author (and artist) Rod Judkins, in his book *The Art of Creative Thinking* makes a most compelling statement: "Doubt what you know." He goes on to say that, "Everything that has been achieved over the last five hundred years is because of doubt." It is his contention that we don't make progress – creative progress – if we accept everything we were taught or everything we have ever learned. He contends that, yes, it's important for us to go out and seek knowledge, but we also need to feel comfortable in doubting some of that knowledge. Accepting things as they are, rather than as they could be is one of the great depressors of creativity. Just because an "expert" said something is so, doesn't necessarily mean that it is right or that is can't be changed. At one time "experts" said that humans would never be able to fly. Keep that in mind the next time you book a plane trip to Hawaii. At one time "experts" said that women would never be able to vote. Keep that in mind the next time your sister, aunt, or grandmother casts her ballot in a national election. At one time "experts" said that wireless communication was an impossibility. Keep that in mind the next time you send a text message to your best friend. Don't always accept what the "experts" say is the truth – doubt them. Most important, take significant time to doubt what you know...and to doubt yourself. You may open a door to creative opportunities.

85. Not An Expert. I am not an expert in paleontology, marine biology, longevity, interviewing, or ancient creatures. Yet, I've written adult nonfiction books on all those topics. I learned about a topic I knew nothing about and then went out and tried to explain it to an audience of readers. I approached my search for new stuff as a child might approach a playground jungle gym: with excitement, anticipation, and a sense of discovery. Experts are those who tend to rely on past experiences - experiences they have collected over time; information rituals that become repetitive and everlasting. All those experiences (all that knowledge) often becomes a solid chuck of stone - keeping them anchored and weighing them down. They have a bedrock of knowledge, but seldom an incentive to move in new directions. They are comfortable with what they're comfortable with. New ideas are a threat. New ideas are a challenge. New ideas are strange, foreign, and, quite possibly, contradictive to what they know. Instead, find something you know little about and work to explain it to someone else. You'll open up new avenues for creative expression.

86. SCAMPER. Elaborate on your ideas by applying a checklist of seven creative-thinking principles that were first formally suggested by Alex Osborn and later arranged by Bob Eberle into the following mnemonic.

> S = Substitute?
> C = Combine?
> A = Adapt?
> M = Magnify? Modify?
> P = Put to other uses?
> E = Eliminate?
> R = Rearrange? Reverse?
> SCAMPER is based on the notion that

everything new is some addition or modification of something that already exists. You can do this by isolating a subject or topic and adding a checklist of questions to see what new ideas and thoughts emerge. Think about a current project you're working on and apply the SCAMPER checklist of questions. You'll discover that ideas will begin popping up almost immediately.

Substitute?
➤ Can I substitute something else? Who else? What else?
➤ Can the rules be changed?
➤ What else instead?
➤ What other element, condition, setting, or fact?

Combine?
➤ What can be combined?
➤ How about an assortment?
➤ What elements are similar?
➤ Who is like who?
➤ What is like what?

Adapt?
➤ What else is like this?
➤ What could I copy?
➤ What idea could I incorporate?
➤ What are some different contexts?
➤ What ideas from another source could I use?

Magnify? Modify?
➤ What can be made larger? Extended?
➤ What can be exaggerated?
➤ What can be overstated?
➤ What can be added?
➤ How can this be altered?
➤ What feature can be changed?
➤ What other form could this take?

Put to other uses?
➤ What else could this be used for?
➤ Are there new ways to use this?
➤ What else can be made from this?
➤ How would this be used by _____?

Eliminate?
➤ What if this was eliminated?
➤ What if this was smaller?
➤ What can I get rid of?
➤ Can I divide this into several parts?
➤ Can this be compacted? Reduced? Condensed?

Rearrange? Reverse?
➤ What other arrangement would be better?
➤ Is there another pattern?
➤ Can I interchange components?
➤ What are the opposites? Antonyms?
➤ What are the negatives?
➤ What if I wrote this backwards?
➤ Can I turn this around?
➤ What's another angle?

The value of SCAMPER is that it gives you a host of creative questions to play with. It implies that there is no such thing as the perfect idea. All ideas are subject to change, modification, and reinterpretation. In doing so, you will be able to take an original idea and look at it from any number of different perspectives and angles. As a result, you will discover a host of creative possibilities that go above and beyond. In short, any idea can be expanded into multiple possibilities through the use of multiple questions.

23.
Adult (Mis) Behaviors

Only those who are capable of silliness can
be called truly intelligent.
- CHRISTOPHER ISHERWOOD

1.

I laughed so hard, milk came out of my nose.

He was the funniest person I ever heard - a comedian's comedian. His ability to improvise characters, do impersonations, and create scenarios out of thin air had me in stiches. I listened to his second comedy album so many times I could recite every line and replicate every character with flawless ease. He made me laugh when I was awake and when I was asleep. To my mind, he was the funniest individual on the planet.

I, along with the rest of America, was in awe of his creative energy and his seemingly inexhaustible collection of made-up stories and silly anecdotes. He could do impressions with comedic precision, create wild characters that were slightly off-center, and bring a smile, guffaw, and spasmodic laugh to every scene. He was the king of improvisational comedy and as a teenager, I loved his mix of irreverence, turns of phrases, and improbable situations. His was a sophisticated absurdity that endeared him to millions of Americans as a comedic talent unlike any other. He once told the New York Times, "I was fighting for the fact that you could be funny without telling jokes."

His was a world populated by the oldest living airline stewardess, Martians with attitude, nervous airline pilots, pesky gas station attendants, voracious cats, angry westerners, and his two favorite characters:

a saucy and quite unpredictable little old lady (Maude Frickert) and a farmer who was just one brick shy of a load (Elwood P. Suggins). He was the inspiration for scores of stand-up comedians including Lily Tomlin, Billy Crystal, Johnny Carson, Steve Martin, Jim Carrey, Jimmy Kimmel, and Robin Williams. He was the most creative comedian I knew and when he passed away in 2013, I thought I had lost a close friend.

His name: Jonathan Winters.

Watch a You Tube video of Jonathan and you'll see a comedian who was king. He could take a simple prop (a hat, a comb, a pen, a shoe) and turn it into a five-minute comedy routine that would have you falling off your chair in exquisite laughter or shooting milk out your nose in uncontrollable guffaws. Robin Williams once said that Jonathan Winters was his comedy mentor and whenever the two of them were on the *Tonight Show with Johnny Carson* you knew you were in for a glorious laugh-fest. It was comedy at its finest.

Many comedians of the 50s, 60s, and 70s told jokes - stories with a punch line. Winters broke that mold by telling stories, stories he made up on the spot with slightly off-center characters and slightly off-center situations. His was comedy of the moment - humor that resonated with audiences because it was familiar, overflowing with edgy stories suffused with a healthy dose of silliness, and punctuated with facial expressions and body movements that made the ride all the more enjoyable.

Watch kids in a happy mood playing together and you'll see the same thing: creative fun.

2.

Journey with me to a third grade classroom. I asked this class of eight-year-olds to generate as many different uses for a paper clip as they could. I wanted to tap into their creative thinking abilities with no restrictions on trying to get right answers (The answers adults want to hear.). Here are a few of the fifty-eight ideas they produced on how to use a paper clip: game spinner, Christmas tree ornament holder, to clean gunk out of a straw, cheap nose ring, ear cleaner, tongue scratcher, mini fishing rod, make metal letters, metal toothpick, ant javelin, a poker (to annoy sister), miniature back scratcher, bookmark, under toe nail scrubber, attach a rubber band and it becomes a musical instrument, zipper pull (on jacket or jeans), earring, weapon against small animals, bracelet, cheese cube holder, fish hook, gun barrel greaser, Easter egg holder, glue bottle unclogger, tie clip, and frame.

I carefully observed this group as they set about their tasks. I was particularly interested in the processes they used to arrive at their list. During our time together, the students grouped themselves into various working teams. There were pairs, triplets, and quadruplets that quickly formed to generate possibilities. Three students decided to each work alone. As I watched the dynamics of this activity, it was clear that certain characteristics were in play. These included the fact that students pursued a creative endeavor without the fear of grades or teacher evaluation. No rules were established and no pre-conceived conditions were set. The kids' motivation came from within, rather than from an adult.

It was equally apparent that a variety of thinking styles was in play. There was no "right way" to pursue this task. Various lists were generated on scraps of paper, on iPads, and on the whiteboard. Divergent thinking was in full gear. In so doing, the students demon-strated a willingness to take some risks; they volunteered responses that were neither right or wrong, rather the possibilities were voiced without restraint.

Just as important was the observation that students were having fun - there was no grade to be assigned, no teacher evaluation, and no standardized test at the end. It was done for the sheer joy of the activity. As a result, there was no limit on the imaginations of the students. Responses were fanciful, imaginative, and free-spirited. They weren't looking for a right answer; rather they were looking for all kinds of answers. There was an amazing divergence of possibilities.

Psychologists note that one of the chief attributes of creativity is plasticity. This term is often defined as a "tendency to explore and engage with novel ideas, objects, and scenarios." Clearly, these young-sters demonstrated a high level of plasticity as they asked questions that began with "What if" rather than those that were practical and staid.

This allowed these kids to take some chances. They eschewed the expected and roamed through the unexpected looking at all manner of possibilities without regard for what someone (an adult perhaps) might think of them.

I (silently) applauded and cheered these students on this quest. Their outlook on problem-solving was refreshing, dynamic, and without limits. But I also knew that these creative souls would change as they grew up. Their inherent creativity would be sublimated, quashed, and trampled as they worked their way through the education system, pursued a career, raised a family, and became functioning members of society. They would shed their childish vestments and become transformed individuals: practical, logical, pragmatic, sensible, and businesslike adults.

3.

Creatively speaking, we often feel hampered and constrained in our everyday activities. Much of our education and most of our professional experiences mitigate against creativity. As we've seen throughout this book, we've been brainwashed by beliefs, myths, contradictions, and practices that have put the skids on any creative output. As a result, being creative is not what we do best. Although we were very creative as kids, being creative as adults is a constant challenge because of hidden forces at work to "standardize" our thinking and direct our mental compliance. Our natural creativity (as adults) is being sublimated in favor of practical and pragmatic thinking. For example, here's part of a "Code of Behavior" as promulgated by an organization with a significant number of employees (~13,000).

All employees will:
➤ Report to work as scheduled and seek approval from their supervisors in advance for any changes to the established work schedule, including the use of leave and late or early arrivals and departures. Review the attendance policy.

➤ Perform assigned duties and responsibilities with the highest degree of public trust.

➤ Devote full effort to job responsibilities during work hours.

➤ Maintain the qualifications, certification, licensure, and/or training requirements identified for their positions.

➤ Demonstrate respect for [the institution] and toward coworkers, supervisors, managers, subordinates, students, and customers.

➤ Use...equipment, time, and resources judiciously and as authorized.

➤ Support efforts that ensure a safe and healthy work environment.

➤ Utilize leave and related employee benefits in the manner for which they were intended.

➤ Resolve work-related issues and disputes in a professional manner and through established business processes.

➤ Meet or exceed established job performance expectations.

➤ Make work-related decisions and/or take actions that are in the best interest of [the institution].

➤ Comply with the letter and spirit of all...agency policies and procedures, the Conflict of Interest Act, and [pertinent] laws and regulations.

➤ Report circumstances or concerns that may affect satisfactory work performance to management, including any inappropriate (fraudulent, illegal, unethical) activities of other employees.

➤ Obtain approval from supervisor prior to accepting outside employment.

➤ Obtain approval from supervisor prior to working overtime....

➤ Work cooperatively to achieve work unit and [the institution's] goals and objectives.

➤ Conduct themselves at all times in a manner that supports the mission of [the institution] and the performance of their duties.

➤ Adhere to the [the institution's] Statement of Business Conduct Standards.

You would certainly agree that this "Code" is extensive, thorough, comprehensive, and all-encompassing. It clearly and definitively lays out a set of expectations that leaves little room for interpretation and little room for experimentation. A rigid and expansive collection of "shoulds" is proffered for all employees...no exceptions. Or, the familiar explanation: "The rules are there for a reason." [The most common reason being to maintain order and discipline.].

Playing by the rules is instilled in us at a very early age. We are told that we "can't color outside the lines," "can't play in mud puddles after a thunderstorm," or "can't make faces at our little sister." As we get older and attend school, we are subjected to another set of rules. These may include, "The teacher is always right," "Your desks must always be in straight rows," or "Always do your own work." When we become adults and engage ourselves in an occupation, we are faced with a new coterie of rules including, "Devote full effort to job responsibilities during work hours," "Obtain approval from supervisor prior to working overtime," and "Meet or exceed established job performance expectations."

Rod Judkins, an art instructor and author of *The Art of Creative Thinking*, points out the significant differences between life in an art college (which he attended) and life in the outside world. "In the art world students experiment, do things that make no sense, make many mistakes, or just do things because they made no sense. The world outside that college was filled with people doing reasonable things or doing things because that the way everyone else did those things, too. It was a conflict between the logic and sensibility of everyday life and the creative expressions of students freed of that logic and practicality."

We are a society of rules and I'm certainly not challenging the need for certain rules. Without them, there would be no order. People could arbitrarily choose which side of the road they want to drive on, they could take items from the corner grocery store without paying for them, or they could punch their server in the nose when he brings you your prime rib well done, instead of medium rare.

However, the plethora of rules we are subjected to over the span of our lives also affects our creative impulses. That is to say, we become comfortable with our adherence to rules and, as a result, less apt to challenge them. The more rules we have in our lives, the more ordered our thinking becomes. The more ordered our thinking, the less inclined we are to alter the status quo. In turn, we are more inclined to be mentally compliant. And that is a problem when we have a challenge to solve.

To use a hackneyed analogy, all the rules in our lives put us in a mental "box." It's difficult for us to break out of that box, because its very "weight" depresses our creative impulses. According to at least one researcher, they create a mental lock on our thinking. We are more inclined to think about things as they currently are, rather than things as they could be.

> *Every act of creation is first of all an act of destruction.*
> —**PABLO PICASSO**

EXERCISE

In the following line of letters, cross out five letters so that the remaining letters, without changing their order, will spell a familiar English word.

C F R I V E E A L T E T I T V E R I T S Y

In the exercise above, you may have been predisposed to follow the rules. That is, you may have searched through the entire line of twenty-one letters to identify five individual letters that could be eliminated, thus leaving a series of letters that spelled a common word. After all, in school, you learned to follow the rules explicitly when answering questions on a standardized test or a teacher-made exam (thus increasing your chances of getting "The Right Answer"). You followed that oft-stated rule, but were frustrated at your inability to obtain a satisfactory answer.

But, let's break that rule. Go back to the line of letters above and cross out the following "five letters": F I V E L E T T E R S. You'll discover that the remaining letters spell: CREATIVITY (a familiar English word). What I'd like you to realize is that your education and professional training have "conditioned" your mind to look at a problem (actually most problems) in a certain way: If you follow the rules, you'll get the answer. That's what your parents said, your teachers said, and your boss(es) said. Play by the rules and you'll be all right. But, as we can see, rule playing often has some negative implications for our creative endeavors. In short, throughout our lives we have been trained to look for the obvious, thus clouding our ability to create the unfamiliar. Or, to put it in other words, the more we adhere to (pre-established) rules, the less disposed we are to generate new ideas.

> *If I'd observed all the rules, I'd never have got anywhere.*
> —MARILYN MONROE

4.

Take a look at this line:

O.K., now take a look at these three lines:

Here is your task. Select the white line (above) that is the same length as the black line. That is, decide whether the first, second, or third white line is the same length as the black line. Should be fairly easy? Go ahead.

Which one did you select? The third one? That's correct!

But, now, let's change the conditions for this little test. Imagine you've been invited to participate in a study conducted by a member of the Psychology Department at your local college. You arrive on campus, park your car in the Visitor's Lot, and amble over to the Psych Building. You walk in and proceed to Room 124. As you enter, you note that there are six other people there, all seated around a rectangular table. There is one remaining chair on the far side or the table and that's where you sit.

You make a quick survey of the other participants in the room. One is a middle-aged man dressed in a business suit. Another is an attractive lady, probably mid-forties, casually dressed. The third is a bearded man about 60 years old in jeans and a t-shirt. The fourth is an older woman who appears to be a retiree. The fifth is a college co-ed absorbed in her cell phone. And the sixth is a thirty-something man in a Coast Guard uniform.

Shortly after you sit down, an examiner arrives, introduces herself to the group and explains the experiment. She tells everyone that she is testing some theories about vision and is looking to gather some preliminary information that will help her begin her study. Using a PowerPoint slide, she shows the group the single black line. Below that line are the three white lines. She tells the group that she will call on each individual separately to say which of the white lines is the same length as the black line. She will record the choice of each individual on a specially designed form.

The experimenter points to the middle-aged man and asks him to begin. "Which of the white lines is the same length as the black line? The first, the second, or the third?" she asks. "The second one," he replies, with a voice of authority. She then moves to the attractive lady and she instantly relies, "The second one." The bearded man also selects the second line, as does the older woman, the college co-ed, and the serviceman. She then turns to you. "Which one do you choose," she asks.

If you are like most people, you'll select the wrong one!

It's been almost seventy years, but a little experiment conducted by Solomon Asch told us a lot about human behavior - particularly with respect to the influence of others in how we make decisions. When we're in a new situation or don't have sufficient information about a topic we often turn to others for clues to help us in our decision-making. What others (who may have more experience) say and do is valuable advice that often helps us wade through unfamiliar waters.[31]

Asch was interested in how other's opinions influenced decision-making, particularly in situations when the answer was obvious and clear. He was curious as to whether we held fast to an opinion even when others disagreed. And, so, he developed the line-length task similar to what you did above. But, Asch's test was rigged. He filled the room with actors - paid participants who were told to give a predetermined answer. At times, his actors gave the right answer (the third white line is the same length as the black line); in other trials, all of them gave the wrong answer (the second white line is the same length as the black line). In every trial a subject, who didn't know the test was "rigged," was brought into the room and made a part of the group.

Asch assumed that even when the answer was very clear, test subjects would "stick to their guns," and give the obvious and very correct answer. It didn't matter if the other people in the room, despite their age or occupation, gave wrong answers, when the answer was obvious, Asch figured, all the subjects would say exactly what they saw, rather than defer to the opinions of people they had never seen or met before.

How wrong he was! So very wrong!

When Asch reviewed the results, he discovered something startling - approximately 75 percent of the participants conformed to the opinions of the actors at least once. Not everyone conformed on every trial, but it was interesting to note that people conformed at least 30 percent of the time. In other words, we tend to go along with others ("power of the pack") even when it may conflict with what we know to be right. If we are a minority of one, our inclination is to defer to the wisdom of the group rather than to set ourselves up for potential condemnation or ridicule. Consequently, we believe that there is more wisdom in a group than there is in a single individual.

We often use other opinions to help us get through our daily lives. We look to the behaviors of others when deciding on which car to buy, which hotel to stay in when vacationing at the beach, which

---

31 How do we behave at a funeral? How do we greet people in a foreign country? What do we wear to a formal dinner on a cruise?

restaurant to eat at when we're away from home on a business trip, or which doctor to use when we've been diagnosed with a serious medical ailment. There is a raft of internet sites that encourage people to give their opinions on everything from the best craft brewery in town to the competence of a local contractor in updating our kitchen. The wisdom of many helps us save considerable time and money when the situation is unfamiliar or infrequent.

We believe that when many opinions are in the mix everything averages out. Sure, there will be a few outliers here and there, but the mass of opinions collectively sends a most powerful message. If, for example, all of the reviewers of a new movie give it an average rating of 16 percent on *Rotten Tomatoes*, we can be fairly certain that the movie is not very good. By the same token, if that hotel in Santa Fe has 1,793 5-star reviews on *Trip Advisor*, we can be equally certain that we will have a most pleasant stay if we book it. This is the power of social pressure.

But, social pressure can also be dangerous - creatively speaking. Particularly when it morphs into a psychological construct known as groupthink.

Imagine you are attending your department's monthly meeting. The top item on the agenda is customer service; or, more specifically, a significant increase in complaints from customers about their inability to resolve issues quickly and fairly. Six other members of the department are arrayed around the rectangular table. There's Big Bob (with the company for 33 years) who is carefully guarding the box of chocolate donuts. There's Mrs. Simpson (with the company for 29 years), and a close associate of Big Bob (who always calls her "Sweet Betty"). There's Harold (27 years) who seldom says much, Louise (25 years) who can't stop talking, Lonnie (16 years) who always wears ties with comic characters, and "Crazy Carol" (9 years), the department gossip. And, then there's you (4 months), the newest member of the team.

You have a great idea about how to deal with the issue. But your boss ("Mad Max"), lays out some of the issues and then turns to Big Bob and asks, "Well, what do you think, Bob?" And Bob replies, "I really don't think there's a problem at all. This is just an aberration - it will go away soon enough." The boss turns to Mrs. Simpson and asks, "Well Mrs. Simpson what do you suggest?" And she says, "Whatever Bob says, I say!" He turns to the other four individuals and ask for their opinions and they all say, "Yeah, I'm with Bob too." Then he turns to you and asks, "Well _____, what do you think?"

What do you say?

First used by social psychologist Irving Janis in 1972, "groupthink" is a psychological term that refers to the how people try to achieve consensus within a group. The default is that in many group situations, people will set aside their own personal opinions or innovative ideas and embrace the opinion of the group. In essence, the group achieves more creative power due to its numbers than would any single individual. The individual's input (or potential input) is sublimated in favor of the harmony of the larger entity.

In turn, when individuals often have a creative idea or opposing idea, they will, quite frequently, keep quiet rather than injecting their minority thought(s). The belief is that it is far better to maintain the uniformity of the group than it is in sticking one's neck out with a contrary view. Individual members of a group are often more interested in securing the overall approval of the group than they are in advancing a new or innovative idea. Security within the group frequently supersedes a creative thought that might conflict the group. In short, dissent is not valued, while harmony and coherence are ("Let's all stay on the same page, people!").

If there appears to be a pervading consensus within the group, individuals will often be reluctant to express any doubts, judgements, or disagreements for fear of reprisal or retribution. "Go with the flow" seems to be the driving force behind many group decisions. Variety and disagreement are often quashed in favor of getting a meeting over with, deferring to a strong and commanding group leader, or maintaining a certain level of camaraderie with one's colleagues (with whom one has to work on a daily basis). Better to be seen as a "team player," rather than as a disruptive influence.

As you might expect, groupthink seriously dampens or permanently extinguishes our creative contributions. Those with a new idea to share or an innovative change to "standard operating procedures" are often pressured into silence. Creative ideas become outliers simply because they are unsettling to the equanimity and overall balance of the group. In the words of Irving Janis, "Direct pressure to conform is often placed on members who pose questions, and those who question the group are often seen as disloyal or traitorous."

Think about all the groups you belong to. These may include social groups, fraternal groups, religious groups, business and professional groups, family groups, volunteer groups, hobby groups, athletic groups...lots and lots of various groups. What happens when someone has a new thought, a creative expression, or a different way of doing things? Does the group's way of doing things or their general thinking predominate? Or does the individual have free rein to inject something different, imaginative, or ingenious? Or, maybe just their own personal opinion?

Now, imagine you have planned a special Friday night dinner with a group of friends at a local restaurant - one known for their exquisitely prepared prime rib. All during the day you've been conjuring up images of a king cut of medium-rare prime rib slathered with a blanket of horseradish and complimented by a heaping mound of mashed potatoes topped with a warm pool of melted butter and a side salad heaped with cascading rivers of blue cheese dressing. Your taste buds have been working overtime just thinking about tonight's dinner. You can hardly wait.

The group arrives at the restaurant at 7:00 and everyone is shown to your reserved table. After filling your drink orders, the server ("Hi, my name is Abigail and I'll be your server tonight.") turns to everyone to take their dinner orders. Your best friend's wife says, "You know I'm ready to sink my teeth into their Chicken Cacciatore, which I hear is absolutely fabulous! Chicken Cacciatore, please." Your best friend says, "Oh, yes, it has to be the Chicken Cacciatore! That's what I'll have, too." The other couple at the table also order Chicken Cacciatore, both agreeing that the aromatic vegetables and tomatoes are beyond compare. Your spouse, with an enormous smile, says, "Oh, I have to have the Chicken Cacciatore, too. All my friends at work have ordered it here and they all say it is better than any New York restaurant. I've just have to have it!"

The server turns to you. What do you order?

5.

When was the last time you played?

_____Earlier today   _____ Roughly a year ago

_____Yesterday	_____ When I was about twelve years old
_____Last week	_____ Never
_____Maybe it was a month ago	

Mention the word "play" to most adults and they will quickly roam their memory banks for a favorite childhood pastime, vacation experience, or youthful free time. Rarely will they come up with a memory of something that occurred last week or last month. We associate play with kids and work with adults (and seldom do the twain meet). It is assumed that when we grow up we give up our playful instincts. After all, isn't that what adults are supposed to do? Work. Play is something that is the sole province of kids - a time of unstructured, free, non-judgmental activities...often without a care in the world.

Work, on the other hand, is what we strive to accomplish in our adult years. We exit school with a set of skills that are focused on a lifetime occupation - an occupation designed to help us pay the bills, keep a roof over our heads, provide for a family, or sock away some funds for our retirement. Work is what adults do - we leave behind our "playful years" and seek comfort (or not) in our working years.

It's interesting, however, that a rash of studies have universally revealed that we, as adults, convince ourselves we are no longer allowed to play; we must work. Kids at play are having fun; people at work are having...well...they're having to survive, endure, and "tough it out." Margarita Tartakovsky, an editor at Psych Central notes, "Our society tends to dismiss play for adults. Play is perceived as unproductive, petty or even a guilty pleasure. The notion is that once we reach adulthood, it's time to get serious. And between personal and professional responsibilities, there's no time to play."

Stuart Brown, head of the National Institute for Play, has spent a lifetime looking at the role of play in the lives of individuals from all walks of life. Included in this assembly of people are Nobel Prize laureates, businesspeople, and, oh yes, kids. He examined more than six thousand case studies that looked at the role of play in the lives of people from around the world. What he discovered will not shock you

- play is an essential ingredient in everyone's life (young AND old) for a wide range of reasons.

Not only is play instrumental in helping us solve problems, so too is it a critical factor in our socialization, our attitude towards work, and our overall productivity. One of the most striking discoveries of Brown's research was when he looked for commonalities among murderers in Texas prisons. His data showed a clear and convincing correlation between criminal behavior and the lack of play in inmates' lives (prompting a possible ad campaign: "More play = less jail!").

Brown defines play as something that should be "purposeless, fun, and pleasurable." The experience should be for the sheer joy of "letting go" and should not involve any competition or external rewards. Most important, he concludes, play is as essential for adults as it is for children.

As you might suspect, play is also essential for our creativity. Play allows us to use and expand our divergent thinking abilities, because in play everything is possible. We look at situations and events without a critical eye, we are less judgmental and less inhibited. In a play situation, we are more apt to ask questions beginning with "What if?" ("What if we threw a Frisbee with an overhand motion, rather than an underhand motion?"), more inclined to take creative chances ("I bet I can swing higher than you can."), and more willing to seek out unknown possibilities ("Hey, let's climb that mountain and see if there are any bears there.").

Part of that comes from the fact that we know that some events will work and others will not. In short, we are more apt to accept failure, since failure shifts our focus from one possibility to another without any fear of retribution or shame. For example, as kids we may be inclined to try and jump over a stream on our bike. Maybe we didn't make it. That's O.K., let's try it again and see what we need to change (distance before the jump, speed, body position) to make it happen successfully. Play gives us permission to experiment - to try things out simply because they might be fun or exciting.

But play also allows us to think without artificial constraints. Play allows us to live in a world where anything goes - a world with few limits and lots of possibilities. Creativity expert Tanner Christensen, puts it this way, "By removing the strain and constraints of the real world, play allows us to more openly explore possibilities in our work. But play offers us more than mere escape from reality, it also offers us more exposure to diversity of perspectives."

The overriding consensus from the research is that play - even in our adult years - is a balm to our creative spirit. It underscores the processes important in looking at the world with a different eye, examining possibilities, not because they are right or wrong, but just because they are possibilities, and loosening up our thinking sufficiently to tackle myriad challenges. Companies known for their creativity and innovative thinking (like Google) have established play stations with ping pong, billiards, and foosball tables to encourage their employees to make play a regular activity of their work day.

So, here's the question one more time: When was the last time you played?

If you want creative workers, give them
enough time to play.
—JOHN CLEESE

6.

Those readers who remember the old TV series, "Star Trek" will also remember one of its most iconic characters - Mr. Spock. Half-Vulcan and half-human, Mr. Spock, as the second in command on the starship Enterprise, would often have a word or two to say about some impending doom, strange invader, or desperate situation. However, one of his most famous quotes (which wasn't spoken until the first episode of the second season), was "That's not logical." It was often said whenever he was frustrated by the imprecision and randomness of human thinking. Uttered with his characteristic unemotional voice, it was a "put-down" of the highest order.

With that in mind, I'd like to invite you to solve the following problem:

You walk into a room. Upon entering, you discover
John and Mary lying dead on the floor.
There is broken glass and water all around them.
How did they die?

Over the years, I have shared this problem with many groups of people. It has been presented to Kindergarten students, elementary and secondary students, college students, and various groups of adults including teachers, social workers, executives, college professors, small business owners, and retired individuals. Guess which group gets the correct answer more often than any other group? Yup, you guessed it - the youngest students. In fact, I've discovered that the ability to solve this problem declines the more people progress through the education system or rise in their chosen professions. Kindergarten kids take less than a minute to solve it; business executives often give up in frustration.

Why? On the surface, it seems to be missing some information. There's a piece or two of data that appears to be left out - as a result, we seem to have insufficient background information necessary to reach a satisfactory conclusion. Or, as Mr. Spock would say, "It's not logical."

Throughout our lives we have been trained to be logical. If you go back into Chapter 6, you will remember that much of our education is geared towards ensuring that we always get the right answer. When you answer a question such as, "In what year did the United States enter WWI?" with a response such as "1917" then you would be right - or, more specifically, you'd be logical. Consequently, when asked more than one million "right answer" questions over your educational career, your mind has been trained to think in logical terms. In a sense, you've been creatively "brainwashed."

As you might imagine, an overemphasis on logical thinking can seriously inhibit our creative thinking. If something is logical, it's accepted. One plus one equals two. That's logical; that's accepted. But, what if I said that one plus one equals seven. That's not logical; consequently, it's not accepted. When something is accepted, it achieves permanency; it becomes concrete and often immovable. It is subject to little change and no alteration. As such, it is inured against any creative possibilities.

This is not to denigrate logical thinking; quite the contrary. Employers often state that they place a high value on logical thinkers - people who use data and facts to prove a point or make a decision.

Businesses, for the most part, don't want to base their economic viability on emotional reactions or sentimental decisions. They desire employees who can use logical thinking and reasoning skills to make sound decisions - decisions based on facts, rather than feelings.

That logic, however, sometimes gets in the way of creativity. According to Roger von Oech, logical thinkers often focus on the differences among things, while creative thinkers look for similarities and connections among things. For example, a logical thinker might say that a brick and a rubber band are members of two completely different sets. A creative thinker, on the other hand, might say that a brick and a rubber band have a lot in common (they are both composed of organic materials, they can both be found in a hardware store, they both have potential energy, they both can be used as projectiles, they both can be used to hold things together, they both come in a variety of colors, they both have a finite lifetimes, they both have 90° edges, etc.)

Throughout our educational experiences, our teachers have focused primarily on developing our logical thinking. An over-emphasis on standardized testing, a reliance of getting the right answer, a propensity to ask a plethora of fact-based questions, a tendency to quash thinking that does not support the status quo, and a relentless fear of failure all combine to create a mental environment that is, most certainly, logical (and, quite often, predictable). In turn, we tend to see logical thinkers as intelligent thinkers (the more facts you have in your head and the myriad ways you can use those facts in everyday life equates to a higher level of intelligence).

On the other hand, we give short shrift to creative thinking throughout our education system. For example, think about how many times you were tested on your musical abilities, your artistic predilections, your decorating skills, your cooking acumen, or your storytelling talents. Not much, I would venture. If you are musically gifted, for example, how much did that talent come into play when the Admissions Department at your college was deciding on whether to admit you or not? If you were logical (and got high scores on the entrance exams) you stood a better chance of admission than if you could compose your own sonatas or do improvisational drum riffs like Ginger Baker (Cream) or John Bonham (Led Zeppelin). As creativity educator Edward de Bono stated, "If someone says he has learned to think, most of us assume that he means he has learned to think logically."

Logic is a valuable thinking commodity and we have been trained to rely on it to solve many, if not all, of life's challenges. However, as von Oech points out, an excessive reliance on logical thinking can short-circuit our creative impulses. That's because logical thinking is focused thinking, while creative thinking is divergent and diverse. Creative thinking asks "What if" questions; logical thinking asks, "What is" questions. Our education, experiences, and interactions with others have placed a premium on logical (adult) thinking while, at the same time modulating or restricting creative (childlike) thinking.

Let's return to our "John and Mary" problem at the beginning of this section. If you had difficulty with this conundrum, then you may well have been over-relying on your logical thinking abilities. In fact, you probably made a logical assumption based on "facts" you had learned early in your life. That is, when two individuals are named John and Mary then they must, by definition, be people. But, what if I told you that John and Mary were the names of two goldfish. They both lived in a small aquarium. But someone accidentally knocked the aquarium over where it crashed on the floor scattering water and glass in all directions. The two fish (John and Mary) eventually died from lack of oxygen.

Here's the reality: We begin life as uninhibited children and then are educated/trained to become logical adults. Along the way, we lose our unrestrained predilections and develop practical predispositions. We begin with unlimited possibilities and wind up with barriers and bonds. We start at a place outside the "box" and are slowly pushed, shoved, and directed to a place inside the "box." We are rigid where once we were free. What happened?

As adults, we often let our logic get in the way of our creativity.[32]

---

32 That said, an article in Forbes Magazine offers us an invitation (and a challenge): "Your level of creativity isn't fixed at birth. Instead, think of creativity as an expandable muscle. You don't become a champion body builder without hitting the gym. Similarly, to build creative capacity requires some focus and practice. There is an overwhelming amount of scientific research confirming that you can grow your creativity at any age."

24.
How to Sizzle: 87 - 95

87. Break Your Habits. We often get into routines or habitual ways of doing things. We eat the same cereal for breakfast every morning. We drive the same route to work every day. We go to the same resort every summer. We socialize with the same people. We buy the same brand of running shoes every year. We read books by the same author over and over. The more routines we have in our lives, the more difficult it is to think about doing things any other way. Break some of those routines, change some of those habits, and you'll start generating new ideas simply because you are looking at the world in new ways. Take a new route to work. Eat something exotic for breakfast. Go camping instead of staying at a chain hotel on your next vacation. Join a different gym. Style your hair differently. Go out to dinner at a Nepalese or Ethiopian restaurant. Do something new/different each day and your mind will also generate new/different ideas.

88. It's Not About Approval. In department meetings, corporate retreats, and group discussions we often share ideas or concepts that we intuitively know will get some form of recognition or approval. That endorsement is a mental elixir; an affirmation of success. We need and desire that approbation to confirm our importance to the organization. But, at what price? Is it more important to get the applause of our colleagues or to share what inspires us...what excites us...what floats our boat? In reality, the opinions of others is less important that our own self-opinion. If we believe in an idea or a new way of completing a task that should matter. If we are truly interested in what we're interested in, then that should take precedence over what others believe. Creative people wrap themselves in a plethora of ideas - their self-initiated ideas - not in the opinions of others. In many cases, those opinions tend to be negative rather than supportive. Hold fast to your internal intensions instead of wasting time on the constant assent of others.

89. Go To The Experts. Give a group of kids some paper clips and ask them what they could be used for (ear wax cleaner, javelin for an athletic insect, cheap earrings, Christmas tree decorations, etc.). Kids have a way of looking at the world without preconceptions or biases. Their thinking is unfettered by conventional wisdom or adult logic. They see possibilities, rather than restrictions. Have a challenge or problem? Share it with a group of kids (be sure they know there is no test associated with your request), and let them run with it. How would they approach the problem? What kinds of potential solutions would they generate? What kinds of things would they think about that you haven't yet considered? How many different responses could they come up with? Listen carefully and you may be surprised at what you hear. Watch carefully and they may give you ideas on how you might approach the whole notion of problem-solving.

90. Laugh It Up. The book *Creativity and Humor* confirms what we all know intuitively; that is, humor stimulates our creativity. What the authors discovered, among other things, was that watching humorous videos (for example) increased the "cognitive flexibility" of participants in the study. In short, humor (or laughing specifically) not only puts us in a positive mood, but it also increases our optimism about future events or possibilities. It frees up our thinking and causes us to look at the world around with a new set of eyes...with a new perspective. For me, I love watching videos and reading books by comedian George Carlin (His book *Braindroppings* is a classic!). He had a decidedly offbeat way of looking at the world – his ability to dissect the English language, create unimaginable similes, redefine familiar euphemisms, and invent improbable situations is just what this writer needs to keep ideas flowing. You Tube videos of Jonathan Winters always bring an enormous smile to my face. His improbable characters, silly comments, and facial contortions are the perfect antidote for the "blues." Find your own comedian, wit, or humorist; listen every now and again; and you'll open up untapped regions of your brain, see the world a little differently, and begin creating a plethora of new ideas.

91. Write It Down. I often get some of my best ideas, not when I'm in front of my computer, but more often when I'm driving, grocery shopping, buying a pack of gym socks at the sporting goods store, in the middle of a prime rib dinner at our favorite restaurant, or even when I'm typing a paragraph about where I get some of my best ideas. I've discovered that ideas can come about almost any time or any place (like the shower, for example). So, I'm always ready to record those ideas no matter the time or place. I keep a small notebook/calendar and a pen in the front pocket of my shirt, I readily use the "Notes" and "Voice Memos" apps on my smart phone when I'm shopping, walking along a trail, or just relaxing on a summer day. I carry a small tape recorder in my car and record random thoughts while I'm waiting for a traffic light to change. I'll often stuff a blank index card in my back pocket in case a brilliant thought hits me while eating a pastrami sandwich at my favorite diner. I've learned that creativity isn't always convenient - it can strike any time of the day.[33] My task is to be ready to write down those brilliant thoughts (as well as a whole bunch of less-than-brilliant thoughts) whenever they strike me. Later, I can sort through them and see which ones are appropriate for a current or future project.

92. Embrace Your Inner Child. As a friend once told me, "You have to grow old, but you don't have to grow up." Reconnect with your inner child, rediscover your once imaginative attitude, don't be so serious so much of the time, and play as much as you work (if not more). If it rains, jump in puddles; if its windy, go fly a kite; if its sunny, kick a ball; and if its hot, jump in a lake. Make fun a regular part of your daily routine. Break away from what is expected and do something out of the ordinary. Playful children are creative children.

---

33 This is not the "Eureka!" myth (an idea that springs out of nowhere). I constantly try to "lubricate" my mind with diverse readings, unusual experiences, assorted trips, varied conversations, and sundry explorations. In short, I'm always trying to sow some new "mental seeds" - some of which may germinate into new ideas; others not so much.

The same holds true for adults. Don't assume that "play" is the sole province of children. Regular play in our adult lives sends a powerful message to our brains that allows creativity to incubate and prosper.

Companies such as Google and Apple offer their employees lots of "play time" or "thinking time" outside of their normal activities. Their thinking (supported by a bank of psychological research) is that the mind cannot operate at "full tilt" for eight hours a day, five days a week, without some form of mental relaxation or escape (Imagine your car engine running non-stop for that length of time.). We all need regular mental "vacations" every now and again to keep the "mental batteries" fully functioning. When managers schedule "open time" into the workday they give their employees opportunities to recharge their mental batteries as well as opportunities to let their minds wander in new directions and explore new territories. The results can often be quite revolutionary.

93. Focused Doodling. You're in a meeting and things are getting boring...very, very boring. You have a piece of paper in front of you and you begin doodling - random, inconsequential, and meaningless doodles. Some of your doodles may be surrealistic, others may be more concrete objects, and still others may be the stuff of science fiction. This is unchecked creativity - you're creating things that may or may not exist.

While we know there's a correlation between daydreaming and creativity, we can put ourselves in a more creative frame of thinking by taking common everyday items and turning them (via focused doodling) into something they are not. For example, I was recently employed by a local excursion/tourist train to develop a series of S.T.E.A.M. activities offering youngsters educational and scientific explorations about trains and train travel. As part of an Art (A.) activity, I presented them with the four random shapes below:

I invited kids to use some focused doodling with each symbol and turn it into a part of the train. For example, the circle could be developed into the smokestack on a steam engine, the diamond could be turned into the logo on the conductor's hat, and the cross could be tipped on its side to become a railroad crossing sign. These are certainly not the only options for those symbols; yet, the freedom to create a multiplicity of "products" for each symbol offered participants various ways of exercising their creativity.

Bring a collection of geometric symbols to your next meeting. Use your pen or pencil to turn one or two of them into a potential product or creative solution to an ongoing challenge. Put your finished drawing in a file and refer to them every so often. You might come up with a design for something different or unusual...something quite creative. For example, while writing this paragraph, I just designed a new breakfast loveseat for two using the last symbol above (the "arrowhead"). Can't wait to share it with my wife!

94. Pair Up! Join with a co-worker or two and form an "action group." Discuss something that may be holding you back creatively and a potential action that might reduce or eliminate that constraint. Write out an action plan and stick to it. Check in with each other occasionally on your individual and group progress. What modifications or changes need to be implemented? You may want to focus on a specific work project, your job in general, or your overall life. By joining forces with others you can share some common creative impediments and investigate recommended "fixes" such as those suggested at the end of each chapter in this book. Which ones work best and which ones can be slightly modified for a particular project or assignment.

95. Read Around. For nearly a half-century, I worked as a professional educator - teaching everything from Kindergarten to college graduate courses. Sure, I read educational journals and books to stay current in my field. But, I also read an eclectic array of books that forced me to look at the world through different sets of lenses. I read business books, books about archeology, environmental studies, social psychology, pop science, commerce, ancient history, paleontology, philosophy, and cartography.

For example, here are a few books I am now reading (or plan to start reading in the next few weeks). You will note that none of them are education titles - rather they are all in fields quite different from how I was trained. But, I also know that reading an eclectic arrangement of titles will lead me into new arenas for discovery and new opportunities for learning.

➤ *Sapiens: A Brief History of Humankind* (Evolution)
➤ *What Got You Here Won't Get You There: How Successful People Become Even More Successful* (Business)
➤ *Turn Right at Machu Picchu: Rediscovering the Lost City One Step at a Time* (Archeology)
➤ *Rivers of Power: How a Natural Force Raised Kingdoms, Destroyed Civilizations, and Shapes Our World* (Hydrology)
➤ *Word by Word: The Secret Life of Dictionaries* (Lexicology)
➤ *Tree Story: The History of the World Written in Rings* (Dendrochronology)
➤ *Decisive* (Decision-making)
➤ *The Perfect Mile: Three Athletes, One Goal, And Less Than Four Minutes to Achieve It* (Sports)
➤ *The Wave: In Pursuit of the Rogues, Freaks, and Giants of the Ocean* (Oceanography)
➤ *Destinations of a Lifetime* (Travel)
➤ *Quiet: The Power of Introverts in a World That Can't Stop Talking* (Psychology)
➤ *Naked* (Humor)
➤ *The Sixth Extinction: An Unnatural History* (Natural History)
➤ *Brain Storms: The Race to Unlock the Mysteries of Parkinson's Disease* (Medicine)

Reading broadly opens your eyes (and your thinking) to new concepts and new ideas:

➤ If you're a businessperson, read a book about teaching. You may alter your staff development program.

➤ If you're a carpenter, read a book about archeology. You may discover a new (or ancient) way of constructing buildings.

➤ If you're an artist, read some books about environmental issues. You may generate some paintings or illustrations with a more naturalistic view of the world.

➤ If you're a professional hair stylist, read some books about the ocean. You may find a new hair style embedded in the motions of waves or the interaction of rivers flowing into the sea.

➤ If you're a landscape architect, read some books about paleontology. You may see some illustrations of ancient landscapes that will help you solve a conundrum with a current project.

In his book *The Creative Curve*, author Allen Gannett discusses the "20 percent principle" – a recommendation that professionals spend 20 percent of their waking hours (three to four hours a day) consuming reading material in their chosen field. While I have no problem with the need to read books and articles on a regular and consistent basis, it has been my experience that that reading should be done in fields away from, or different from, one's chosen profession. In doing so, you get to see something from a different point of view while offering your brain new and varied perspectives from different angles and different points of view. 20 percent is an ideal; but, what is even more critical is that you expose your mind to varied ways of thinking: looking at the world through – not rose-colored glasses – but vermilion-colored glasses, gingerline-colored glasses, cerulean blue-colored glasses, or coral-pink-colored glasses. Exposing yourself to new and varied fields also exposes you to new and varied thinking. In short, broad reading outside your comfort zone often leads to new ways of conceptualizing familiar problems.

25.
One or the Other

There are two kinds of people in this world:
those who divide everything into
two groups, and those who don't.
- KENNETH BOULDING, ECONOMIST

1.

Let's gather a couple of historical figures together in a room - say a cocktail party in advance of a formal dinner. Included in this august group are the following folks: Descartes, Michelangelo, Marie Curie, Leonardo da Vinci, Vincent van Gogh, Benjamin Franklin, Archimedes, Albert Einstein, and Mozart.

All nine of those individuals are standing around the hors d'oeuvre table sampling the fire-roasted Vienna sausages and smearing globs of brie on whole wheat crackers. Their drinks are positioned across an ornate mahogany table covered with a flowered tablecloth. All nine are chatting away - discussing all manner of artistic, musical, or scientific possibilities. Now, how likely would it be for you to step up to this group of individuals and join in the conversation? Or, would you be like most folks and forego any social interaction with these creative types for fear of being made to look like someone who couldn't generate a single new idea to save your soul.

If the prevailing research is correct, then less than five percent of us would join that distinguished group for any type of meaningful conversation. In short, many people are "afraid" of creative folks. "Creative folks are those who are brilliant, generate earth-shaking ideas at the drop of a hat, and are recorded by legions of history scholars as some of the brightest individuals on the planet. They're in a different class; a different league; a different universe. I'm not one of them...I'll never rise to their level," you might respond.

2.

Although we dealt with some of the most common and most persistent myths regarding creativity in Chapter 12, there is one overriding myth that refuses to go away. In fact, it is so ingrained in our collective consciousness, that it is blindly accepted as concrete proof that most of us are permanently confined to a non-creative existence. And, that is a deep-seated belief that some of us are born creative and others are gifted with a set of genes that mitigates against any sort of creative output. A few folks were gifted with creativity; the rest of us - not so much!

Truth be told, creativity is not something that is genetically determined. It is not something you inherit from your parents nor is it some "special gene" that your great-great-grandfather from Denmark passed down to you. Creativity is NOT some kind of Las Vegas magic trick, ancient Egyptian secret, or long-ago Norse legend. Nope! Quite simply, creativity is an inherent and natural sequence of actions leading to the production of dynamic ideas. Most of us are creative souls early in our lives and it is our upbringing, schooling and work environment that often determine the degree or comfort we have with matters creative. What we have experienced (in formalized settings) frequently determines what we can create. Creativity is never a matter of chance or genetics; it is always a matter of incubation.

The rise of this persistent myth is often attributed to the psychological reality that, as humans, we have a tendency to compare ourselves to others. When we are at a social function we compare our clothing to those worn by others ("See that woman? I'm sure she doesn't shop at the same stores I do!"). In a work environment, we wonder how much someone makes if they are engaged in the same job or position as us ("How come Janice drives a BMW? She's doing the same job I am."). In your neighborhood, you may compare your lawn to that of your neighbor's ("Hey, look at Jake's lawn. It doesn't even begin to compare with mine.").

By the same token, when it comes to matters creative, we frequently compare ourselves to creative giants - those individuals who are celebrated for their creative discoveries, inventions, or contributions:

Georgia O'Keefe and her majestic and iconic paintings, John Steinbeck and his quintessential, yet down-to-earth, novels, Steven Spielberg and his prototypical movies, the "get up and dance in the aisle" songs of Elton John,[34] Jane Goodall and her groundbreaking studies of primates, and the overwhelming gracefulness of ballet dancer Misty Copeland are all ceremoniously raised upon a pedestal of creative expression and creative thinking that few can ever hope to achieve. They are icons, celebrities, idols, and modern-day gods. We'll never rise to their level; we'll never achieve their creative greatness. They are a different breed, in a different universe, and products of a different gene pool. "They are the creative people" and "I am not creative" thus become two clearly defined groups. If we don't belong in the first, then it stands to reason that we must certainly belong to the other.

The unfortunate consequence of this mindset is that we significantly diminish our individual creative ability. By casting people into two distinct (and highly unequal) categories, we have a psychological tendency to assign ourselves to the "lower" of the two groups. If we like to draw, we may compare ourselves to van Gogh and convince ourselves that, "I'll never be as creative as he was." If we are freelance writers, we may tell ourselves, "Well, I guess I'm never going to be as creative as Steven King." If we are in the business world, we may bemoan the fact that, "I'm certainly no Bill Gates...and probably never will be."

Our mantra often becomes, "If (van Gogh, Steven King, Bill Gates) are creative, then I am not!"

We frequently put those "famous creatives" on an altar that we can never ascend. We tend to see ourselves in their shadow; celebrating their works, but never attaining their glory. Often, it looks as though creativity is so far away - a concept honored, but infrequently (if ever) attained. And that opens a door, a door that allows fear, insecurity, and negative self-judgement to enter. We begin to believe that we will seldom generate new and innovative ideas, that any ideas that we do spawn will wither and die when presented to our colleagues and friends, and that we are burdened with a significant disability that will internally quash any creative endeavors for all of our lives.

---

34 Try not to create an image of a way-past-middle-age author acting as though he were a hormone-fueled teenager: jumping up and down and flailing his arms at, not one, but two Elton John concerts (and yelling the lyrics to "Rocketman" - off-key, no less). It's not a pretty picture, but it has been known to happen.

Part of this enormous myth is based on the reality that we are a comparative society (Are you: a Republican or a Democrat, short or tall, young or old, urbanite or suburbanite, female or male, blond or brunette, gay or straight?) , But, by the same token, the myth is also supported by the belief that creativity is mutually exclusive. It's a province of a few, but unavailable to the many. To extend this concept even further, there are some who believe that the words "creativity" and "creative" should only be used when referring to inventions and ideas that are totally new to the world. That thought, as you might imagine, further cements this myth in our consciousness - so much so, that it becomes a self-defeating prophecy.

3.

"If given the choice, would you rather room with a creative person or with a smart person?" was a question I posed to my undergraduate students at the start of one semester. Almost universally, the responses were in favor of "the creative person." When pressed, students indicated that a creative person would be "more interesting," "more fun to be with," "more off the wall," and "more likely to come up with new and innovative ideas." Then, when I asked them, "How many of you would consider yourselves to be a creative person?" virtually nobody raised their hand. When queried further, they told me that they've never been taught to be creative; the standard high school curriculum is based almost exclusively on memorization, rather than creative thinking; school is geared more towards getting good grades (products) than in innovation or creativity (processes); and they're simply not sure where to begin in order to be creative. Many of them turned to an all-too-common response, "I'm just not a creative person."

Out of habit, custom, or convenience, we often assign ourselves to the "I'm just not a creative person" group. We find comfort in that group simply because there are so many others who have also self-assigned themselves into that body. To be sure, it's a substantial and ever-expanding population. We are also on friendly terms with many of the members. We work with them, we live with them, we marry them, we move into neighborhoods with them, and we socialize with them. If there is, indeed, "safety in numbers," then our membership in this group is cemented by its very size. It's "one big happy family."

We are also a dichotomous society - we often see things in contrasting pairs. We tend to see ourselves as belonging to one group to the exclusion of those folks who belong to an opposing group. And, once we assume "membership" in one group we assume the features or characteristics of all the other members of that group and shun the characteristics of an opposing group. Democrat vs. Republican. Pro-choice vs. pro-life. Gun control vs. gun advocate. Coke vs. Pepsi. McDonalds vs. Burger King. Los Angeles Dodgers vs. San Francisco Giants.

As a society, we also have a tendency, nay a compulsion, to place others into categories. This is, quite often, done for the convenience of identification. We assign labels to people as a way of understanding them - more specifically, how they are similar to, or (more often) different from, ourselves. This process begins early in our lives (boys vs. girls. smart vs. dumb) and continues straight through to adulthood (rich vs. poor. liberal vs. conservative). This predilection to group separates people into categories that are easily recognizable, although not always clearly defined.

As you might imagine, it is also an arena fraught with danger.

Once we assign people - or ourselves - to a group several things happen. First of all, the group (and the members within that group) assume an identity. A label is placed on them; a label that, over time, achieves a level of permanency. Once you are a member of a recognized group, you seldom escape the inevitable label that goes along with that group. For example, if you are a "tree hugger", you will forever and ever be a "tree hugger" - at least as long as you remain in the local community. Once a label has been "assigned," either by the members of the group or by others not affiliated with the group, it frequently achieves status or permanency.

In fact, you may recall times in your academic life - particularly in elementary school - when you were assigned to a specific reading group (the "Redbirds," the "Bluebirds," and the "Yellow Birds" or the "Tigers," the "Panthers," and the "Bobcats"). Teachers often assign students into groups, not only for the sake of convenience, but also for instructional purposes. The prevailing thinking is that if a teacher has a small group of students with similar academic abilities, she is better able to meet their instructional needs, than if the group was composed of individuals with a wide range of abilities. This is often done as a matter of academic convenience - a practice that puts students with similar reading skills into an artificial hierarchy (For example, the "Redbirds " were those students who, presumably, were the best readers; the "Bluebirds" were the average readers; and the "Yellow Birds" were those with some reading deficiencies). This allowed the teacher to tailor her instruction based on the perceived reading level and competency of each individual group.

The danger, of course, is that once you were a member of a certain group there was little or no upward mobility. In short, if you were assigned to the "Bluebirds" at the beginning of the school year, you (typically) remained a "Bluebird" through the year, irrespective of how well you may have progressed (or not) in your reading skills. Take it from a former "Bluebird," once you have been assigned a reading label, you typically maintain that label for an infinite amount of time (until the end of the school year...or beyond). You have achieved a designation that is difficult to alter.

Let's advance that argument one step further. If, for example, you have assigned yourself as someone who belongs to the "I'm really not creative" group, you tend to view yourself as primarily and permanently uncreative. The more you self-advocate that label, the more that label becomes a constant part of who you are (in your own eyes). The longer you bemoan your "station" in life as someone who is seldom, if ever, creative, the more that label becomes enduringly attached to your psyche. The longer it is in place (as determined by others or by yourself) the more difficult it is to escape.

Another issue surfaces when we paste a label on someone or on ourselves: the label dominates to the exclusion of other personality dynamics. For example, we may know a group of people in our local community as LGBTQ advocates. Their primary and singular designation is "that LGBTQ group." The group achieves a singular and permanent designation. Unknowingly, we tend to view that group by its label, rather than by other personality dynamics such as occupation (engineers, teachers, architects, landscapers), personalities (introspective, humorous, cerebral, conversationalist), or avocations (runner, stamp collector, gardener, sailor) that reveals more of their character and personality. A single label is semantically more convenient than a coterie of skills and attributes.

We may have colleagues who belong to a different political party than we do. Whenever a political discussion ensues, the lines of demarcation may surface rapidly. We takes sides, we stand our group, we are intractable...as are they. We see things in shades of black and white, rather than in all the possible permutations of an issue or agenda. They belong to one group and we belong to another (and that's the way it will always be). Groups conveniently separate people, rather than enjoin them. Grouping often allows us to create artificial barriers that protect our beliefs, ensure our commonality, and solidify our standing.

Groups also give us an opportunity to be content. If we have self-assigned ourselves to the "I'm not creative" group, then we have also conveniently protected ourselves from moving beyond the borders of that group into new, and often unfamiliar, territory. Over time, we have become comfortable, contented, and snug in this group. We have eschewed any desire to move out of the group, not only because we have so many like-minded "associates" in the group, but also because it offers a safe environment in which to work and play. We have achieved a comfort that is often difficult to overcome and challenging to change. We have labeled ourselves into complacency.

There's another force at work here - one I've noticed over the course of the research for this book. Sometimes, we are nudged into the "I'm not creative" group by forces that are often subtle and seemingly beyond our control. These "forces" frequently surface in the tens of thousands of books and millions of articles on creativity. And that is the tendency of many authors to systematically edge us into either the "I'm not creative" group or "I am creative" group through the use of linguistic manipulations.

Throughout my research, I encountered numerous books and articles that used language such as the following: "Creative people are individuals like Leonardo, Edison, Picasso, or Einstein [who] have changed our culture in some important respect," "Creative people are the ones who get ahead in their jobs, start new businesses, invent products,...paint pictures, and make things of beauty." and "...creative people need to know a lot about a little and a little about a lot." Go back and re-read each statement and you'll note a disconcerting term in each one: "Creative people." In using that designation, each author has quietly and subtly injected the idea that there are, indeed, two groups of people on the planet - the creative class and the non-creative class. That is to say, we either identify with one group or the other.

Many of those same authors go on to expound on all the qualities, dynamics, and features - often in glowing terms - of those folks who are part of the "Yes, I'm a creative person" group. The appellations and compliments are rampant and it is clear that this is a singularly unique group inhabited by individuals who not only get a lot of press, but who have skills that the rest of us could never aspire to. In reading about these intellectual "Masters of the Universe," we often, by default, create and assign ourselves to that "other group," knowing that we lack comparative abilities or a similar intellect. As we have shared throughout the pages of this book, creativity is not the province of a few, but rather the inheritance of all. So, be careful what you read; someone may be grouping you without your knowledge...or consent.

4.

Please duplicate the following form on a separate sheet of paper. Then, I'd like to invite you to take a few minutes and complete the entire questionnaire. Please know that there are no right or wrong responses to any of the questions (thus, there is no scoring guide).

First name: _____

Today's date: _____

Age: _____

Sex: **M   F**

On a scale of 1 (low) to 10 (high) please rate your level of creativity [circle one]:

---

1   2   3   4   5   6   7   8   9   10

Birthplace:_____
Occupation:_____
Marital status:_____
Educational Level: _____

1. Write down as many different uses for a spoon as you can.
(5 minutes)

———————   ———————   ———————   ———————
———————   ———————   ———————   ———————
———————   ———————   ———————   ———————
———————   ———————   ———————   ———————
———————   ———————   ———————   ———————

2. In what ways are a bulldozer and a pencil similar? (5 minutes)

———————   ———————   ———————   ———————
———————   ———————   ———————   ———————
———————   ———————   ———————   ———————
———————   ———————   ———————   ———————
———————   ———————   ———————   ———————

3. How many different words can you create that include these
three letters: N C A (5 minutes)

———————   ———————   ———————   ———————
———————   ———————   ———————   ———————
———————   ———————   ———————   ———————
———————   ———————   ———————   ———————
———————   ———————   ———————   ———————

4. Write down as many objects as you can that are orange.
(5 minutes)

———————   ———————   ———————   ———————
———————   ———————   ———————   ———————
———————   ———————   ———————   ———————
———————   ———————   ———————   ———————
———————   ———————   ———————   ———————

Two psychologists - Claude Steele and Joshua Aronson - conduced a most interesting research project a few years ago. They assembled a group of black college students and gave them a set of questions extracted from the Graduate Record Examination (GRE), a test used to determine one's qualifications for graduate school. The students were all asked to identify their race on a pre-test questionnaire. What the researchers discovered was that the simple act of identifying one's race was enough to prime individuals with (negative) academic stereotypes associated with African Americans and their (perceived) scholastic achievement. As a result of that priming, the number of correct answers on the test was reduced by half.

As we saw in an earlier chapter, standardized tests are a ubiquitous component of American education. They are as common as a chocolate smear on a child's face on Halloween night. We assume that those tests (created by professional educators) are an accurate and reliable measure of academic achievement. But, as Steele and Aronson's research indicates, they may indicate a hidden factor not anticipated by the test-makers. They also raise some interesting questions.

If a black student from an urban school gets a low score on a standardized test, is it because she is not as academically prepared as a white student from a suburban school? Or, is it because the black student perceives herself as a lower performing student because of her race and all the negative stereotypes that are sometimes associated with that designation? And, what about the white student? Does she see herself as a better performing student (consequently getting better scores on standardized tests) because she is white and attends a high-performing suburban school?

If students classify themselves as either "Black" or "White" do they perform (on standardized tests) according to societal expectations of the group they identify with? In other words, is the test measuring something it was never intended to measure?

Let's examine that concept using the results of the questionnaire you completed above. You will note that before you completed any of the four questions, I invited you to identify your level of creativity. For the sake of discussion, let's assume you identified yourself as someone with a low level of creativity (You rated your level of creativity with a number lower than 5). How did that identification affect your performance on the test. Were you able to fill in all 20 blanks following each of the four questions or did you leave a lot of them blank?

Perhaps you self-identified yourself with a "creativity score" higher than 5. As such, did you find it relatively easy to generate responses to each of the four questions? By "announcing" that you thought you were a highly creative individual, did you match that identification with a robust array of responses for each of the four questions?

Were you primed? Yes! You may have discovered that the "priming" had an effect on how many creative responses you were able to generate. If you identified yourself as a member of the "I'm just not creative" group, did you "prove" it by doing poorly on the four questions? On the other hand, if you self-assigned yourself to the "Yes, I'm a creative person" group, did you find it relatively easy to produce a host of responses?

Think about this: The group to which you pre-assign yourself ("I'm just not creative" or "I'm a creative.") may have a significant influence on how well you are able to engage in creative endeavors.

5.

How often have you heard the following statements? Alternatively, and more specifically, how often have you said these statements yourself?: "I couldn't draw a straight line if my life depended on it." "If you're looking for a creative person, you might as well look somewhere else." "Me? Creative? No way, José." "I'm probably the least creative person you'll meet." "Go see Jack (or Jill) if you want a creative solution."

There is a persuasive tendency of people to downplay their creative talents or place limits on their creative output. Many people believe they aren't creative simply because they weren't born with a creative gene or with a "basket" of creative attributes. Not having those attributes becomes a self-fulfilling prophecy. As a result, their confidence dwindles, erodes, and is washed away. We often fall into the all too common perception that we are either creative or we're not. We belong to either one group or the other. There is no middle ground - we are one or the other. "If I wasn't born creative, I'll never be creative."

As you would expect, that's a myth!

Truth be told, the "I'm creative" and "I'm just not creative" groups are imaginary - we're not one or the other. As shared throughout the pages of this book, we are all creative individuals as children, it's just that that creativity has been steam-rolled into submission as we get older and begin to deal with the realities of everyday living. David Perkins, a psychologist at Yale University has convincingly demonstrated that creativity results from ordinary cognitive processes that virtually every person uses in the normal course of life. His research findings have been substantiated by legions of other psychological experts whose research also support a universal contention that the processes of creativity are not that extraordinary.

Perkins has proven that there are everyday cognitive processes that are an integral part of creative invention. One such process is *directed remembering*. This is the ability to channel your memory in order to make conscious some past experience or knowledge that meets various constraints. For example, think of as many countries as you can that begin with the letter **S**. To do this you have to engage in the same kind of thinking as do scientists, historians, and mathematicians.

A second relative cognitive process is *noticing*. This is when we become aware of the similarity between one problem and another. Watch a child construct a tower of wooden blocks. She is aware that some arrangements work better than others (based on prior experiences with blocks) and will often make corrections based on prior experiences.

A third cognitive process consistent with everyday thinking and creative thinking is known as *contrary recognition*. This is the ability to recognize objects, not for what they are, but as something else, in another important creative process. For example, you may step outside and notice a cloud that looks just like a particular animal (cow, dog, "Jabba the Hutt" from the Star Wars movies). Or, you may be at a social engagement and see someone who looks just like your brother-in-law or your great aunt Sophie. This ability engages our imagination and allows us to interpret events in fanciful or imaginative ways.

The conclusion to be drawn from this bank of research is that the same cognitive processes used to create innovative inventions and dynamic new approaches in fields as diverse as medicine, education, architecture, business, agriculture, and engineering are similar to those you and I use, quite frequently, in our everyday lives.

Kaufman and Gregoire further cement the similarities between those often self-designated as "Creative" and those who self-select the "I'm not creative" moniker. In fact, as you review their list of characteristics you will, not only notice similarities to the earlier work by Perkins, you will also note that many of these beliefs and personality dynamics are also those that have been an inherent part of your own life. It could well be said, that the characteristics of "Creatives" are the same characteristics that are part and parcel of your past as well as your present. As this book seeks to share, however, some of those features have been systematically crushed, pummeled, mashed, and trampled as we have grown up, gone to school, and gotten a job.

Here are their ten attributes of creative types. Note how many of these attributes apply to you now or were once an element of your younger years:

1. I played imaginative games as a child.
2. I have, or have had, a passion for something important in my life.
3. I've been known to daydream about things unrelated to my work.
4. I enjoy doing things on my own or by myself.
5. I sometimes "just know" something is right; I've been intuitive at times.
6. I'm open to learning new things and having new experiences.
7. I've meditated or engaged in mindfulness activities.
8. I'm sensitive to the needs and feelings of others.
9. I've been able to turn adversities into advantages.
10. I sometimes think about things others do not.

I suspect you have more than one or two attributes from that list. I also suspect that you would embrace Perkins three attributes of creativity (*remembering, noticing, recognition*). Thus, it seems reasonable to assume that almost all of us, at one time or another in our lives, have engaged in common practices and shared performances emblematic of creative thinking. That is to say, no matter your perceived station in life, you have the components of creative thinking already "in your system." In short, you are more similar to those arbitrarily classified as "Creative People" than you are different.

6.

A few years ago, *Inc.* Magazine ran a special feature about hiring for creativity. The authors presented a case for companies to do a better job of hiring more people who think outside the box. Several corporations have taken this thinking to the extreme by utilizing a battery of exams to assess the creativity of potential workers. That is to say, assessed (vs. potential creativity) creativity is often viewed as one of the most significant factors in the hiring process.

This argument, however, misses the point. It assumes that there is a "creative class" of potential employees and a non-creative group of potential employees. As we saw in an earlier chapter, hiring the "creative class" will not produce a plethora of creative ideas if the conditions and environment of the work place is not conducive to generating ideas in the first place. It also rails against the notion of two classes. Having creative minds in place won't solve problems if, for example, a traditional hierarchy is in place thwarting those ideas. Sir Ken Robinson put an exclamation point on this when he states, "Everybody has huge creative capacities. The challenge is to develop them. A culture of creativity has to involve everybody, not just a select few."

What is evident is that we all can be more creative, no matter what our occupational field or professional endeavor. Realizing the creative obstacles, addressing those impediments, and engaging our common habits - irrespective of age, education, socio-economic status, gender, race, religion or any other societal determinant - gives us opportunities to creatively contribute, in both large and small measure, to everyday tasks as well as problems much larger. In essence, creativity is not a matter of genetics, but more a matter of what we do with our innate talents.

> *One of the myths of creativity is that very few*
> *people are really creative. The truth is that*
> *everyone has great capacities, but not*
> *everyone develops them.*
> —SIR KEN ROBINSON

26.
How to Sizzle: 96 - 103

96. Your Potential. Do you have the potential to be more creative? Although you and I have never met, I'm pretty sure I know the answer to that query. In fact, the overall theme of this book is that EVERYBODY has the potential to be more creative - no matter what their field, what their endeavors, or what their challenges. One of the absolutes of this book is that if you think you're creative, you'll act creatively. I'm often reminded of the Greek philosopher Epictetus who said, "[It's] not the way things are, but rather the way people think things are." In short, if we believe ourselves to be creative, we'll act in a creative manner. On the other hand, if we think we're part of a class of people who aren't "born creative," then we'll never realize our full potential. It's a self-fulfilling prophecy: we act as we believe. All of the ideas, techniques, and strategies in the "Sizzle" section of each chapter in this book will be ineffective and unproductive unless we embrace them as part of an ongoing (and lifelong) creative reformation.

97. Dismiss The Comparison Mindset. Stop comparing yourself to Georgia O'Keefe, Steve Jobs, or Einstein. They were unique in their own way. And, guess what? You are unique in your own way. Everybody has the potential to make a creative contribution. Changing the design of the company letterhead is just as creative as painting a multi-million dollar work of art. "Small" acts of creativity need and use the same creative thinking processes as do "large" acts of creativity. When you compare yourself to the Bill Gates of the business world or the Jeff Koons of the art world, you are diminishing your own potential.

98. One More Myth. There is a lingering myth whenever people talk about creativity - specifically when they self-assign themselves to either the "I'm creative" class or the "I'm not creative" category. That is the overwhelming and fundamental belief that we are either born one or the other. Our fate is predetermined at birth; our creative future (or lack of it) is tied into our genetics, heritage, or family history. Well, I'm going to let you in on a little secret: creativity is often the result of lots of work. In short: no input, no output. One of the things we seldom see behind a great painting, a magnificent invention, a dynamic piece of music, an architecturally-rich building, or a best-selling book is all the "blood, sweat and tears" that went into its inception, development, and construction. We often envision creativity as overnight wonders - one day there's nothing; the next day there is this marvelously magnificent and wildly successful creation. Here's the ultimate key to being a creative person: you need to put a lot of time into it. In short, it's a 24/7 endeavor, not a one-time response to an isolated work project.

99. Doing What Comes Naturally. Throughout this book there is a deep and abiding philosophy - namely that everyone was creative once in their lives (when we were young). Over time, that natural creative spirit has diminished due to our upbringing, our education, our work environment, and our personal beliefs. Over time, we begin to believe that we are not creative souls any longer and that that youthful spirit of creativity is something out of reach as adults. But, let's look at this concept with different eyes. What are some of the things that you do quite naturally? Are you someone who can whip up the world's greatest margarita? Can you tell stories to children that have them gasping with wide-eyed wonder? Do you have a sense of humor that keeps your friends laughing at every social occasion? Can you cook up an Italian meal that has all your friends on Facebook begging for the recipes? Can you write a poem for your lover that brings tears to his eyes? What other creative skills or talents do you have that come quite naturally? The point is that you are already creative. You have retained vestiges of your creative youth. The foundation is there...the challenge now is to expand it; take it in new directions; discover new possibilities. Are you creative? Damn right you are!

100. Inside Out. A few years ago, I was working on a children's book about majestic redwood trees (*Tall Tall Tree*). The book – a counting book – focused on the various critters that lived in the canopy of these botanical skyscrapers. But, near the beginning of the writing process, I was stuck – I couldn't seem to generate any imaginative ideas. So, I decided to do something different. I imagined that, instead of observing these iconic trees as an outsider, I would mentally crawl inside a towering redwood tree and look at the surrounding environment as if I was that tree. What creatures would be crawling over my surface, how would the wind feel against my bark, what birds would be roosting in my branches, and what kinds of insects would be creeping up my trunk. In short order, the ideas began to flow like warm syrup on a stack of Sunday morning pancakes. I couldn't write fast enough. Long story short: the book was published and eventually went on to garner several national book awards including the *Outstanding Science Trade Book for Children* in 2018. So, if your creativity wheels are getting rusty or are slowing down, crawl inside your subject matter and look at it from the inside out, rather than the outside in. In short, imagine you are the subject of a current project. For example, if you are trying to design a new coffee table, pretend you are that table. Where will you be placed? What objects will be arranged on your surface? How tall will you be? What shape will you be? What type of wood will be used in your construction? How heavy should you be? In short, crawl inside your subject...become your subject... and take a look from the inside out.

101. Create A Metaphor. One of the best ways to stimulate your latent creativity is to generate metaphors about a current problem or issue. Metaphors are, by definition, a comparison between two seemingly unlike items. In crafting a metaphor we are showing the similarities - rather than the differences - that exist between two thoughts or two ideas. For example, the first locomotives were referred to as "iron horses" - in other words a familiar object (a horse) was compared with an unfamiliar object (a locomotive) to enhance the comprehension of the new item. Or, how about a metaphorical question: What are some of the similarities between a mouse (the animal) and a toaster. Well, they both have compartments for food, they both have a tail, they both come in different colors, they both generate heat, and they both work at all hours of the day. Now, let's say you are the product manager for a company that produces razor blades. You are about to come out with a brand new blade, but aren't sure all the elements are in place. Generate a random metaphor and see what you discover. For example, what are the similarities between a razor blade and a skyscraper? A razor blade and a jar of strawberry jam? A razor blade and a walrus? A razor blade and the word at the end of this question?

102. Good & Bad. As humans, we have a tendency to see the world in black and white. In other words, we see things as either being good or bad. In essence, judgement becomes more important than creativity ("That's a really ugly car!" instead of "Wow, can you see what they incorporated into the design of those lug nuts?). We're comfortable with judgement because we're exposed to it regularly throughout our lives. Yet, judgement and creativity are two different concepts. You can't be creative when you are judging the "rightness" or "wrongness" of an object or idea. Once you have assigned a label to something ("That is a terrible idea! What were you thinking of?") its utility (or lack of) is forever locked in place. However, when you defer or eliminate judgement, you open up the creative floodgates and look at possibilities, rather than absolutes. Deferring judgement is always preferable to making judgements.

103. Cross-Breeding. One way to create new ideas to crossbreed two subjects from two different worlds. By actively merging two separate subjects into the same space, you articulate a new identity. This new identity will encourage you to think of connecting links and plausible circumstances to express them. Here are the guidelines:

1. Take an item, object or concept and crossbreed it with an item, object or concept from some other domain to create a "new creation." What happens when you crossbreed X with Y? What happens when you crossbreed a car with an apple? Or a clam with a radio? Suppose you wanted to write some nonfiction and the first word you saw in this morning's newspaper was "factory." Think about what happens when you crossbreed:

   ➤ A factory with a pickle
   ➤ A factory with a hang glider
   ➤ A factory with a sparrow
   ➤ A factory with a horse trainer
   ➤ A factory with a stamp
   ➤ A factory with a barn

2. Draw a picture of your "creation." Consider the following:

   ➤ How does it look from the side?
   ➤ What is its most distinguishing feature?
   ➤ What is it good at?
   ➤ In what area does it need to improve?
   ➤ Where does it live?
   ➤ What is its most serious problem?
   ➤ Who is important in its life?

3. Write a 2-4 sentence description of your "creation."
4. What are three of its unique weaknesses?
5. What are three of its most unique strengths?
6. Create ideas from these crossbreed strengths.

Steve Jobs probably said it best, "Creativity is just connecting things. When you ask creative people how they did something, they feel a little guilty because they didn't really *do* it, they just saw something."

27.
Jumping Backwards, Mindsets, and Toilet Paper

The creative is the place where no one else has ever been. You have to leave the city of your comfort and go into the wilderness of your intuition.
—ALAN ALDA, ACTOR

1.

He stood on the run-up to the high jump pit in the Estadio Olímpico Universitario in Mexico City. Eighty thousand pairs of eyes were focused on this lanky 21-year-old American in white shorts and a blue singlet with **USA** emblazoned in bold red letters. He was rocking back and forth on his long legs, holding his arms in an "L" pattern, and clenching his fists. His eyes were clearly focused downward; his breathing was rhythmic and his demeanor calm.

A hush swept through the crowd and an air of anticipation filled the stadium. Few spectators had actually seen him in competition and yet he was rumored to be one of the most innovative athletes on the entire U.S. Olympic track and field team.

He began his approach. Slowly at first and then with increasing speed. He was like a mature gazelle loping over the rubberized surface - smooth, intentional, and absolutely fluid. He gained more speed and then suddenly planted his right foot and leapt into the air with deliberate grace and absolute calmness.

In a matter of seconds, he did something no human being had ever done before - eventually winning an Olympic gold medal in the process.

He jumped - backwards!

Dick Fosbury was a most unlikely hero. With a passion for civil engineering, this six foot, four inch athlete, who couldn't even make his high school basketball team, decided to try out for the high jump - one of the premier events in track and field. In the 40s, 50s, and 60s high jumpers cleared the crossbar using a complex jumping technique known as the "Straddle." To do the Straddle, jumpers ran up to the bar, planted their inside foot, and swing their outside foot (like a moving pendulum) up and over the bar. The trailing leg followed a somewhat different arc. As a result, each leg had to be lifted individually over the bar. Then, in clearing the bar, the athlete would rotate her or his entire body and land sideways in a pit filled with sawdust. It was the accepted practice and every high jumper from elementary school beginners to world class athletes practiced this standardized technique religiously. In the minds of high jumpers it was the most efficient way to get up and over a high jump bar.

However, Fosbury found it difficult to coordinate all the motions involved in the straddle, and began to experiment with other ways of getting over the bar. Instead of jumping face forward like everyone else, Fosbury began his jumps off the "wrong" foot, arching his back and clearing the bar backwards. Not surprisingly, his high school coaches in Medford, Oregon and his mentors at Oregon State University tried to dissuade him from this radical maneuver. His fellow athletes even branded him as a lazy athlete. But, he persisted in refining his technique and mastering the arc of his body as it sailed over the bar. In 1964, local reporters dubbed his new method the "Fosbury Flop" because he looked like "a fish flopping in a boat."

Slowly, he began winning competitions and when he qualified for the United States Olympic team in 1968, the national buzz about this innovative athlete now became an international interest. In Mexico City, he stunned the athletic world by setting a new Olympic record of 2.24 meters (7 feet, 4¼ inches) - earning him the honor of standing on the highest tier of the awards platform and hearing the "Star Spangled Banner" played. His jumping style has since been used by every female and male high jumper from the early 1970s to the present day to set an array of high school, college, Olympic, and world records. As this is written, the current world record in the high jump of 2.09 meters (6 feet, 10¼ inches) for women, and 2.45 meters (8 feet, ¼ inch) for men, were both set using the "Fosbury Flop."[35]

Dick Fosbury ran up to the status quo and creatively leapt over it... backwards!

---

35 Dick Fosbury was accorded many honors after winning the gold medal in Mexico City. He was inducted into the US Olympic Hall of Fame, the USA Track and Field Hall of Fame, and the National High School Hall of Fame, among many other awards. One of the most interesting, at least in terms of the theme of this book, occurred in Dubai in 2011. There, he was presented the Mohammad bin Rashid Al Maktoum Creativity in Sport Award.

2.

I'm certain Carol Dweck would be a most enthusiastic fan of Dick Fosbury. Dweck, a Stanford University researcher, wrote a pivotal and ground-breaking book in 2006 - *Mindset: The New Psychology of Success*. In it, she presents compelling evidence from her own studies as well as those of other psychologists, that we each select one of two mindsets to govern our lives. The first, the fixed mindset, is an internal belief that our talents and abilities are fixed and unchanging - they are carved in stone - unchangeable and unmovable. As a result, we spend much of our lives trying to prove how good we are; how well we are living up to our "assigned role."

Those of us with a growth mindset, however, believe that our abilities can be improved with effort and practice. We work to improve ourselves - <u>not prove ourselves</u> - striving to overcome any handicaps or shortcomings and pushing ourselves into new areas ripe for exploration and discovery. The "Fosbury Flop" is a perfect example of a growth mindset - one athlete's realization that his true potential was unknown, but that it was possible to reach for it with some creative modifications and passionate determination. Dweck emphatically supports this notion when she writes, "People in a growth mindset don't just *seek* challenge, they thrive on it. The bigger the challenge, the more they stretch. And nowhere can it be seen more clearly than in the world of sports. You can just watch people stretch and grow."

Many politicians[36] embrace the fixed mindset - they boost, they bluster, they pontificate. They engage in a constant affirmation of not only how good they are, but also by downplaying the successes of others. Perhaps you know some "politicians" at work - people who are stuck in a personality that is as unmovable or unchangeable as the Rock of Gibraltar. "It's my way or the highway," they are often fond of saying. They spend large amounts of time trying to validate their "position": they have a large amount of native talent and everybody else doesn't! They need to establish and prove their superiority over all the "nobodies" in their lives. They are famous for standing their position - come hell or high water - and will not change for fear of appearing weak and indecisive.

---

36 "Politicians are people who, when they see light at the end of a tunnel, go out and buy some more tunnel." - John Quinton.

But, the fixed mindset is not exclusive to politicians or bosses who hold fast to the philosophy that "If it ain't broke, don't fix it." We often bump into people from all walks of life who embrace the fixed mindset as their way of dealing with an uncertain world or the inevitable challenges of everyday living. Perhaps you've met some of these people: A college student who gets a less that satisfactory grade on an assignment and considers herself a failure, a colleague at work who gives up early on a project because it's nothing but a never-ending series of frustrations, a child trying out for the local Little League baseball team who repeatedly strikes out and throws the bat away in disgust, or a friend who is afraid of trying something new simply because he's afraid of failing. These are the people who fervently believe that they only have a certain amount of talent, a certain amount of skill, and a certain amount of expertise and that they'd better hang on to those (limited) abilities rather than risking anything new or untried.

In her two decades of research with both children and adults, Dweck discovered that intelligence and talent are not necessarily immutably ingrained traits; rather they can be developed and expanded with effort. She writes:

> "For twenty years, my research has shown that the view you adopt for yourself profoundly affects the way you lead your life. It can determine whether you become the person you want to be and whether you accomplish the things you value. How does this happen? How can a simple belief have the power to transform your psychology and, as a result, your life?
>
> Believing that your qualities are carved in stone — the fixed mindset — creates an urgency to prove yourself over and over. If you have only a certain amount of intelligence, a certain personality, and a certain moral character — well, then you'd better prove that you have a healthy dose of them. It simply wouldn't do to look or feel deficient in these most basic characteristics.
>
> [...]

I've seen so many people with this one consuming goal of proving themselves — in the classroom, in their careers, and in their relationships. Every situation calls for a confirmation of their intelligence, personality, or character. Every situation is evaluated: Will I succeed or fail? Will I look smart or dumb? Will I be accepted or rejected? Will I feel like a winner or a loser? ...

There's another mindset in which these traits are not simply a hand you're dealt and have to live with, always trying to convince yourself and others that you have a royal flush when you're secretly worried it's a pair of tens. In this mindset, the hand you're dealt is just the starting point for development. This growth mindset is based on the belief that your basic qualities are things you can cultivate through your efforts. Although people may differ in every which way — in their initial talents and aptitudes, interests, or temperaments — everyone can change and grow through application and experience.

Do people with this mindset believe that anyone can be anything, that anyone with proper motivation or education can become Einstein or Beethoven? No, but they believe that a person's true potential is unknown (and unknowable); that it's impossible to foresee what can be accomplished with years of passion, toil, and training."

Maria Popova cements Dweck's research findings when she writes, "At the heart of what makes the 'growth mindset' so winsome is that it creates a passion for learning rather than a hunger for approval. Its hallmark is the conviction that human qualities like intelligence and creativity, and even relational capacities like love and friendship, can be cultivated through effort and deliberate practice. Not only are people with this mindset not discouraged by failure, but they don't actually see themselves as failing in those situations - they see themselves as learning."

Thus, it could be reasonably expected that people with a growth mindset would say something like, "I wonder if there's another way I could get over the high jump bar?" Those with a fixed mindset would be those content with exclaiming, "I'll just do what everyone else is doing!"

3.

One of the elements of the creative process is our ability to dislodge or remove absolutes from our mind. In other words, to mentally let go of the "status quo" and free our mind to examine things with fresh new eyes. I'll admit, that's sometimes difficult. We get used to doing things in certain ways, thinking about things in certain ways, and processing information in certain ways. We get into a "mental comfort zone" - it's reliable and it's predictable. We know what we should be getting and we're O.K. with that.

But, there are times when we need a change of thinking. This change, albeit temporary, is often satisfied by the plethora of published books on "How to be more creative in ten easy steps," and "You can change your life with these 1001 creativity strategies that will guarantee you exceptional and unconditional wealth, multiple appearances on national TV, and an endless supply of tropical drinks (with the requisite tiny umbrellas) on a Caribbean island of your choice." Are these books popular? Do they satisfy a basic need? As I write this, scores of brand new books on creativity are being published every year. So, the answer to those two questions must be 'Yes.'"

But, is it? Many of those tomes offer a predictable collection of admonitions such as "Always do more than is expected." "Change your mind, change your thinking," "Be your best self," and "Risk more, learn more." Unfortunately, those platitudes are isolated bits of advice; it's never made clear how they are connected or how they, collectively, change one's thinking. Without that integration, the suggestions all last for a few days and then we revert back to our usual (and very comfortable) ways of thinking. Dweck puts a decided exclamation mark on the "value" of these books when she writes, "Sure, people with the fixed mindset have read the books that say: Success is about being your best self, not about being better than others; failure is an opportunity, not a condemnation; effort is the key to success. But they can't put this into practice because their basic mindset— their belief in fixed traits— is telling them something entirely different: that success is about being more gifted than others, that failure does measure you, and that effort is for those who can't make it on talent."

Do mindsets affect our creativity? Absolutely!

Consider a poll conducted with more than 140 creativity researchers. When asked about the number one ingredient in creative achievement they all identified the perseverance and resilience generated by the growth mindset. Dweck writes:

> "When you enter a mindset, you enter a new world. In one world – the world of fixed traits – success is about proving you're smart or talented. Validating yourself. In the other – the world of changing qualities – it's about stretching yourself to learn something new. Developing yourself.
>
> In one world, failure is about having a setback. Getting a bad grade. Losing a tournament. Getting fired. Getting rejected. It means you're not smart or talented. In the other world, failure is about not growing. Not reaching for the things you value. It means you're not fulfilling your potential.
>
> In one world, effort is a bad thing. It, like failure, means you're not smart or talented. If you were, you wouldn't need effort. In the other world, effort is what makes you smart or talented."

In *What the Best College Students Do* author Ken Bain writes that the idea that intelligence is static - either you're born smart or your aren't - is simply not true. Creative, successful people have something in common, he discovered: they all believed that intelligence is expandable. People who believe they can "grow" their brainpower demonstrated more curiosity and open-mindedness and took more professional and intellectual risks, and as a result became very successful adults.

As Dweck would say, the growth mindset is focused more on the process than the outcome. So, too, is creativity. Creatives embraces the concept that looking for ideas is considerably more important and more productive than believing you already have the idea in the first place. In essence, creativity is a continual process of growth and discovery as opposed to a stationary and immovable belief that "I'm just not creative."

In truth, one of the major factors that differentiates creative people (those with a growth mindset) from less creative people (those with a fixed mindset) is that creative people give themselves a license to actively look for and thus, pay attention to, ideas of every size and shape. Even though they don't know where one of those ideas will lead, they know that even a small idea can lead to a big breakthrough... and they search for them. "I'm just not creatives," by contrast, prevent themselves from that search process because it's just too risky...because it's prone to potential failure. As a result, if you think you are creative, then you'll put yourself in situations where you can use your creativity, take a few risks, try some new approaches, and come up with new ideas.

On the other hand, the "I'm just not creatives" self-assign themselves to a permanent perception and encase themselves in a mental shroud that is not only "safe," but often impenetrable. If we believe ourselves to be uncreative, we avoid challenges, give up early, see effort as fruitless, condemn the ideas of others, ignore useful negative feedback, seek to accumulate lots of "gold stars," eschew failure as a learning tool, focus only on getting the "right answer," eliminate play from our lives, hold fast to myths...

...and forever embrace a fixed mindset.

4.

Here are two terms you don't often see in the same sentence: "funeral director" and "creative individual." Add in "passionate SCUBA diver" and you have a fairly accurate description of Ernie Heffner, the president and owner of Heffner Funeral Chapel and Crematory in York, Pennsylvania. Heffner has been in business for more than four decades and is known throughout the funeral industry as "an innovative leader."[37]

---

[37] In 2019 Heffner was presented with the Lasting Impact Award by The International Cemetery, Cremation and Funeral Association.

In a profession often perceived as conservative, staid, and traditional, Heffner breaks the mold with his keen attention to customer needs and his embrace of all the "little things" that make a difference in the services his firm offers. "There are too many people in end-of-life care that own a lifestyle, not a business," he states. "They're in it for the money. So, consequently, they're not paying close enough attention to their customers and their changing perceptions, desires, and wishes. And, then, as those customers change, and change in their selections, they don't understand why people moved away from them."

Here is the growth mindset in business terms.

As an example, Heffner notes that there has been a major change in society with regards to religious standards. "[The funeral] business was based on religious ceremony followed by burial. Yet, that reality has changed dramatically, simply because the second largest faith group in America now is the 'Nones' - that is, people with no religious affiliation. As a result, they find no comfort in a sermon. Thus, we need a ceremony that's relevant for them. Subsequent to the ceremony, burials are no longer meaningful for more than 50 percent of the population. Well, if families are choosing cremation and our business is based on religious ceremony and burial, there's a horrendous disconnect. So, if the providers are not creative, flexible, and paying attention to their customer base they are becoming nothing more than biohazardous waste haulers."

That Heffner keeps his finger on the ever evolving pulse of his clientele is clear via his voracious reading habit. He gets up early every morning to read an eclectic array of newspapers, assorted trade journals, biographies, and history books - all with equal fervor. For Heffner, creativity is as much about preparation and research as it is about actually going out and doing something different. For him, creativity is not simply the generation of new ideas; it also involves the establishment of a "seedbed" of thoughts, perceptions, and data to prepare himself for that discovery process. Heffner's view is that creativity doesn't spring from a vacuum; the mind has to be sufficiently prepared in advance.

His view is further accentuated by his desire to talk with people and listen to their views of the world around. He often cites a critical lesson he learned in his mid-twenties: "You will be the same person in five years as you are today - except for the people you meet and the books you read." Clearly, Heffner is an individual who welcomes and endorses the growth mindset as an essential element of his business model.

What is equally apparent is that Heffner is a master of noticing little things - items that create a satisfying experience for his clients. In Chapter 12, we examined several creativity myths that have crept into our consciousness. One of the most persistent is the belief that creativity is a large event - a massive mental undertaking only possible by great minds (and "great" individuals). The invention of the telephone, the eradication of yellow fever, manned exploration of the moon, the creation of a massive telecommunications empire such as MTV, or the invention of penicillin are significant creative events. The prevalent thinking, then, is that creative people are simply those who generate big ideas or big concepts.

Many "I'm just not creatives" stifle themselves because they think that creativity belongs exclusively to the Einsteins, Rembrandts, and Shakespeares of the world. To be sure, these are some of the super luminaries of the creative firmament; but, by in large, these people didn't get their big ideas right out of the blue. Most often the big ideas came from paying attention to the medium-sized ideas, playing with them, and turning them into big ideas. The same thing holds for most medium-size ideas. These came from small ideas their creators focused on - gradually massaging them into bigger things.

When we think of creativity as "Big" people generating "Big" ideas, we get trapped in a fixed mindset. We erect a psychological "Everest" - a personal mountain we may never scale. As a result, we frequently retreat into a safe, secure, and isolated environment ("I'm just not creative!"). On the other hand, when we shift our focus to little things, we give ourselves permission to collect some important "pebbles" along the creativity highway. Often, an accumulation of "pebbles" (notice the plural) turns into a great big idea that clarifies our work or answers our questions.

Heffner is known for paying attention to "pebbles." As a result, his funeral business is always evolving; always ready to meet the changing needs and expectations of his clientele. As he puts it, "Creativity is all about customer service and creativity is all about research. So, anytime

I'm walking into a hotel or restaurant, I'm on research. I'm always looking for things I don't have to ask for, the things that give me an 'Ah Ha' moment."

Heffner mentions a specific incident from years ago when he was visiting a funeral home in Arizona. His wife exited the Ladies Room and motioned to Heffner, "Come here." The rest room was empty, and his wife led him inside and pointed to several items on the counters. There were fingernail files, special mirrors so women could look at their hair from the back, bottles of hand lotion, a can of cling-free spray, a container of tampons, and even clear fingernail polish to repair stocking runs. "And my wife just gave me 'The Look' and I knew what she was getting at! And, so, we've stepped it up!"

Now, Heffner makes sure there's cling free spray in all the rest rooms of his funeral home. This is helpful for men who haven't worn a suit for some time, particularly in the winter. He also has a decided opinion about toilet paper. "I've long said that you can judge a funeral home - and you can judge a restaurant, too - as to the attitude towards their customers and their staff by checking out the toilet paper. Is it single-ply, course, or crummy toilet paper? The quality of toilet paper speaks volumes. It should be the finest toilet paper. And, when you walk in a rest room do you have to change the toilet paper? If it's a premium business, I think somebody should be checking that - making sure the toilet paper isn't an almost empty roll."

Heffner is quick to defend his "little things" philosophy. For him, it clearly separates his business from the competition. According to Heffner, if the business model is "same old, same old," then it is seldom responsive to customer needs and is more fixated on the comfort and convenience of management. An accumulation of little things can result in a "big thing" - a business that is innovative and dynamic. That said, Heffner is quick to point out, "I don't like to take credit for being innovative, so much as taking the time to look around and seeing what others are doing and how that might be applied to the families we're serving."

Heffner's philosophy echoes that of Sam Walton, the patriarch of the commercial goliath Walmart. Walton, too, kept his eyes open for the ideas and practices of competitors - not just in tiny Bentonville, Arkansas - but across the country. He traveled (by bus) to Minnesota to see the innovative checkout lines instituted in Ben Franklin variety stores. Most department stores (in the 1950s) had several checkout stations so that a customer had to pay for toiletries at one counter, dog food at another counter, and corn flakes at a third. Ben Franklin stores had a centralized checkout line that not only was more convenient for customers, but reduced the number of checkout clerks and minimized errors. Walton quickly adopted this new procedure for his stores - a practice clearly in place today.

Walton made it his mission to keep abreast of what his competitors were doing. He crisscrossed the country in search of both new ideas as well as ideas tried and true. In so doing, he advanced a more efficient distribution of merchandise (a signature element of Walmart "borrowed" from FedMart in California). The characteristic mix of displays and merchandise in Walmarts today was based on a business model in place at Kmarts in Michigan. Walton knew that creativity was not necessarily the creation of something original, but also the constant search for innovative ideas "test-driven" by others. He once said, "most everything I've done I've copied from someone else."

Sam Walton collected "pebbles" from across the country.

5.

It's important to note that the "Looking For Little Things" philosophy is a passionate embrace of the growth mindset - a way we have of breaking through the educational, cultural, and personal forces that frequently squelch our creative impulses. By contrast, those with a fixed mindset often miss all the small ideas. Frustrated by their inability to locate large ideas (often few and far between) they retreat into the "I'm just not creative" zone and, consequently, languish in a permanent state of staid practices and beliefs. As both Sam Walton and Ernie Heffner have proven over the years, actively looking for and gathering seemingly minor additions to their businesses has the potential for creating a grand and meaningful experience for their customers. Or, to use Heffner's words, "Innovation is simply doing more for clients - more than the competition might do. Whether that's because the competition is too lazy or simply unwilling to do more for the customers or because of specific service enhancements that never crossed the minds of that competitor."

Researchers have found that the transition from a "I'm just not Creative!" (fixed) mindset to a "I'm working on being more creative." (growth) mindset involves a continuous commitment to improvement. No matter the amount or intensity of the lifelong factors that have depressed our natural creative spirit, they can always be overcome.

With tiny steps.

This commitment - an ongoing series of small changes - may well be one of the most defining features of a creative life. Discovering a new way home from work that bypasses the usual 5:00 traffic jam, augmenting your favorite Sloppy Joe recipe with the addition of a teaspoon of chili powder, helping your child discover an interesting way of multiplying two-digit numbers, adding hosta plants to the perimeter of your garden to give it more green, and putting on a new pair of silver earrings to compliment an equally dazzling new outfit are all innovative "pebbles." True, they won't win any Nobel prizes or get your face on the cover of Time Magazine, but they are no less creative.

If you knew you could begin changing your mindset - like replacing a roll of crummy toilet paper - simply by shifting your focus from "Large Events" to "Small Events," would you do it?

28.
How to Sizzle: 104 - 110

104. Eliminate The "I'm Just Not Creative" Mindset.
Re-route your thinking from "I'm not creative" to "I have the potential to alter my mindset because I now know what's been holding me back." Society will continue to exert its influence on our brains - shaping us into a way of thinking that satisfies the status quo and maintains a societal equilibrium. In other words, it's easier to assign ourselves to the "uncreative" class; much more challenging to face the forces that negatively impacted our creative spirit as kids and overcome them. Challenging - yes; but certainly not impossible. Consider this quote from Arthur Koestler, "Creativity is the defeat of habit by originality."

105. Developing A Growth Mindset.

➤ Recognize that failing is part of the learning process; rather than the end of a project or challenge.
➤ Acknowledge, accept, and celebrate your imperfections. It's what makes you unique!
➤ Effort is much more important than talent. Reward your hard work, not your final product.
➤ Self-approval is much more important than approval from others. Working to gain the acclimation of others can produce a fixed mindset and inhibit a growth mindset.
➤ It's been said before - read lots of biographies. Learn from the successes and failures of others. How did

they solve their problems? How did they meet their
challenges?

➤ Take a risk; take a chance. Try new things just because...
just because they're new - not because they're safe.

➤ Don't aim for perfection; rather, aim for the learning
that's involved. Far better to be a constant learner than
one who rests on her/his laurels.

➤ Reflect: What is one new thing you learned today? If
you can't answer that query, then you have some work to
do.

➤ Learning shouldn't end with graduation or a diploma.
Learning is a constant lifelong process; not a means to
an end.

➤ If you are wrestling with a challenge or struggling with a
problem, tell yourself that you haven't quite mastered it
"yet." Perseverance is just as important as effort.

106. Shoot More. As famous hockey player Wayne Gretzky
once said, "You miss 100% of the shots you don't take." Instead of
looking for the single right answer, generate lots of answers. The more
ideas you produce the more opportunities you have to find an answer
that helps solve your problem. Don't focus on the one perfect shot,
take lots of shots. You'll increase your chances of scoring a goal. Or,
to paraphrase Thomas Edison, "Get lots and lots of ideas and then just
throw the bad ones away."

107. Practice Mindfulness. Take time each day to be
alone. Get away from the hustle and bustle of everyday living (and
everyday habits). Mindfulness is active, open attention on the present.
It is a quiet time that allows us to focus, non-judgmentally, on what we
are thinking, feeling, and doing. It is a time for both contemplation
and reflection. It is also an opportunity to consider where we are and
where we might want to be. Psychological research also demonstrates
that it can actually remodel the physical structure of your brain.

108. Meditation. Research from Erasmus University in
Rotterdam, Netherlands has found that just 10 minutes of meditation

a day can positively increase your creative powers. This held true even for participants who had never had any formal meditation training. The simple act of "taking time off" is sufficient to calm your mind and offer opportunity for you to create and innovate. The key is to make meditation a regular part of your daily activities - not something you do when it's convenient or when you can't find anything else to do. Meditation's benefits lie in its regularity - a commitment to find a quiet place and devote 15-30 minutes to letting your thoughts flow. No cell phones, no texts, no emails, no Facebook, no Spotify, no tweets, no Instagram, no nothing. The time of day is not particularly important. I find early afternoon works best for me - before I go out for my daily walk. You may discover meditation time in the early morning, after the kids are down for the night, right after breakfast, or as soon as you get home from work. Pick a time and place that works for your schedule. Tell the family that this is "Me Time" and that they need to leave you alone for a designated time. Make it a regular part of your daily routine and you'll notice some significant changes taking place.

109. Mental Imagery. In 1986, I wrote an article for a professional journal about a teaching concept known as mental imagery. By definition, mental imagery is the creation of pictures in one's mind prior to beginning a cognitive task such as reading. Research at the time showed that forming mental images produces higher levels of comprehension for students of all ability levels. Subsequent research and professional experience has shown a direct relationship between the regular practice of mental imagery and higher levels of creative thinking. Mental imagery helped Albert Einstein generate the general theory of relativity: Does a person who falls freely in an enclosed chamber feel his own weight? He also used it to visualize lightning strikes, moving trains, accelerating elevators, and falling painters. Leonardo da Vinci also used it when he doodled various thought experiments in his notebooks - sketching a random assortment of engineering designs formulated in his mind. Simply put, mental imagery has been proven to energize our "creativity quotient" and readies us to address various mental challenges.

One way you can engage in mental imagery is to find a comfortable and quiet place to sit, close your eyes, and imagine yourself doing creative things, being more creative, or being congratulated for developing a creative solution for a perplexing problem at work. Create mind pictures of yourself in any number of situations - solving problems, finding solutions, discovering innovative way of doing familiar tasks, developing a new product, or generating a unique and distinctive invention. Make this a regular element of any problem-solving activity - something done both before and during any new project - and you just might see some of those proverbial "light bulbs" flashing over your head.

110. Looking For Little Things. We often have this mistaken idea that a creative idea is a big idea. The invention of manned flight, the cure for polio, the creation of the World Wide Web, and the development of a vaccine for COVID-19. True, those are big creative concepts; but true creativity is founded on a principle of little discoveries...the small treasures we find when we envision creativity as "looking for the small, not just the big." Discovering a synonym for "said" in the novel we're writing. Mixing three colors together for the sunset in a landscape painting we're working on. Purchasing a new tie, not because it's fashionable, but because it's "cool." Discovering that a paper clip can be used to repair a broken toy. Looking for little acts of creativity is just as significant (if not more so) than the big creative projects. Lots of little creative acts gets us in the habit of making creativity a normal and natural part of our daily lives, rather than just an event that happens on rare occasions.

Stephen Guise in his book *Mini Habits: Smaller Habits, Bigger Results* makes a case for the power of small habits, rather than our over-reliance on large, wieldy, and often weighty big habits (How many of your New Year's resolutions are you still embracing?). He makes a valid point when he says, "Big intensions are worthless if they don't bring results." For example, we may make a resolution to lose 50 pounds this year, but we often find ourselves giving up (sooner, rather than later) because the perceived goal was much too large. Guise emphatically states that most people "have big ambitions, but overestimate their ability to make themselves do what it takes to change."

Early in the book (p. 11) he makes two clear and penetrating points: "1) Doing a little bit is infinitely bigger and better than doing nothing, and 2) doing a little bit every day has a greater impact than doing a lot on one day." Now, let's put that in terms of our personal creativity: 1) Looking for one little piece of creativity is better than doing nothing at all, and 2) looking for a little (creative) thing every day is much more effective and practical than trying to generate a very large idea every so often. The point is clear - a determination to make creativity a regular and normal part of our daily activities prepares our mind to be ready for those times when we need a REALLY LARGE (AND/OR PROFITABLE) IDEA in our work or our everyday lives. The same holds true for our children. When we offer them opportunities to make creativity a regular part of their development and education, we send a powerful signal that creativity doesn't just happen every so often, but can be a normal (even daily) part of our intellectual functioning.

Best of all, a tiny creative act every day puts us in the growth mindset and begins to shatter all those unseen forces that have influenced our thinking for so long. We move away from the fixed mindset and into new realms of creative expression. Like the vitamin, we can all profit from <u>one a day</u>.

Conclusion: Reactive or Proactive?

*The world needs dreamers and the
world needs doers.
But, above all, the world needs
dreamers who do.*
- Sarah Ban Breathnach

1.

Several years ago, a businessman stayed at a well-known hotel in Sarasota, Florida. In a hurry to get to the airport for his return flight home, he inadvertently left his laptop charger in his hotel room. Realizing his error, he planned to call the hotel soon after he returned to his office the next day.

I'm sure that if you spend considerable time "on the road," you have, on occasion, left important items (cell phone, business documents, car keys, a shoe, teddy bear) behind in your hotel room. It's a most common occurrence, so much so that many hotels have a dedicated location to store any found items recovered by Housekeeping or other members of the staff. In some cases, items are designated as "Valuable," "Non-Valuable," or "Perishable" to denote their level of importance.

The hotel staff in Florida, when it discovered the wayward charger, had one of two choices: 1) They could place the item in a designated cardboard box in the back of the manager's office and wait until the customer contacted them for instructions on how to return the item (The hotel would, of course, add on "necessary" fees for the handling and/or the shipping of the item.). Or, 2) the hotel could do something proactive to ensure that the customer would be reunited with his charger in the shortest amount of time and with the least amount of inconvenience.

The hotel chose the latter.

The next day, the customer received an overnight package containing his charger. Also included was a note from an employee in "Loss Prevention." The note read: "Mr. D_____, I wanted to make sure we got this to you right away. I am sure you need it, and, just in case, I sent you an extra charger for your laptop."

Guess which hotel that customer now uses exclusively?

2.

We have always embraced creativity...indeed, celebrated creativity. We have cheered those who have advanced scientific frontiers, those who have conquered previously unconquerable diseases, and those who have improved society through their actions and deeds. We've also applauded a unique flower arrangement at our child's wedding, an exquisite version of a classic soup prepared by a neighbor, or a dynamic new logo for the company letterhead sketched by an administrative assistant. From the earliest reaches of recorded history, we have celebrated those among us who have forged new trails and established new outlooks that have enlightened, improved, and enabled us to move in new directions or solved unique challenges. It is a universal mantra; part of our *raison d'etre*.

That creativity has had, and will continue to have, a profound effect on the economic, social, and personal fabric of all citizens, irrespective of country, is a certainty. However, past practices are no guarantee that current challenges will be met with the same level of "solvability." Or, as Roger von Oech puts it, "When things change and new information comes into existence, it is no longer possible to solve current problems with yesterday's solutions. [People] can either bemoan the fact that things aren't as easy as they used to be, or they can use their creative abilities to find new answers, new solutions, and new ideas."

Although we have embraced creativity as both a right and an obligation, we have also ingrained it with a certain note of admiration, if not adulation. We applaud the accomplishments of selected women and men - elevating them to often mythological positions in history texts and erecting mental statues of them as paragons of high intelligence and free spirit. We pen tens of thousands of books on how to emulate these creative luminaries - tomes filled with a panoply of techniques and strategies destined to make our lives more productive, more satisfying, and more complete. And, we have highlighted creativity as a psychological temple available to but a few.

Nevertheless, the overriding consensus of most psychologists is that we all have creative capacities. We come into this world with an innate curiosity about how things work (or don't). We want to know more, we want to examine a problem and seek an answer. It is part of the human psyche to know what is around the corner or just over the next hill. So, too, is creativity an essential element and natural component of how we interact with the world. Solving problems is part of our evolutionary heritage. As Shelley Carson, a Harvard researcher states, "We are all in possession of a fantastic creativity machine - our human brain. In fact, creativity is our survival tool. If it wasn't for creativity, we wouldn't be here. Think of all the different ways our ingenuity has extended and enriched our lives on this planet." Whether we're a Paleolithic human attempting to capture a beefy mammoth or a modern day office worker arranging a desk to increase our personal productivity, creativity has always been part of our attempt to address challenges of every size, shape, and dimension.

You may look at the factors and events profiled throughout this book and assume that there has been an insurmountable mountain of negative events acting on your life that make it nearly impossible for you to climb out of a very deep hole. Suffice it to say, most of us have experienced an array of personal events that have annulled our creative instincts. However, to assume that this mass of negative experiences will have a lasting and permanent effect on our creative possibilities is to cave in to one of the most persistent of creativity myths: Once you have become "noncreative", there is little to no chance of becoming "re-creative" again.

Such a feeling is generated in part because of all the times when we needed to be creative and couldn't drum up a creative idea to save our souls. We've wrestled with ideas only to draw a blank mind; we've tried to generate an original concept only to find that our brain is sometimes our enemy; and we've looked at a challenge face to face only to find that the problem was much bigger than our ability to solve it. These are the times when we've cried out, "But, I'm just not creative!" We've self-assigned ourselves into that group of people discussed throughout this book - a group that expands exponentially with the challenges of an increasingly more complex society along with the frustrations of mastering a world around us moving at light speed and in diverse directions.

Ultimately it comes down to a question of whether we are content to accept a reactive position ("I've been affected by a ton of negative experiences and will never be able to escape.") or engage in a proactive attitude ("Sure, I've been pummeled by many factors in my life, but let's see what I can do to overcome them."). A particular employee at a hotel in Florida decided on a proactive stance - placing a customer's needs before the ease of tossing a misplaced item in a cardboard box to be subsequently forgotten and/or discarded. That single creative act ensured a customer's loyalty to the hotel brand and its way of doing business. Instead of accepting, "Well, let's do it like it's always been done," that employee *made* something happen. His proactivity made a difference; it made a change.

It was a small act of creativity; but one with large implications.

Unsurprisingly, we often default to beliefs, practices, and perceptions that negate or diminish our creative spirit. We maintain a myth that creative ideas spring from a bolt of lightning with no forewarning or preparation. We become the "victims" of a questioning system that while easy to implement in our classrooms, has serious ramifications for our creative future. We seldom take occupational chances because of an innate fear of failure...because failure may mean have economic loss or termination. We continually participate in brainstorming sessions in a search for "the ultimate solution" only to discover that we've wasted a considerable amount of time and achieved little progress.

These influences may all be invisible, but they are also substantial. They are constantly below the surface - working against us as we seek to address issues and concerns that we often discover to be uncomfortable or frustrating.

Throughout this book we have examined those processes and practices - some intentional, some not - that have deeply affected each of our lives. We now know what has been holding us back; what has prevented us from our natural creative aspirations in our journey from childhood to a contributing member of society. We now have critical information - a personal diagnosis - that can provide us with the necessary tools to change.

Just as important, this book has shared over one hundred different ways where we can creatively "sizzle." We've examined strategies that can provide our children with the skills and talents to use their natural sense of creativity at home and throughout their growth years. We've looked at techniques that emphasize the creative side of education - in both public and private schools as well as corporate retreats and professional conferences. We've introduced various ways of reinforcing a creative work environment so that innovation takes precedence over the "same old, same old" ways of doing business. And, we've seen how easy-to-implement changes in our personal thinking can have a major impact on how we embrace creativity as a natural element of our everyday lives.

Now armed with all that information, what will you do? Will you remain in a fixed mindset or embrace a growth (or creatively-oriented) mindset? Will you toss a laptop charger into a cardboard box or FedEx it to its owner with a personal note?

Epilogue:
Hurting Your Head

Like professors at most colleges and universities, I was required to administer end-of-course evaluations every semester. Those evaluations were typically done during the last two weeks week of a semester, long before final grades were issued. Every college course I taught was evaluated by students using one of several different instruments. Some instruments were numerical in nature ("On a scale of 1 [low] to 10 [high] how would you rate the instructor's competence to teach this course.") and some were open-ended ("Using the space below explain how this course was important [or not] to your field of study.").

I always preferred the open-ended evaluation forms believing that they gave me much more information about how well I taught, how well students learned, and how a course might be improved in the future. Students were not restricted to the topics on the form (as with a numerical rating system), rather they had opportunities to inject their feelings, impressions, likes and dislikes (anonymously, of course) without any restrictions on length or topic.

Over the years, my courses were frequently designated by students as "creatively intense," "worked my butt off," "most certainly high-level," "passionately engaging," "challenging...yeah, definitely challenging," and "incredibly thought-provoking." However, at the conclusion of one course a few semesters ago, one individual took it to the extreme when she or he penned the following review:

*"He made me think so much that I actually
had a headache at the end of every class!"* [38]

I certainly hope that by this point in the book your head "hurts," too (but, in a most positive way!). I hope your eyes have been opened to some of the reasons why your innate creativity has diminished over the years. I also hope you've seen new ways of overcoming those creative "depressants" with a vast array of innovative habits, dynamic strategies, and powerful suggestions for a more productive life. If you would like to continue the journey, I invite you to log on to my website for additional insights and possibilities. That site is refreshed every so often and will offer worksheets, challenges, exercises, and fresh ideas you can use at home and at work to "punch up" your C.Q. (Creativity Quotient). I look forward to your visit!

www.anthonydfredericks.com

---

38 Dear Readers: I am so enamored of that statement that I'm seriously considering it as my epitaph.

Acknowledgments ||||

I'm a member of that class of people who enjoy reading the Acknowledgments section of the books I buy. In doing so, I discover unique insights into the personality of the author, how expansive or thorough her background research is, and some of the unique places she may have traveled, and people she met along the way - particularly during an often lengthy writing process. Apparently, in reading these mentions; you, too, are also a member of that distinguished group.

For me, the citations in this sector give credence to the fact that most books "take a village to write." It verifies that books are ultimately dependent on the creative insights of many people - friends, colleagues, associates, family, and a whole lot of strangers - who ensure that the author is sharing information that is relevant and informative (and, hopefully, entertaining), instead of promoting a mishmash of philosophical diversions that meander across the intellectual universe like pub-crawling crowds of inebriated undergraduates on Spring Break.

In this book's long journey from a nascent idea lodged in the farthest reaches of my brain to the bound product you now hold in your hands, I was influenced by a glorious assembly of supporters (or conspirators) who contributed immeasurable advice, research, guidance, inspiration, insights, and hand-holding that prevented me from embarrassing myself...or you from sliding it back on the bookshelf and moving on to the "Romance" or "International Travel" sections of your local bookstore.

I am particularly indebted to the entire team at Blue River Press who championed this venture from the outset and continually gave both counsel and encouragement every step of the way. Tom, Adriane, Thomas, Ginger, and Dani all deserve a rousing cheer for their work on my behalf. They are professionals of the highest order and truly one of the most "author friendly" crews to be found anywhere in the world of publishing.

My fellow band of R.O.M.E.O.s (Retired Old Men Eating Out) - Pete Piepmeier, Bob Lindsay, and Mike McGough - each month, over heaping plates of home fries and looming stacks of pancakes at Mary Jane's Restaurant, offered equally prodigious quantities of support and insight that sharpened my focus and broadened my perspectives. I am forever indebted for their astute counsel and rampant creativity. They are friends and colleagues of the highest order.

Former associates Dave Griesler and Josh DeSantis opened up their classrooms and allowed me to survey their undergraduate students with their usual brand of collegial generosity. As usual, they ignited many creative sparks. I am incredibly appreciative for the contributions of Ernie Heffner. As you noted, Ernie is one of the most amazing businesspeople around. He clearly knows what a creative enterprise is all about, and he willingly and enthusiastically shares his insights with any and all who seek to infuse their own professional ventures with equal measures of spirit, inventiveness, and a fervent embrace of customer service. He is truly one of a kind!

No thank-you would seem adequate for all the support I've received from Jack and Linda Sommer. That this book has been dedicated to them is a testament to their boundless friendship, constant respect, and joyous camaraderie. They truly deserve a standing ovation!

During the writing of this book, our cat of eighteen years (Tubby) passed away. Tubby was my constant writing companion and steadfast supporter. Each morning, he curled up under my computer table where I would talk to him about misplaced synonyms, dangling modifiers, and run-on sentences; ask him for advice about the utility of a research article; or complain to him about a disjointed paragraph. He took it all in stride with his usual air of feline indifference (and persistent snoring). He instinctively knew what his job was and he accepted his responsibilities without complaint or protest. I miss him.

Special thanks go out to my sisters Chris and Holly, whose support is always celebrated and cheered. A very "high five" to all my former students at York College who frequently plied me with tough questions, shared personal anecdotes, and discussed their own creativity demons during our many in-class discussions. A particular note of appreciation to my former teachers at the Orme School in Mayer, AZ who opened my eyes to the possibilities of a creative lifestyle and the magic of innovative thinking. Thanks, also, to the Class of '65 for their 55+ years of fellowship, friendship, and camaraderie.

A celebratory ovation is due Greenwell Farms of Kealakekua, Hawaii who produce the finest coffee to be found anywhere! Their Macadamia Nut flavored 100% Kona coffee sustained me and my creative intentions through many long mornings of writing and equally long afternoons of editing during the three years of this most incredible journey. Trust me when I tell you that their coffee will instill all sorts of creative inspirations in your own work - it is, most assuredly, a treat for both taste buds and mind.

My children, Rebecca (professional artist) and Jonathan (landscape architect), constantly amaze me with their creative interpretations and innovative ideas. Each of their respective endeavors resonate with imagination and flair - reminding me that creativity can be nurtured and promoted in a variety of ways, particularly when the growth mindset is embraced as the *modus operandi* of one's personal and professional life. They were a constant inspiration for this book - proving that creativity is always a process and seldom a product. That their children (Isabelle, Amelia, Lara) will be the ultimate beneficiaries of their parents' creative perspectives is a reality I will long cherish.

This book would never had been were it not for the love and encouragement of my wife, Phyllis. She celebrated when the book proposal was accepted, she cheered when I announced the final selection for a title, she listened patiently as I described progress on a particular chapter and then gently told me that I had completely lost my way (as well as my mind), she held my hand when an idea I had been working on for months literally disintegrated in front of me, she soothed my aching muscles when I hunched over a particular section for hours on end overloading both my brain and my hard drive, and she inspired me to create a tome that had equal measures of philosophy and passion, anecdotes and research, and desire and intrigue. As a professional (and celebrated) artist, she knows creativity first-hand. Her insights and love are part of every sentence, thought, and concept. She is my creative muse.

Notes

1. Creativity Blues

Article in the Harvard Business Review: Jeff Dyers, Hal Gregersen, and Clayton M. Christensen. "Crush the 'I'm Not Creative' Barrier." *Harvard Business Review* (May 7, 2012). https://hbr.org/2012/05/crush-the-im-not-creative-barr.

This conclusion is supported by another study: For the quintessential book on creativity strategies you can't do much better than Roger von Oech, *A Whack on the Side of the Head*. (New York: Grand Central Publishing, 2008). It's a book everyone should read at least once a year.

Hidden forces firmly entrenched: For a most fascinating journey inside creative minds you need to check out Scott Barry Kaufman & Carolyn Gregoire. *Wired to Create: Unraveling the Mysteries of the Creative Mind*. (New York: Penguin Random House, 2015).

2. Invisible Influences

2.5 million years ago the cranial capacity: Yuval Noah Harari. *Sapiens: A Brief History of Humankind* (New York: Harper, 2015). This book has been translated into more than fifty languages and has sold over ten million copies worldwide. Read it and you'll understand why.

In his seminal book: Edward O. Wilson. *The Origins of Creativity*. (New York: W.W. Norton, 2017).

Creativity is the greatest gift: Ken Robinson. *Out of Our Minds: Learning to be Creative*. (New York: Wiley, 2011). If there was a "King of Creativity," then Robinson would be the one. Read this book and see his TED talk ("Do Schools Kill Creativity?") - you'll be all the better for it.

Torrance Tests of Creative Thinking: Paul Torrance. *Torrance Tests of Creative Thinking*. (Bentenville, IL: Scholastic Testing Services, 2018).

272,000 scores of both children and adults: Kyung Hee Kim. *The Creativity Challenge: How We Can Recapture American Innovation*. (Amherst, NY: Prometheus Books, 2016).

John Barrel, an educator in New Jersey: cited in Anthony D. Fredericks, *The Teacher's Handbook: Strategies for Success* (Lanham, MD: Rowman & Littlefield, 2010).

In 2012, the research firm Strategy One: cited in (no author), *Study Reveals Global Creativity Gap* (San Jose, CA: Adobe Systems, April 23, 2012) (https://www.adobe.com/aboutadobe/pressroom/pressreleases/201204/042312AdobeGlobalCreativityStudy.html).

Ken Robinson puts it this way: Ken Robinson. *Out of Our Minds: Learning to be Creative*. (New York: Wiley, 2011).

Conclusions drawn from several research studies: Michael A. Rober o. *U th ck.ng Creativity: How to Solve Any Problem and Make the Best Decisions by Shifting Crea ivi N 'i dis ts.* (New York, Wiley: 2019). Here's a book that will open your eyes and open your mi d :o o n of the most egregious mistakes made in corporate America. Be forewarned!

In the past 60 years something strange has happened: Derek Thompso . 'G o k X and the Science of Radical Creativity", *The Atlantic*, November 2017 (https://www.the tl in ic. com/magazine/archive/2017/11/x-google-moonshot-factory/540648/).

In 2011 GE interviewed a thousand: (no author) *GE Global Innovation Barometer 2011: An Overview on Messaging, Data and Amplification* (Boston: General Electric, 2011). (http://files. gereports.com/wp-content/uploads/2011/01/GIB-results.pdf).

U.S. employers rate creativity/innovation among the top five: The Conference Board staff. "Ready to Innovate: Key Findings." *The Conference Board*, 2008 (https://www.americans-forthearts.org/sites/default/files/ReadyToInnovate_KeyFindings_0.pdf).

Unfortunately, our society increasingly: Scott Barry Kaufman & Carolyn Gregoire. *Wired to Create: Unraveling the Mysteries of the Creative Mind.* (New York: Penguin Random House, 2015).

Teachers [regard creativity] as dangerous: Rod Junkins. *The Art of Creative Thinking: 89 Ways to See Things Differently.* (New York: Perigree, 2016). This is a most delightful collection of everyday practices that will re-energize and re-invigorate your creative impulses.

Our schools may be discouraging: Michael A. Roberto. *Unlocking Creativity: How to Solve Any Problem and Make the Best Decisions by Shifting Creative Mindsets.* (New York, Wiley: 2019).

84 percent of executives say "innovation is extremely or very important: McKinsey and Company staff. "Innovation and commercialization, 2010: McKinsey Global Survey results." *McKinsey and Company*, 2010 (https://www. mckinsey.com/business-functions/strategy-and-corporate-finance/our-insights/ innovation-and-commercialization-2010-mckinsey-global-survey-results?reload).

Researchers at the Cornell Food and Brand Lab: Aviva Musicus, Aner Tai, Brian Wansink. "Eyes in the Aisle: Why is Cap'n Crunch Looking Down at my Child?" (Cornell, NY: Cornell Food and Brand Lab, April 2, 2014). (https://journals.sagepub.com/doi/10.1177/0013916514528793).

Researcher George Land administered: George Land & Beth Jarman. *Breaking Point and Beyond: Mastering the Future Today.* (San Francisco, CA: Harper Business, 1993).

3. Parental Persuasion

Isidor Issac Rabi: Isidor Isaac Rabi – Biographical. *NobelPrize.org*. Nobel Media AB 2019. Fri. 5 Apr 2019. (https://www.nobelprize.org/prizes/physics/1944/rabi/biographical).

There is a strong message in our society: Carol D. Dweck. *Mindset: The New Psychology of Success.* (New York: Random House, 2006). Run, don't walk, and get a copy of this book. Put it at the top of your reading list and pay attention to her arguments. You will be changed!

Here are some of the things parents sometimes say to their children: The comments here came from a variety of resources including conversations with friends and colleagues, my own "boo-boos" as a parent, and a wealth of articles in various parent magazines and online sites. If interested in additional parental comments, the following offer an incredible variety: Rachel Lynette. "8 Ways That Could Crush Creative Thinking in Children" *Minds-in Bloom* (https://minds-in-bloom.

com/8-ways-to-destroy-creative-thinking-in/), Peter Gray. "As Children's Freedom Has Declined, So Has Their Creativity" *Psychology Today* (https://www.psychologytoday.com/us/blog/freedom-learn/201209/children-s-freedom-has-declined-so-has-their-creativity), Sarah Crow. "40 Things You Should Never say to Your Kid". *Best Life on Line* (https://bestlifeonline.com/phrases-no-parent-should-use/), Paula Spencer. "Positive Reinforcement: 9 Things You Shouldn't Say to Your Child" *Parenting* (https://www.parenting.com/child/things-you-I-say-to-your-child/), David Marquet. "5 Things Good Parents Never Say to Their Children", *Forbes* (https://www.forbes.com/sites/davidmarquet/2017/02/25/5-things-good-parents-never-say-to-their-children/#343ff-3304beb), (no author) "9 Things Parents Should Never Say to Their Children", *All Pro Dad* (https://www.allprodad.com/9-things-parents-should-never-say-to-their-children/).

Assigning labels to children: Pam Nicholson. "Freeing Your Children from Disabling Labels." *Center for Parenting Education* (no date). (https://centerforparentingeducation.org/library-of-articles/self-esteem/freeing-your-children-from-disabling-labels/).

Creativity can't thrive in an atmosphere: Thomas Armstrong. "The Natural Genius of Children." *American Institute for Learning and Human Development*. No date (http://www.institute4learning.com/resources/articles/the-natural-genius-of-children/).

Oftentimes we put verbal or psychological barriers: Some of these ideas emanated from two articles: Sara Langer. "Raising a Creative Child" Mother Magazine (https://www.mothermag.com/raising-a-creative-child/) - an overview of some penetrating research from various magazines and books, and Jennifer King Lindley. "10 Secrets to Raising Creative Kids" Parents (https://www.parents.com/parenting/better-parenting/advice/secrets-to-raising-creative-kids/).

In 1987 a group of researchers in California: D.M. Harrington, J.H. Block, & J. Block, 1987. "Testing aspects of Carl Rogers's theory of creative environments: Child-rearing antecedents of creative potential in your adolescents." *Journal of Personality and Social Psychology* 52, 851-856.

Homes that nurture creative children: Teresa M. Amabile. *Growing up Creative: Nurturing a Lifetime of Creativity* (Amherst, MA: C.E.F. Press, 1989).

Mihaly Csikszentmihalyi, a distinguished and respected psychologist: Mihaly Csikszentmihalyi. *The Systems Model of Creativity* (New York: Springer, 2015).

Additional research conducted in 2012: Angie L. Miller, Amber D. Lambert, Kristie L. Speirs Neumeister. "Parenting Style, Perfectionism, and Creativity in High-Ability and High-Achieving Young Adults." *Journal for the Education of the Gifted*, Vol. 35, No. 4 (December 2012).

According to at least one children's counselor: Kathryn J. Kvols. *Redirecting Children's Behavior* (Seattle, WA: Parenting Press, 1998).

5. Creative Endeavors

This is elastic thinking: Leonard Mlodinow. *Elastic: Flexible Thinking in a Time of Change*. (New York: Pantheon Books, 2018).

In one classic study, researchers divided ninety preschool children: Dorothy G. Singer, Roberta Michnick Golinkoff, and Kathy Hirsh-Pasek. *Play = Learning: How Play Motivates and Enhances Children's Cognitive and Social-Emotional Growth* (Oxford: Oxford University Press, 2006).

Creative thinking has been validated by other researchers: Anthony D. Pellegrini,

Danielle Dupuis and Peter K. Smith. "Play in Evolution and Development." *Developmental Review*, Vol. 27, No. 2, pps 261-276 (June 2007).

The American Academy of Pediatrics: Michael Yogman, Andrew Garner, Jeffrey Hutchinson, Kathy Hirsh-Pasel, and Roberta Michnick Golinkoff (Committee on Psychosocial Aspects of Child and Family Health, Council on Communications and Media). "The Power of Play: A Pediatric Role in Enhancing Development in Young Children." *Pediatrics*. Vol. 142, No. 3 (September 2018).

There is convincing evidence that a play-deprived childhood: Melinda Wenner Moyer, "The Serious Need for Play" in *The Mad Science of Creativity - Scientific American Mind* (Spring 2017), 27, no. 1: 78-85.

According to psychologist Eric Klinger: Eric Klinger as quoted in Josie Glausiusz. "Living in an Imaginary World" in *The Mad Science of Creativity - Scientific American Mind* (Spring 2017), 27, no. 1: 70-77.

In one study, researchers asked 122 students: Benjamin W. Mooneyham and Jonathan W. Schooler. "The Costs and Benefits of Mind-Wandering: A Review." *Canadian Journal of Experimental Psychology*, 67, no. 1, 11-18.

Another study, this from the Georgia Institute of Technology: Georgia Institute of Technology. "Functional Connectivity Within and Between Intrinsic Brain Networks Correlates with Trait Mind Wandering." *Neuropsychologia*, Vol. 7, No. 6, pps 140-153, (August 2017).

A classic children's book: Judith Viorst. *Alexander and the Terrible, Horrible, No Good, Very Bad Day* (New York, Atheneum, 1972). Ever have "one of those days?" If so, you'll enjoy this book yourself as much as you will enjoy sharing it with kids.

According to at least one expert: Valeriya Metla. "School Art Programs: Should They Be Saved?" *Law Street Media* (May 14, 2015) (https://lawstreetmedia.com/issues/education/cutting-art-programs-schools-solution-part-problem/).

The multiple advantages of arts education has been cited by numerous researchers: (no author) "10 Salient Studies on the Arts in Education" Center for Online Education (no date). Accessed on June 25, 2019. (https://www.onlinecolleges.net/10-salient-studies-on-the-arts-in-education/).

In a novel experiment: Jill Suttie. "How Music Helps Us Be More Creative" *Greater Good Magazine* (November 17, 2017) (https://greatergood.berkeley.edu/article/item/how_music_helps_us_be_more_creative).

Other studies have reported similar findings relative to arts education: Valeriya Metla. "School Art Programs: Should They Be Saved?" *Law Street Media* (May 14, 2015) (https://lawstreetmedia.com/issues/education/cutting-art-programs-schools-solution-part-problem/) and (no author) "10 Salient Studies on the Arts in Education" Center for Online Education (no date). Accessed on June 25, 2019. (https://www.onlinecolleges.net/10-salient-studies-on-the-arts-in-education/).

Public investment in K-12 schools has declined dramatically: Michael Leachman, Kathleen Masterson and Eric Figueroa. "A Punishing Decade for School Funding." *Center on Budget and Policy Priorities* (November 29, 2017) (https://www.cbpp.org/research/state-budget-and-tax/a-punishing-decade-for-school-funding).

According to some recent data: (no author). "Hispanics and Arts Education" White House Initiative on Educational Excellence for Hispanics. (no date) (https://sites.ed.gov/hispanic-initiative/files/2015/03/Hispanics-and-Arts-Education-Factsheet-Final-121814.pdf).

A recent survey by the National Endowment for the Arts (NEA): cited in (no author).

"Hispanics and Arts Education" White House Initiative on Educational Excellence for Hispanics. (no date) (https://sites.ed.gov/hispanic-initiative/files/2015/03/Hispanics-and-Arts-Education-Fact-sheet-Final-121814.pdf).

The consensus of researchers is that the reduction: (no author) "Ready to Innovate: Are Educators and Executives Aligned on the Creative Readiness of the U.S. Workforce?" *The Conference Board*, Research Report R-1424-08-RR.

A study by Darya L. Zabelina and Michael D. Robinson: Darya L. Zabelina and Michael D. Robinson, "Child's Play: Facilitating the Originality of Creative Output by a Priming Manipulation," *Psychology of Aesthetics, Creativity, and the Arts* 4, No. 1 (2010): 57-65.

A recent study in England - commissioned by the National Trust: cited in Rebecca Kennedy. "Children spend half the time playing outside in comparison to their parents" (January 15, 2018) (https://www.childinthecity.org/2018/01/15/children-spend-half-the-time-playing-outside-in-comparison-to-their-parents/?gdpr=accept).

Or, consider this quote from Albert Einstein: Walter Isaacson. *Einstein: His Life and Universe*. (New York: Simon & Schuster, 2007).

According to researchers at the University of California, Santa Barbara: Claire Zedeelius. "Daydreaming Might Make You More Creative - But It Depends on What You Daydream About," *Behavioralscientist.org* (November 2, 2020). (https://behavioralscientist.org/daydreaming-might-make-you-more-creative-but-it-depends-on-what-you-daydream-about/)

7. Images: Natural and Artificial

Remote Associates Test: S. A. Mednick and M. T. Mednick. Examiner's manual: Remote Associates Test. (Boston: Houghton Mifflin, 1967). [NOTE: an online version of the R.A.T. can be accessed at https://www.remote-associates-test.com/.].

In 2012 a fascinating study was conducted with the RAT: Ruth Ann Atchley, David Strayer, and Paul Atchley. "Creativity in the Wild: Improving Creative Reasoning through Immersion in Natural Settings." PloS ONE 7(12):e51474 (2012). (https://doi.org/10.1371/journal.pone.0051474).

Robin Moore, an expert in the design: Robin Moore and Herb H. Wong, *Natural Learning: Creating Environments for Rediscovering Nature's Way of Thinking* (Berkeley, CA: MIG Communications, 1997).

Consider our early human ancestors: Yuval Noah Harari. *Sapiens: A Brief History of Humankind* (New York: Harper, 2015).
Researchers in the United States, Sweden, Canada, and Australia: Karen Malone and Paul; J. Tranter, "School Grounds as Sites for Learning: Making the Most of Environmental Opportunities," *Environmental Education Research*, 9, No. 3 (2003): 283-303.

A series of qualitative interviews with Danish professionals: Trine Plambech and Cecil C. Konijnendijk van den Bosch. "The Impact of Nature on Creativity - A Study Among Danish Creative Professionals," *Urban Forestry & Urban Greening*, 14, no. 2, (2015): 255-263.

Nature is the great visible engine of creativity: Terrance McKenna as quoted in "Opening the Doors of Creativity." *Ask TMK* (October 20, 1990) (https://www.asktmk.com/talks/Opening+the+Doors+of+Creativity).

It quickly became evident: cited in Candice Gaukel Andrews. "Want a Creativity Boost? Take a Walk in Nature." *Natural Habitat Adventures*. (October 16, 2018) (https://www.nathab.com/blog/want-a-creativity-boost-take-a-walk-in-nature/).

There is certainly ample evidence to support: Florence Williams. *The Nature Fix: Why Nature Makes Us Happier, Healthier, and More Creative*. (New York: Norton, 2017). This book is packed with powerful research and compelling evidence to support why we need to open the front door and get outside.

In 2005 Richard Louv published a groundbreaking book: Richard Louv. *Last Child in the Woods: Saving Our Children From Nature-Deficit Disorder*. (Chapel Hill: NC: Algonquin Books, 2008). One of the most compelling and important books of our lifetime. If you have kids, you must read this book. Now!

According to a study by researchers at the University of Maryland: Sandra L. Hofferth and J. F. Sandberg, "How American Children Spend Their Time," *Journal of Marriage and Family*, 63, no. 3 (2001): 295-308.

Another team of researchers at Manhattenville College: Rhonda L. Clements, "An Investigation of the State of Outdoor Play," *Contemporary Issues in Early Childhood*, 5, No. 1 (2004): 68-80.

Erika Christakis, in her penetrating piece in *The Atlantic*: Erika Christakis. "School Wasn't So Great Before Covid, Either." *The Atlantic* (December 2020), p. 22.
   What happens to the nation's intrinsic creativity: Richard Louv. *Last Child in the Woods: Saving Our Children From Nature-Deficit Disorder*. (Chapel Hill: NC: Algonquin Books, 2008).
   There are approximately 4.88 billion mobile users: (no author) "How Many Smart Phones are in the World?" Bank My Cell (2021) (accessed March 23, 2021) (https://www.bankmycell.com/blog/how-many-phones-are-in-the-world).

American children spend an unbelievable seven hours a day: cited in Liraz Margalit. "What Screen Time Can Really Do to Kids' Brains." *Psychology Today* (April 17, 2016) (https://www.psychologytoday.com/us/blog/behind-online-behavior/201604/what-screen-time-can-really-do-kids-brains) and Chandra Johnson. "How Digital Media Has Changed Creativity." *Desert News* (November 23, 2016) (https://www.deseretnews.com/article/865667716/How-digital-media-has-changed-creativity.html).

Dr. Aric Sigman, an associate fellow of the British Psychological; Society: cited in: Liraz Margalit. "What Screen Time Can Really Do to Kids' Brains." *Psychology Today* (April 17, 2016) (https://www.psychologytoday.com/us/blog/behind-online-behavior/201604/what-screen-time-can-really-do-kids-brains).

The American Academy of Pediatrics (AAP) has issued: (no author) "American Academy of Pediatrics Announces New Recommendations for Children's Media Use." *American Academy of Pediatrics* (October 21, 2016) and Pam Lathbury. "Is Viewing the Same as Doing? What Parents Need to Know About How Screen Time is Affecting the Growing Brains of Their Children." *The Center for Parenting Education* (no date).

Melissa Bernstein: Melissa Bernstein. "How We're Endangering Our Kid's Imaginations." *Time* (October 25, 2016).

According to a 2016 report by Common Sense Media: Reported in Mike Brooks, "How Much Screen Time is Too Much," *Psychology Today.com* (December 26, 2018). (https://www.psychologytoday.com/us/blog/tech-happy-life/201812/how-much-screen-time-is-too-much).

...walking improves the generation of novel yet appropriate ideas: May Wong, "Stanford study finds walking improves creativity," *Stanford News* (April 24, 2014). (https://news.stanford.edu/2014/04/24/walking-vs-sitting-042414/#:~:text=Stanford%20researchers%20found%20that%20walking%20boosts%20creative%20inspiration.,claim%20they%20do%20their%20best%20thinking%20while%20walking).

Shane O'Mara in his book *In Praise of Walking*: Shane O'Mara. *In Praise of Walking* (New York: W.W. Norton, 2019). In this compelling and far-reaching book, neuroscientist O'Mara extolls the psychological, sociological, personal, and creative benefits of walking. You will look at the (seemingly) simple act of walking with new eyes after reading this tome.

Empirical research and anecdotal evidence have shown: Daniel Kahneman. *Thinking Fast and Slow*. (New York: Farrar, Straus & Giroux, 2011). This book is a classic on thinking and cognition. Read it and you'll see why.

For an excellent example, check out "Old Movie Stars Dance to Uptown Funk": (no author) Old Movie Stars Dance to Uptown Funk, *You Tube* (4:53). (https://www.youtube.com/watch?v=M1F0lBnsnkE) . This is one of the most innovative videos you'll ever see. If you view it, you'll be in good company - as of this writing, it has been seen more than 58 million times (Full disclosure: at least two dozen of those viewings are mine).

Compelling research shows that the constant onslaught of text messages: Nicholas Carr. *The Shallows: What the Internet Is Doing to Our Brains*. (New York: W.W. Norton, 2020).

9. The Limits of Right Answers

Our passion for the right answer: Kathryn Haydon. "When You Say You're Not Creative..." *Psychology Today.com* (January 4, 2019). (https://www.psychologytoday.com/us/blog/adventures-in-divergent-thinking/201901/when-you-say-you-re-not-creative).

By some estimates: cited in Anthony D. Fredericks. *Ace Your First Year Teaching: How to be an Effective and Successful Teacher* (Indianapolis, IN: Blue River Press, 2017).

There are various types of federal legislation: There are numerous articles (and a rash of books) that have tackled the subject of standardized tests and their effects (both positive and negative) on the American education system. This is frequently a "black and white" situation - you're either for them or against them. Those considerable arguments are beyond the scope of this book; however, if you'd like some additional insights, here are some resources to get you started: Daniel Luzer. "What Kills Creativity" Pacific Standard Magazine (https://psmag.com/education/kills-creativity-standardized-testing-children-69137). Jonathan Supovitz. "Is High-Stakes Testing Working?" *University of Pennsylvania GSE* (https://www.gse.upenn.edu/review/feature/supovitz), Ken Robinson and Lou Aronica. "How Schools Kill Creativity: Forget Standardized Tests, Here's How We Really Engage Our Kids" *Salon* (https://www.salon.com/2015/04/26/how_schools_kill_creativity_forget_standardized_tests_heres_how_we_really_engage_our_kids/), Batten Institute University of Virginia School of Business. "How America's Education Model Kills Creativity and Entrepreneurship" *Forbes* (https://www.forbes.com/sites/darden/2015/03/19/how-americas-education-model-kills-creativity-and-entrepreneurship-2/#1a99edd73e49), Valerie Strauss. "Confirmed: Standardized Testing Has Taken Over Our Schools. But Who's to Blame?" *The Washington Post*. (October 24, 2015).

As University of San Diego professor Jennifer Meuller explains: Jennifer S. Mueller, Shimul Melwani, and Jack Goncalo, "The Bias Against Creativity: Why People Desire but Reject Creative Ideas," *Psychological Science*, 23(1), 2011, 13-17.

My "Marshmallow Challenge" has been verified dozens of times: Tom Wujec. "Build a Tower, Build a Team," *TED Talk* (February 2010). (https://www.ted.com/talks/tom_wujec_build_a_tower).

Ken Robinson puts this all into perspective: Ken Robinson. *Out of Our Minds: Learning to be Creative*. (New York: Wiley, 2011).

Dr. Robert Sternberg, a psychologist: Robert J. Sternberg and T.I. Lubert. *Defying the Crowd: Cultivating Creativity in a Culture of Conformity*. (New York: Free Press, 1995).

Michael Roberto, in his book *Unlocking Creativity*: Michael A. Roberto. *Unlocking Creativity: How to Solve Any Problem and Make the Best Decisions by Shifting Creative Mindsets*. (New York, Wiley: 2019).

Simon Kashchock-Marenda: The story of this young man and his fascinating experiments was brought to my attention by an article in *The Philadelphia Inquirer*. Check it out: Tom Avril. "Boy Scientist in Manayunk Finds Sweetener That Kills Fruit Flies" *The Philadelphia Inquirer* (June 4, 2014).

As a result of all those "right answer" questions: Anthony D. Fredericks. *Ace Your First Year Teaching: How to be an Effective and Successful Teacher*. (Indianapolis, IN: Blue River Press, 2017).

Or, as famed management guru Peter Drucker once wrote: Peter Drucker. *The Practice of Management*. (Abington, UK: Routledge, 2012).

The No Child Left Behind Act: D.S. Renter, C. Scott, N. Kober, N. Chudowsky, V. Chudowsky, D. Joftus, and D. Zabala. *From the Capital to the Classroom: Year 4 of the No Child left Behind Act* (Washington DC: Center on Education Policy, 2006), Ken Robinson. *Out of Our Minds: Learning to be Creative*. (New York: Wiley, 2011), and Jonathan Supovitz. "Is High-Stakes Testing Working?" University of Pennsylvania GSE (2019) (https://www.gse.upenn.edu/review/feature/supovitz).

Teachers are often prone to "teach to the test": B. Stecher and R.T. Brennan. "Mirror, Mirror on the Wall, Which is the Fairest Test of All? An Examination of the Equitability of Portfolio Assessment Relative to Standardized Tests." *Harvard Educational Review*, 67(3), 472-506.

According to the Pennsylvania Department of Education website: Pennsylvania Department of Education. "Pennsylvania System of School Assessment (PSSA)" (no date) (https://www.education.pa.gov/K-12/Assessment%20and%20Accountability/PSSA/Pages/default.aspx).

As Ken Robinson writes: Ken Robinson. *Out of Our Minds: Learning to be Creative*. (New York: Wiley, 2011).

Or, as Scott Barry Kaufman and Carolyn Gregoire state: Scott Barry Kaufman & Carolyn Gregoire. *Wired to Create: Unraveling the Mysteries of the Creative Mind*. (New York: Penguin Random House, 2015).

Well, that's what the folks at Amazon do: Jeff Dyer and Hal Gregersen, "How Does Amazon Stay at Day One?," *Forbes*, August 8, 2017.

I'm also aware that there is some anecdotal evidence that demonstrates: Ed Catmull. *Creativity, Inc.: Overcoming the Unseen Forces That Stand in the Way of True Inspiration*. (New York: Random House, 2014).

The value of "What-iffing" is further substantiated by some compelling research: Jessica Stillman. "Follow the 70-20-10 Rule to Produce Your Best Work." *Inc.com*. (March 24, 2021). (https://www.inc.com/jessica-stillman/success-jerry-uelsmann-70-20-10-rule.html).

11. It's All in the Questions

Why do teachers ask questions?: Anthony D. Fredericks. *Ace Your First Year Teaching:*

How to Be an Effective and Successful Teacher. (Indianapolis, IN: Blue River Press, 2017).
In one intriguing study: E. Susskind. "Encouraging Teachers to Encourage Children's Curiosity: A Pivotal Competence." *Journal of Clinical Child Psychology*, 8, 101-106.

Advancing Educational Leadership (AEL) Academy: Jackie Acree Walsh and Beth Dankert Sattes. *Quality Questioning: Research-Based Practice to Engage Every Learner.* (Thousand Oaks, CA: Corwin Press, 2005). This is a book every teacher should read. It will transform your instructional practices as much as it will transform your students' minds.
Even research conducted more than a half-century ago: M. Gall. "The Use of Questions in Teaching." *Review of Educational Research*, (1971) 40, 707-721; and M. Gall. "Synthesis of Research on Teachers' Questioning." *Educational Leadership*, (1984) 42(3), 40-47.

A large proportion of the questions teachers ask: D.L. Redfield & E.W. Rousseau. "A Meta-analysis of Experimental Research on Teacher Questioning Behavior." *Review of Educational Research* (1981) 51, 237-245.

Questions are answered by a small minority of students: D. Sadker & M. Sadker. "Is the OK Classroom OK?" *Phi Delta Kapan* (1985), 66(5), 358-361.

Prevailing research and teacher observations: Mary Budd Rowe. *Teaching Science as Continuous Inquiry: A Basic* (New York: McGraw-Hill, 1978).

Another interesting point that arose: Jackie Acree Walsh and Beth Dankert Sattes. *Quality Questioning: Research-Based Practice to Engage Every Learner.* (Thousand Oaks, CA: Corwin Press, 2005).

Finally, the authors underscore the dearth: Jackie Acree Walsh and Beth Dankert Sattes. *Quality Questioning: Research-Based Practice to Engage Every Learner.* (Thousand Oaks, CA: Corwin Press, 2005).

Yet, many authors have written persuasively: cited in Jackie Acree Walsh and Beth Dankert Sattes. *Quality Questioning: Research-Based Practice to Engage Every Learner.* (Thousand Oaks, CA: Corwin Press, 2005) and Anthony D. Fredericks. *Ace Your First Year Teaching: How to be an Effective and Successful Teacher.* (Indianapolis, IN: Blue River Press, 2017).

Bloom's Taxonomy: Benjamin Bloom. *Taxonomy of Educational Objectives, Book 1: Cognitive Domain.* (New York: Longman, 1987).

The system (revised in 2001): L.W. Anderson & D.R. Krathwohl (Eds). *A Taxonomy for Learning, Teaching, and Assessing: A Revision of Bloom's Taxonomy of Educational Objectives.* (New York: Addison Wesley Longman, 2001).

A significant study completed more than forty years ago: D.L. Redfield & E.W. Rousseau. "A Meta-analysis of Experimental Research on Teacher Questioning Behavior." *Review of Educational Research* (1981) 51, 237-245.

And, yet, additional studies have conclusively shown. (no author) *Deeper Learning through Questioning.* American Institutes for Research [TEAL Center Fact Sheet No. 12]. (Washington, DC: U.S. Department of Education, 2013).

According to Ozan Varol in his book *Think Like a Rocket Scientist*: Ozan Varol, *Think Like a Rocket Scientist: Simple Strategies You Can Use to Make Giant Leaps in Work and Life.* (New York: Public Affairs, 2020), p. 89.

In support of that idea, two British researchers: Teresa Belton and Esther Priyadharshini, "Boredom and Schooling: A Cross-Disciplinary Exploration," *Cambridge Journal of Education*, December 1, 2007.

Recall that kids are frequently bombarded with up to 400 questions every school day: Anthony D. Fredericks. *Ace Your First Year Teaching: How to Be an Effective and Successful Teacher.*

(Indianapolis, IN: Blue River Press, 2017).

Convincing research has shown that most teachers ask far too many questions: Anthony D. Fredericks. *The Adjunct Professor's Complete Guide to Teaching College: How to Be an Effective and Successful Instructor*. (Indianapolis, IN: Blue River Press, 2019).   .

"without boredom, our creativity muscles begin to atrophy....: Ozan Varol. *Think Like a Rocket Scientist: Simple Strategies You Can Use to Make Giant Leaps in Work and Life*. (New York: Public Affairs, 2020).

A few years ago, I began writing a children's book on rainforests: Anthony D. Fredericks. *A is for Anaconda: A Rainforest Alphabet* (Chelsea, MI: Sleeping Bear Press, 2009).

13. Rewards and Punishments

Consider a research study: Alfie Kohn. *Punished by Rewards: The Trouble with Gold Stars, Incentive Plans, A's, Praise, and Other Bribes*. (Boston: Houghton Mifflin, 1999). You'll never use gold stars again after reading this book.

Those results were confirmed: cited in Carol D. Dweck. *Mindset: The New Psychology of Success*. (New York: Random House, 2006).

In another well-known experiment: cited in Megan McArdle. *The Up Side of Down: Why Failing Well is the Key to Success* (New York: Penguin, 2014).

In his pivotal book: Alfie Kohn. *Punished by Rewards: The Trouble with Gold Stars, Incentive Plans, A's, Praise, and Other Bribes*. (Boston: Houghton Mifflin, 1999).

In the first, young creative writers and **Then, the researchers conducted**: both cited in Alfie Kohn. *Punished by Rewards: The Trouble with Gold Stars, Incentive Plans, A's, Praise, and Other Bribes*. (Boston: Houghton Mifflin, 1999).

That was a question psychologists Erik Westby and V.L. Dawson asked: Erik L. Westby & V.L. Dawson (1995) "Creativity: Asset or Burden in the Classroom?" *Creativity Research Journal*, 8:1, 1-10, DOI: 10.1207/s15326934crj0801_1.

A discovery made by the well-known: E. Paul Torrance and Dorothy Sisk. *Gifted and Talented Children in the Regular Classroom* (Buffalo, NY: Creative Education Foundation, 1998).

First, teachers' unwelcoming attitudes: Erik L. Westby & V.L. Dawson (1995) "Creativity: Asset or Burden in the Classroom?" *Creativity Research Journal*, 8:1, 1-10, DOI: 10.1207/s15326934crj0801_1.

In her book *Mindset: The New Psychology of Success*: Carol D. Dweck. *Mindset: The New Psychology of Success*. (New York: Random House, 2006).

One research study in 2017 tested the link between curiosity and creative problem-solving: Wilma Koutstaal. "Creativity—What's Curiosity Got to Do With It?" *Psychology Today. com* (July 5, 2017). https://www.psychologytoday.com/us/blog/our-innovating-minds/201707/creativity-whats-curiosity-got-do-it.

They announced on Facebook that they would toss a parking ticket: (no author) "A Utah City Has Been Forgiving Parking Tickets in Exchange for Food Donations." *CNN - The Good Stuff* (February 21, 2021). https://www.cnn.com/2021/02/21/us/utah-parking-tickets-food-donations-trnd/index.html.

15. "What a Stupid Idea!"

At least one study has confirmed that, on average, children receive: cited in Amy McCready, "Simple Words to Avoid Power Struggles." *Positive Parenting Solutions* (no date (https://www.positive-parentingsolutions.com/parenting/simple-words-to-avoid-power-struggles).

In April 2019, the Cyberbullying Research Center reported: (no author) "Cyberbullying." National Bullying Prevention Center. *Pacer.org.* (https://www.pacer.org/bullying/info/cyberbullying)

Some people are locked into a "fixed mindset.": Carol D. Dweck. *Mindset: The New Psychology of Success.* (New York: Random House, 2006).

In my conversations with business leaders: Chic Thompson. *What a Great Idea! 2.0: Unlocking Your Creativity in Business and in Life.* (New York: Sterling, 2007). This is the book that got me started on a most incredible voyage of discovery. I began with Thompson's list (p. 47-48) of "killer phrases" and used it to ask people in various occupations for some of their favorite phrases. Suffice it to say, I got more than I bargained for - sufficient for an entire stand-alone book. I tried to keep the final list to a reasonable length.

According to one report: (no author) "Global Fraud Survey 2016", *EY.com* (no date) (https://www.ey.com/gl/en/services/assurance/fraud-investigation).

In one study of business teams: cited in Phillip Sandahl. "Breaking the Code on High Performing Teams." Team Coaching International (March 12, 2015), (https://teamcoachinginternational.com/breaking-the-code-ob-high-performing-teams).

A subsequent review of this research: Jack Zenger and Joe Folkman. *The Extraordinary Leader: Turning Good Managers Into Great Leaders* (New York: McGraw-Hill, 2009).

Some compelling research conducted by John Gottman: (no author listed). "Marriage and Couples." (2019) The Gottman Institute blog (https://www.gottman.com/about/research/couples).

Is it any wonder then that the Society for Human Resource Management: Rebecca R. Hastings. "SHRM Poll: Employee Suggestion Programs Underutilized" *SHRM Newsletter* (Alexandria, VA: SHRM, November 17, 2010).

In his book *Think Again*, author Adam Grant makes a strong case: Adam Grant, *Think Again: The Power of Knowing What You Don't Know* (New York: Viking, 2021).

According to Robert Half, the world's largest specialized staffing firm: Robert Half. "7 Elements of a Highly Creative Work Environment." *Robert Half* (May 14, 2019). https://www.roberthalf.com/blog/management-tips/7-elements-of-a-highly-creative-work-environment#:~:text=%207%20Elements%20of%20a%20Highly%20Creative%20Work,Creative%20work%20rarely%20happens%20in%20a...%20More.

17. Fear of Failure

Englishman James Dyson: (no author) "#303 James Dyson." *Forbes* (https://www.forbes.com/profile/james-dyson/#4dafa2e22b38).

In an interview in Fast Company: Chuck Salter. "Failure Doesn't Suck" *Fast Company Magazine* (May 2007).

Dyson's company now has more than sixty consumer products: (no author) "Dyson

Revenue" *Craft* (https://craft.co/dyson/revenue).

An interesting body of research has underscored and **The psychologist Carol Dweck**: Carol Dweck. *Mindset: The New Psychology of Success.* (New York: Ballantine Books, 2006).

Former rocket scientist Ozan Varol: Ozan Varol. *Think Like a Rocket Scientist: Simple Strategies You Can Use to Make Giant Leaps in Work and Life.* (New York: Public Affairs, 2020).

In his book *Failing Forward*: John C. Maxwell. *Failing Forward: Turning Mistakes into Stepping Stones for Success.* (Nashville, TN: Thomas Nelson, 2000).

Psychologist Guy Winch: Guy Winch. "10 Signs That You Might Have a Fear of Failure" *Psychologytoday.com* (June 18, 2013) (https://www.psychologytoday.com/us/blog/the-squeaky-wheel/201306/10-signs-you-might-).

Sara Blakely, the woman who founded Spanx: The material in this section was pulled from several sources including: Gillian Zoe Segel. *Getting There: A Book of Mentors* (New York: Abrams, 2015), a most delightful video (https://www.inc.com/sara-blakely/how-spanx-founder-turned-5000-dollars-into-a-billion-dollar-undergarment-business.html), a Forbes Magazine profile: (no author) "#23 Sara Blakely" *Forbes* (https://www.forbes.com/profile/sara-blakely/#46ffcfce76bb), and a timeline of the company's history (http://www.spanx.com/years-of-great-rears).

In 2012, Blakely was also named to Time Magazine's: Couric, Katie. "The 100 Most Influential People in the World". *Time Magazine.* (April 18, 2012).

Psychologists list fear of failure as one of the biggest stumbling blocks: (no author) "Fear of Failure The Biggest Block to People's Creativity" Triple Helix (accessed March 15, 2019) (https://www.3xcorp.com/fear-of-failure-to-peoples-creativity/); (no author) "How a Fear of Failure is damaging to Creativity" *Viral Solutions* (accessed March 15, 2019) (https://viralsolutions.net/fear-failure-damaginbg-creativity); and R.L. Adams. "5 Ways Fear of Failure Can Ruin Your Business." *Entrepreneur.com* (September 19, 2017) (https://www.entreprenuer.com/article/299403).

Lawrence Lehman Ortega: cited in Karen Higginbottom. "Why the Ability to Fail Leads to Innovation." *Forbes. com* (August 3, 2017). (https://www.forbes.com/sites/karenhigginbottom/2017/08/03/why-the-ability-to-fail-leads-to-innovation/#652451f136f6).

The successful executive is faster to recognize: Hal Gregersen, "Bursting the CEO Bubble," *Harvard Business Review*, April 2017, (https://hbr.org/2017/03/bursting-the-ceo-bubble).

Tom Peters, coauthor of In Search of Excellence: Tom Peters and Robert H. Waterman. *In Search of Excellence: Lessons From America's Best Run Companies* (New York: Harper Business, 2006).

Creativity researcher Bob McKim: You can watch a most intriguing TED talk that describes McKim's unique project at the following site: https://www.ted.com/talks/tim_brown_on_creativity_and_play/transcript?language=en.

Quote from his interview in Fast Company Magazine: Chuck Salter. "Failure Doesn't Suck" *Fast Company Magazine* (May 2007).

I went on to write *Horseshoe Crab: Biography of a Survivor*: Anthony D. Fredericks. *Horseshoe Crab: Biography of a Survivor.* (Washington, DC: Ruka Press, 2012).

If you're a writer, one of the classic books you should have: Natalie Goldberg. *Writing Down the Bones: Freeing the Writer Within.* (Boston, MA: Shambhala, 1986).

19. Corporate Killers

For years Avis had lagged behind Hertz: Seth Stevenson. "We're No. 2! We're No. 2!" *Slate* (August 12, 2013).

Several years ago IBM conducted a Global CEO Study: cited in: Michael A. Roberto. *Unlocking Creativity: How to Solve Any Problem and Make the Best Decisions by Shifting Creative Mindsets*. (New York, Wiley: 2019).

In his pivotal book: Steven Johnson. *Where Good Ideas Come From: The Natural History of Innovation*. (New York: Riverhead Books, 2010). Another book that should be part of your library. Johnson knows how to explain complex ideas in clear, persuasive language. Well worth your time! **Several organizational mindsets that tend to inhibit**: Michael A. Roberto. *Unlocking Creativity: How to Solve Any Problem and Make the Best Decisions by Shifting Creative Mindsets*. (New York, Wiley: 2019).

In an article on *Money Watch*: Margaret Heffernan. "Why Aren't People Creative?" (January 28, 2013) *Money Watch - CBS Interactive* (https://www.cbsnews.com/news/why-arent-people-creative).

There is a persistent myth that the only way: David Burkus. *The Myths of Creativity: The Truth About How Innovative Companies and People Generate Great Ideas*. (San Francisco, CA: Josey-Bass, 2014).

Nicholas Kohn and some colleagues: cited in Andrew Tate. "5 Creativity Myths You Probably Believe." (2019). *Canva* (https://www.canva.com/learn/5-creativity-myths-probably-believe).

R. Keith Sawyer, a professor of education: R. Keith Sawyer, *Zig Zag: The Surprising Path to Greater Creativity* (San Francisco: Jossey-Bass, 2013) and *Explaining Creativity: The Science of Human Innovation* (Cambridge: Oxford University Press, 2012).

Harvard Researcher Shelley Carson postulates that a shower: cited in Leo Widrich. "Why We Have Our Best Ideas in the Shower: The Science of Creativity" *Buffer.com* (September 7, 2018).

Where Good Ideas Come From: Steven Johnson. *Where Good Ideas Come From: The Natural History of Innovation*. (New York: Riverhead Books, 2010).

To assess that disconnect: I was honored to have been invited into the classroom of my friend (and former colleague) Dr. Dave Greisler on March 21, 2019. The class was composed primarily of freshmen and sophomores who were taking one of their first business courses. Dave allowed me to address them in addition to tapping into some of their perceptions of the creative process. I sincerely hope I left them in the same condition in which I found them.

They polled 400 "creatives" and discovered: cited in Anne Fisher. "How Companies Kill Creativity" (October 17, 2013), *Fortune.com* (http://fortune.com/2013/10/17/how-companies-kill-creativity).

"Creativity Under the Gun": by Teresa Amabile, Constance Noonan Hadley, and Steven J. Kramer. "Creativity Under the Gun" *Harvard Business Review*, (August 2002).

"Organizations routinely kill creativity with fake deadlines....": Teresa Amabile, Constance Noonan Hadley, and Steven J. Kramer. "Creativity Under the Gun" *Harvard Business Review*, (August 2002).

Employees spend 20 percent of their working time: Adam Robinson. "Encourage Your Employees to Work on Side Projects." *Inc.* (March 20, 2018).

"It is forgotten that risk can be a good thing.": (no author) "The Dangers of Playing It Safe" *American Management Association*. (January 24, 2019) (https://www.amanet.org/articles/the-dangers-of-playing-it-safe/).

"If you punish employees that don't immediately deliver....": (no author) "5 Ways Your Company is Killing Creativity" (November 3, 2015), *Relation Edge* (https://relationedge.com/5-ways-your-company-is-killing-creativity).

Out of their Minds: Learning to be Creative: Ken Robinson. *Out of Our Minds: Learning to be Creative*. (New York: Wiley, 2011).

Several recent research studies have shown conclusively: Hjalmar Gislason. "Don't Be the Boss Who Talks Too Much." *Harvard Business Review* (May 3, 2019).

Michael Hvisdos, founder and CEO of Inquizo: Michael Hvisdos. "How to Foster Curiosity and Creativity in the Workplace." *Training Magazine* (June 8, 2016) https://trainingmag.com/how-foster-curiosity-and-creativity-workplace.

The Secret Life of Clams: The Mysteries and Magic of Our Favorite Shellfish: Anthony D. Fredericks. *The Secret Life of Clams: The Mysteries and Magic of Our Favorite Shellfish* (New York: Skyhorse Press, 2014). One individual, in her review of the book, even used a simile to compare me to her favorite geology professor from years ago. A most enjoyable compliment.

21. "Here Be Dragons!"

The mythological island of California: Edward Brooke-Hitching. *The Phantom Atlas: The Greatest Myths, Lies and Blunders on Maps*. (San Francisco: Chronicle Books, 2018).

One day in 1666, Sir Isaac Newton: James Clear. "Creativity is a Process, Not an Event." (no date). *Creativity* (https://jamesclear.com/creative-thinking).

One of the most persistent illusions about creativity: David Burkus. *The Myths of Creativity: The Truth About How Innovative Companies and People Generate Great Ideas*. (San Francisco, CA: Josey-Bass, 2014).

Creativity guru Roger von Oech: Roger von Oech, *A Whack on the Side of the Head*. (New York: Grand Central Publishing, 2008).

The threshold hypothesis: Jonathan Wai. "If You Are Creative, Are You Also Intelligent?" Psychology Today (April 12, 2011) (https://www.psychologytoday.com/us/blog/finding-the-next-einstein/201104/if-you-are-creative-are-you-also-intelligent).

The relationship between intelligence and creative potential: Emanual Jauk, Mathias Benedek, Beate Dunst, and Aljoscha C. Neubauer. "The relationship between intelligence and creativity: New support for the threshold hypothesis by means of empirical breakpoint detection" (July 2013) *Intelligence* (https://www.researchgate.net/publication/245030070_The_relationship_between_intelligence_and_creativity_New_support_for_the_threshold_hypothesis_by_means_of_empirical_breakpoint_detection).

Creativity expert Tanner Christensen further solidifies a connection: Tanner Christensen. "The Relationship Between Creativity and Intelligence" *Creative Something* (January 21, 2013) (https://creativesomething.net/post/41103661291/the-relationship-between-creativity-and).

Other researchers have acknowledged that: Roger von Oech, *A Whack on the Side of the Head*. (New York: Grand Central Publishing, 2008), David Burkus. *The Myths of Creativity: The Truth About How Innovative Companies and People Generate Great Ideas*. (San Francisco, CA:

Josey-Bass, 2014), Mitch Resnick. "4 Myths About Creativity." (November 20, 2017), *Edutopia. org* (https://www.edutopia.org/article/4-myths-about-creativity), Margarita Tartakovsky, "3 Myths About Creativity That Just Won't Quit." (July 8, 2018), *Psych Central blog* (https://psych-central.com/blog/3-myths-about-creativity-that-just-wont-quit), and (no author) "The 6 Myths of Creativity." (March 1, 2008). *Harvard Business School* (https://www.alumni.hbs.edu/stories/Pages/story-bulletin.aspx?num=671).

Bette Nesmith: cited in Allyn Freeman and Bob Golden. *Why Didn't I Think of That?: Bizarre Origins of Ingenious Inventions We Couldn't Live Without.* (New York: Wiley, 1997).
"We have a saying in the innovation industry": Phil McKinney. "The 5 Most Common Myths of Creativity." (November 21, 2011), *Phil McKinney Blog* (https://philmckinney.com/the-5-most-common-myths-of-creativity).

One of the most persistent myths is that a creative idea: David Burkus. *The Myths of Creativity: The Truth About How Innovative Companies and People Generate Great Ideas.* (San Francisco, CA: Josey-Bass, 2014).

"Creativity is just connecting things": Quoted in Warren Bennis, *Organizing Genius: The Secrets of Creative Collaboration* (New York: Basic Books, 1998), 66.

History also records these interesting combinations: Paul Sloane. "How Unusual Combinations Lead to Breakthrough Ideas." Innovation Management (no date) (https://innovationmanagement.se/imtool-articles/how-unusual-combinations-lead-to-breakthrough-ideas/).

I give my manuscripts fermentation time: Anthony D. Fredericks. "Fermentation Time" (January 17, 2019), *Navigating Nonfiction* column - *Eastern Penn Points* blog (https://easternpennpoints.wordpress.com/page/6).

In one piece of research: cited in David Burkus. *The Myths of Creativity: The Truth About How Innovative Companies and People Generate Great Ideas.* (San Francisco, CA: Josey-Bass, 2014).

The environment in which those people work: David Burkus. *The Myths of Creativity: The Truth About How Innovative Companies and People Generate Great Ideas.* (San Francisco, CA: Josey-Bass, 2014) and Steven Johnson. *Where Good Ideas Come From: The Natural History of Innovation.* (New York: Riverhead Books, 2010).

"Across all talent levels, people have peaks and valleys....": Teresa M. Amabile and Steven Cramer. *The Progress Principle: Using Small Wins to Ignite Joy, Engagement, and Creativity at Work* (Cambridge, MA: Harvard Business Review Press, 2011).

Creative individuals alone are the key to improving a company's bottom line: David Burkus. *The Myths of Creativity: The Truth About How Innovative Companies and People Generate Great Ideas.* (San Francisco, CA: Josey-Bass, 2014).

Creative ideas are generated in an environment: Steven Johnson. *Where Good Ideas Come From: The Natural History of Innovation.* (New York: Riverhead Books, 2010).
Austin Kleon, author of *Steal Like an Artist* makes a case: Austin Kleon, *Steal Like An Artist: 10 Things Nobody Told You About Being Creative* (New York: Workman, 2012).

Author (and artist) Rod Judkins, in his book *The Art of Creative Thinking* makes a most compelling statement: Rod Junkins, *The Art of Creative Thinking: 89 Ways to See Things Differently* (New York: Random House, 2016).

Elaborate on your ideas by applying a checklist: Alex Osborn (arranged by Bob Eberle) as cited in Michael Michalko. *Cracking Creativity: The Secrets of Creative Genius.* (Berkeley, CA: Ten Speed Press, 1998).

23. Adult (Mis) Behaviors

He was the funniest man I ever heard: (no author). "Jonathan Winters - Biography". *IMDb* (no date). (https://www.imdb.com/name/nm0005565/bio).

Psychologists note that one: Leonard Mlodinow. *Elastic: Flexible Thinking in a Time of Change*. (New York: Pantheon Books, 2018).

Code of Behavior: (no author). "Statement of Business Conduct Standards." (2014) *Virginia Polytechnic Institute and State University*. (https://www.provost.vt.edu/content/dam/provost_vt_edu/faculty_affairs/leadership_development/bus_conduct_stds.pdf).
Rod Junkins, an art instructor: Rod Junkins. *The Art of Creative Thinking: 89 Ways to See Things Differently*. (New York: Perigree, 2016).

According to at least one expert, they create a mental lock: Roger von Oech, *A Whack on the Side of the Head*. (New York: Grand Central Publishing, 2008).

A little experiment conducted by Solomon Asch: Solomon E. Asch. "Opinions and Social Pressure: *Scientific American* 193 (1955): 31-35, and "Studies of Independence and Conformity: A Minority of One Against a Unanimous Majority," *Psychological Monographs* 70 (1956): 1-70.

First used by social psychologist: Irving Lester Janis. *Victims of Groupthink: A psychological study of foreign-policy decisions and fiascoes*. (New York: Houghton Mifflin, 1972). See also: (no author). "What is Groupthink?" (no date) *Psychology Today*. (https://www.psychologytoday.com/us/basics/groupthink); Kendra Cherry. "How to Recognize and Avoid Groupthink" (March 16, 2019). *Very Well Mind*. (https://www.verywellmind.com/what-is-groupthink-2795213); and Marlene E. Turner & Anthony R. Pratkanis, "Twenty-Five Years of Groupthink Theory and Research: Lessons from the Evaluation of a Theory" (1998) *Organizational Behavior and Human Decision Processes*, 73, 105–115.

A rash of studies have universally revealed: Melinda Wenner Moyer. "The Serious Need for Play," *Scientific American Mind: The Mad Science of Creativity* (Spring 2017), Vol. 26, No. 1, pp. 78-83.

Margarita Tartakovsky, an editor at Psych Central: Margarita Tartakovsky. "The Importance of Play for Adults." *Psych Central*. July 8, 2018.

Stuart Brown, head of the National Institute for Play: Stuart Brown. *Play: How it Shapes the Brain, Opens the Imagination, and Invigorates the Soul* (New York: Avery, 2010).

Tanner Christiansen: Tanner Christensen. "Why Play is Essential for Creativity." (April 28, 2014). *Creative Something*. (https://creativesomething.net/post/84134598535/why-play-is-essential-for-creativity).
An overemphasis on logical thinking: Roger von Oech. *A Whack on the Side of the Head* (New York: Grand Central Publishing, 2008).

However, as von Oech points out: Roger von Oech. *A Whack on the Side of the Head* (New York: Grand Central Publishing, 2008).

An article in Forbes magazine: Josh Linker. "5 Common Myths About Creativity." (October 19, 2015). *Forbes*. (https://www.forbes.com/sites/joshlinkner/2015/10/19/the-5-myths-of-creativity/#3dee303d11d9).

In his book *The Creative Curve*, author Allen Gannett discusses the "20 percent principle": Allen Gannett, *The Creative Curve: How to Develop the Right Idea at the Right Time*. (New York: Currency, 2018).

The book *Creativity and Humor* **confirms what we all know**: edited by Sarah R. Luria, John Baer and James C. Kaufman. *Creativity and Humor* (Waltham, MA: Academic Press, 2018).

Companies such as Google and Apple: Adam Robinson. "Encourage Your Employees to Work on Side Projects." *Inc.* (March 20, 2018).

In his book *The Creative Curve*, **author Allen Gannett**: Allen Gannett. *The Creative Curve: How to Develop the Right Idea at the Right Time.* (New York: Currency, 2018).

25. One or the Other

Less than five percent of us: Mitch Resnick. "4 Myths About Creativity." (November 20, 2017). *Edutopia.org.* (https://www.edutopia.org/article/4-myths-about-creativity); Andrew Tate. "5 Creativity Myths You Probably Believe." (2019). *Canva* (https://www.canva.com/learn/5-creativity-myths-probably-believe); and Kathryn Haydon. "When You Say You're Not Creative..." *Psychology Today.com* (January 4, 2019) (https://www.psychologytoday.com/us/blog/adventures-in-divergent-thinking/201901/when...).

The psychological reality that, as humans, we have a tendency: Daniel Pink. *A Whole New Mind: Why Right-Brainers Will Rule the Future.* (New York: Riverhead Books, 2006) and Kathryn Haydon. "When You Say You're Not Creative..." *Psychology Today.com* (January 4, 2019) (https://www.psychologytoday.com/us/blog/adventures-in-divergent-thinking/201901/when...).

But, we are also a dichotomous society: Daniel Pink. *A Whole New Mind: Why Right-Brainers Will Rule the Future.* (New York: Riverhead Books, 2006).

In fact, you may recall times in your academic life: Anthony D. Fredericks. *Guided Reading in Grades 3-6: 300+ Guided Reading Strategies, Activities, and Lesson Plans for Reading Success* (New York: Rigby Best Teachers Press, 2001) and Anthony D. Fredericks. *Guided Reading in Grades K-2: Guided Reading Strategies, Activities, and Lesson Plans for Reading Success* (New York: Rigby Best Teachers Press, 2003).

I encountered numerous documents: Obviously, the citations for this finding would encompass a complete encyclopedia set (Does anyone still read encyclopedias?). You might want to keep an eye out for the term "creative people" as you read various creativity tomes. You may, as did I, discover that the term is more prevalent than not. Be aware, also, of its implications for you personally.

A most interesting research project a few years ago: Claude M. Steele and Joshua Aronson. "Stereotype Threat and the Intellectual Test Performance of African Americans" *Journal of Personality and Social Psychology*, 1995, Vol. 69, No. 5, 797-811.

There is a persuasive tendency of people to downplay: Ken Robinson. *Out of Our Minds: Learning to be Creative.* (New York: Wiley, 2011); David Perkins. *The Mind's Best Work.* (Cambridge, MA: Harvard University Press, 1981); and J.C. Kaufman and R.A. Beghetto. "Beyond Big and Little: The Four C Model of Creativity." (2009) *Review of General Psychology*, 13, 1, 1-12.

David Perkins: David Perkins. *The Mind's Best Work.* (Cambridge, MA: Harvard University Press, 1981).

Kaufman and Gregoire further cement: Scott Barry Kaufman & Carolyn Gregoire. *Wired to Create: Unraveling the Mysteries of the Creative Mind.* (New York: Penguin Random House, 2015).

Inc. Magazine ran a special feature about hiring for creativity: Inc. Staff. "How to Hire for Creativity." *Inc.*, October 1, 2010 (www.inc.com/magazine/20101001/guidebook-how-to-hire-for-creativity.html).

Ken Robinson put an exclamation point on this: Ken Robinson. *Out of Our Minds: Learning to be Creative.* (New York: Wiley, 2011).

Steve Jobs probably said it best: Gary Wolf, "Steve Jobs: The Next Insanely Great Thing," *Wired*, February 1, 1996.

A few years ago, I was working on a children's book about redwood trees: Anthony D. Fredericks. *Tall Tall Tree* (Nevada City, CA: Dawn Publications, 2017).

27. Jumping Backwards, Mindsets, and Toilet Paper

Dick Fosbury: In order to tell the story of Dick Fosbury's Olympic victory I relied on two sources: Bob Welsh with Dick Fosbury. *The Wizard of Foz: Dick Fosbury's One-Man High-Jump Revolution* (New York: Skyhorse, 2018) [An excellent biography track fans will find both absorbing and compelling.] and Mayo Oshin. "The Dick Fosbury Flop: How to Think Outside the Box and Innovate New Ideas." *Mayo Oshin* (accessed June 7, 2019) (https://mayooshin.com/dick-fosbury).

Carol Dweck: Carol D. Dweck. *Mindset: The New Psychology of Success.* (New York: Random House, 2006).

For twenty years my research has shown: Carol D. Dweck. *Mindset: The New Psychology of Success.* (New York: Random House, 2006).

Maria Popova cements Dweck's research findings: Maria Popova. "Fixed vs. Growth: The Two Basic Mindsets That Shape Our Lives." *Brain Pickings* (January 29, 2014) (https://www.brainpickings.org/2014/01/29/carol-dweck-mindset).

Many of those tomes offer a predictable collection of admonitions: You may want to do as I did and visit your local bookstore and/or public library. Check out all the self-help books dealing with creativity and initiate a running list of the suggestions, techniques, and strategies suggested in those books. Although the words and structure may be different from book to book, you will undoubtedly note lots of similarities and comparisons. [I decided against including a list of those 60,000+ books for fear of creating a "bibliographic monster" much bigger and more terrifying than Godzilla.]

When you enter a mindset, you enter a new world: Carol D. Dweck. *Mindset: The New Psychology of Success.* (New York: Random House, 2006).

In *What the Best College Students Do*: Ken Bain. *What the Best College Students Do.* (Cambridge, MA: Harvard University Press, 2012).

Ernie Heffner: On June 16, 2019, I had both the pleasure and honor of interviewing Ernie Heffner - one of the most dynamic and engaging business persons I met on my travels. Section 4 of this chapter is a distillation of that interview.

Sam Walton: Two sources provided the information for this section: Richard S. Tedlow. *Giants of Enterprise: Seven Business Innovators in the Empires They Built.* (New York: Collins, 2003) and Sam Walton and John Huey. *Sam Walton: Made in America* (New York: Doubleday, 1992).

Researchers have found that the transition from: (no author) "Carol Dweck: A Summary of the Two Mindsets and the Power of Believing That You Can Improve." *Farnam Street* (March 2015) (https://fs.blog/2015/03/carol-dweck-mindset); Gary Klein. "Mindsets." *Psychology Today.com* (May 1, 2016) (https://www.psychologytoday.com/us/blog/seeing-what-others-I/201605/mindsets); and Ash Buchanan. "The Nature of Mindsets," *Medium* (March 16, 2017) (https://mediumj.com/benefit-mindset/the-nature-of-mindsets-18afba2ac890).

Mental imagery helped Albert Einstein generate the general theory of relativity: Walter Isaacson. *Einstein: His Life and Universe.* (New York: Simon & Schuster, 2007).

Leonardo da Vinci also used it: Walter Isaacson. *Leonardo da Vinci* (New York: Simon & Schuster, 2017).

Research from Erasmus University in Rotterdam, Netherlands has found: Emma Schootstra, Dirk Deichmann, and Evgenia Dolgova. "Can 10 Minutes of Meditation Make You More Creative?" *Harvard Business Review* (August 29, 2017). (https://hbr.org/2017/08/can-10-minutes-of-meditation-make-you-more-creative).

In 1986, I wrote an article for a professional journal about a teaching concept: Anthony D. Fredericks. "Mental Imagery Activities to Improve Comprehension", *The Reading Teacher* (Vol. 40, No. 1; October 1986, p.78-81).
Stephen Guise in his book *Mini Habits: Smaller Habits, Bigger Results*: Stephen Guise. *Mini Habits: Smaller Habits, Bigger Results.* (Monee, IL: Minihabits.com, 2013).

Conclusion

Several years ago, a businessman stayed: cited in John R. DiJulius. *What's the Secret?: To Providing a World-Class Customer Experience.* (New York: Wiley, 2008).

Or, as Roger von Oech puts it: Roger von Oech, *A Whack on the Side of the Head.* (New York: Grand Central Publishing, 2008).

"We are all in possession of a fantastic creativity machine....": Shelley Carson. *Your Creative Brain: Seven Steps to Maximize Imagination, Productivity, and Innovation in Your Life.* (San Francisco, CA: Jossey-Bass, 2012).

Index

About the Author

Anthony D. Fredericks was born and raised in southern California. He obtained his undergraduate degree from the University of Arizona and his Doctorate from Lehigh University. He is currently Professor Emeritus of Education at York College of Pennsylvania where he taught for thirty years. Additionally, he is an award-winning author of more than 170 books. His numerous and best-selling children's books include *Tall Tall Tree, The Tsunami Quilt, A is for Anaconda,* and *Desert Night, Desert Day.* In addition, he has written many celebrated adult nonfiction books such as *The Secret Life of Clams, Writing Children's Books, Horseshoe Crab: Biography of a Survivor,* and *Ace Your Teacher Interview* (3rd Ed.). Additionally, he has authored more than 600 articles for journals as diverse as *Hawaii Magazine, High Country News, Susquehanna Life Magazine, Teaching K-8, The Writer Magazine,* and *Harrisburg Magazine.* Fredericks is a popular presenter at schools, universities, and professional associations throughout North America and has delivered keynote speeches and conference presentations to both small (5) and large (5,000+) groups on writing strategies, teaching, and (of course) creativity. In addition, he writes on ongoing blog ("Creative Insights") for *Psychology Today.com* that examines the nature and nurture of creativity (https://www.psychologytoday.com/us/contributors/anthony-d-fredericks-edd). Fredericks and his wife live in York, Pennsylvania and divide their time between their granddaughter in England, their two grandchildren in Colorado, and numerous camping adventures in parks and forests throughout the Keystone State.

For more information about Anthony D. Fredericks and his books & presentations go to: **www.anthonydfredericks.com.**